"A gripping read about .... ew
authors h... to
his topic." .... lay

"A master ....
the body l ....

"As he pro... ue
talent for .... nd
will play si .... at
surrounds .... ne

"A thrilling .... or
understand ....

.... ist

"*The Unkn* .... ar
finest milit .... ly
a tribute to .... ly
reminder o ....

.... d
.... fe

"This unkn .... d
timely tribu .... d
War. Super ....

.... 'r

"*The Unkno* .... e
unknown co .... y
combat are ....

—................ Williams, PhD, U.S. Army Center of Military History

"Brilliant in conception and style, *The Unknowns* presents the awe-inspiring and profoundly moving story of The Great War from the viewpoint of the men who fought, sacrificed and bled to win it. A 'must read,' an incredible story related by a master storyteller!"

—James Lacey, author of *Pershing* and *The Washington War*, director of USMC University

Also by Patrick K. O'Donnell

Washington's Immortals:
The Untold Story of an Elite Regiment
Who Changed the Course of the Revolution

First SEALs:
The Untold Story of the Forging of America's Most Elite Unit

Dog Company:
The Boys of Pointe du Hoc—The Rangers Who Accomplished D-Day's
Toughest Mission and Led the Way Across Europe

Give Me Tomorrow:
The Korean War's Greatest Untold Story—The Epic Stand
of the Marines of George Company

They Dared Return:
The True Story of Jewish Spies Behind the Lines in Nazi Germany

The Brenner Assignment:
The Untold Story of the Most Daring Spy Mission of World War II

We Were One:
Shoulder to Shoulder with the Marines Who Took Fallujah

Operatives, Spies, and Saboteurs:
The Unknown Story of the Men and Women of World War II's OSS

Into the Rising Sun:
World War II's Pacific Veterans Reveal the Heart of Combat

Beyond Valor:
World War II's Ranger and Airborne Veterans
Reveal the Heart of Combat

THE
UNKNOWNS

THE UNTOLD STORY OF AMERICA'S UNKNOWN SOLDIER AND WWI'S MOST DECORATED HEROES WHO BROUGHT HIM HOME

PATRICK K. O'DONNELL

Grove Press

New York

Published simultaneously in Canada
Printed in the United States of America

This book was set in 11 pt. Janson by Alpha Design & Composition of Pittsfield, NH.

First Grove Atlantic hardcover edition: May 2018
First Grove Atlantic paperback edition: May 2019

Library of Congress Cataloging-in-Publication data is available for this title.

ISBN 978-0-8021-4717-2
eISBN 978-0-8021-4629-8

Grove Press
an imprint of Grove Atlantic
154 West 14th Street
New York, NY 10011

Distributed by Publishers Group West

groveatlantic.com

19 20 21 22   10 9 8 7 6 5 4 3 2 1

To the doughboys, America's unknown generation
who changed our world

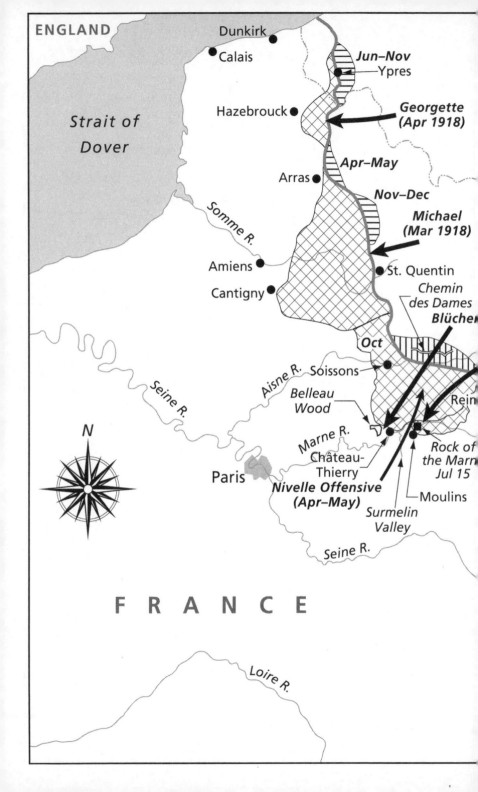

BELGIUM

Brussels

Western Front
April 1917 to July 15, 1918

———— Line of Apr 6, 1917
(Hindenburg Line)

British attacks

French attacks

German attacks

1 Janson/
   49th Company

2 Janson/
   49th Company

3 Razga
   (Oct–Nov 1918)

0   25   50   75

Miles

LUXEMBOURG

Sedan

Reims

Blanc Mont

Cunel

Aug

Meuse R.

Mosel R.

GERMANY

Verdun

Argonne Forest

2

Lemmes

Metz

Chalons

St. Mihiel

Thiaucourt

CHAMPAGNE

Seicheprey

Bar-le-Duc

Toul

Naix-aux-Forges

1

Nancy

Gondrecourt

Meurthe-et-Moselle

3

Domblain

Neufchâteau

Moselle R.

Rhine R.

Chaumont

Breuvannes

Colmar

Mulhouse

Belfort

SWITZERLAND

CONTENTS

VIII AMERICA'S UNKNOWN SOLDIER

PREFACE

Scars of war.

Cratered shell holes so large they could hold a small house.

A moonscape crisscrossed with ghostly depressions, remnants of trenches where men fought hand to hand to the death with knives, clubs, pistols, and bayonets.

Artillery shells, still bearing deadly mustard gas, entombed in dense hardwood that swallowed them long ago.

Over the last hundred years, the world has moved forward from the most important event of the twentieth century. World War I marked the death of the Old World and the emergence of the modern era.

But the Great War remains forever trapped in time at Belleau Wood.

Outside the wood, as far as the eye can see on a clear spring day, golden fields of wheat, rolling hills, and bucolic pastures testify to decades of peace and tranquility.

However, looming in the foreground is the dense patch of woods the French renamed Bois de la Brigade de Marine. In that dark and bloody forest, men of the United States Marine Corps sacrificed themselves to stop the great German drive toward Paris in the final weeks of spring 1918. The somber ground surrounding that wood still bears the marks left by some of the bloodiest days of the USMC. Yet through this crucible of battle emerged the modern Corps.

In 2013, Marines of the Wounded Warrior Regiment, men whose bodies were racked and savaged by war, solemnly traversed this hallowed ground. Many of these veterans were missing limbs; all bore the invisible mental, emotional, and spiritual scars known only to those touched by the fire of combat. I had fought house-to-house with some of these men, including Colonel Willy Buhl, in Fallujah, and I was honored to accompany them for the third time as their volunteer guide* on this special journey to France.[1] Together, we followed in the footsteps of the generation of Americans who landed on the beaches of Normandy in World War II, and then we went back even further in time to revisit the sacrifices made at Belleau Wood.

The trip was meant to help heal these wounded warriors. They hoped that fellowship, brotherhood, and sharing the history of their forebears might soothe and restore their spirit.

Two generations of Marines met at the wood. Nearly one hundred years separated the wounded warriors from their historic brethren. Veterans of Iraq and Afghanistan connected profoundly with those who had fought in World War I. They shared a bond of valor, agony, and losses suffered in battles fought in the former Ottoman Empire, now a patchwork of artificial countries sewn together in the aftermath of the Great War. The doughboys who fought in WWI are a forgotten generation. Many of their sacrifices have gone unnoticed and unrecognized, much like those of Americans who fight in today's seemingly never-ending wars. The current generation is the living embodiment of the fallen and their sacrifices. Only veterans truly know their war; they lived it.

Every Memorial Day, the commandant of the US Marine Corps and small contingents of Marines travel to Belleau Wood to honor the fallen buried in an American cemetery. The graveyard sits on a hill near the ancient hunting lodge that weathered shells, mortars, and bullets as the battle raged. In the nearby town lie the ruins of a centuries-old château the Germans used as their headquarters. Before they leave, the Marines also visit the château and seek an old stone fountain set in a wall adorned with moss and ivy. As a rite of passage, the Marines drink from the

---

* In 2010, I went to Normandy and Belleau Wood as a volunteer guide with the 5th Marines. It was the first time in ninety-three years that the 5th had gone back to France. That trip planted the seeds for this book. I returned with the 5th in 2011, and later, in 2013 and 2014, I accompanied the Wounded Warrior Regiment. On these occasions, I served as a guide to the battlefields at Normandy.

fountain's cool stream, which ironically and fittingly pours from the head of a bulldog (the mascot of the Marine Corps) into a heavy stone basin.

On that day in 2013, after imbibing the cool waters of the fountain, the Marine entourage of wounded combat veterans maneuvered through a golden wheat field still damp from a fresh spring shower. Then they slowly trundled up a muddy path to the crest of Hill 142—crucial high ground during the epic battle.

Lance Corporal Ray Shearer, the great-nephew of the Marine officer who cleared the final northern section of Belleau Wood with his battalion, served as our esteemed guide. After weeks of bloody, unrelenting combat, the elder Shearer had proclaimed, "Woods now US Marine Corps entirely."

On top of Hill 142, the vortex of war raged. At this key inflection point, the Marines took to the offensive for the first time in the Great War. Shearer related the story of one of the heroes of Hill 142: Gunnery Sergeant Ernest August Janson. Considered an "old-timer" by some for his age and experience, the thirty-nine-year-old Janson made a one-man bayonet charge, killing several German machine gunners poised to unleash their deadly weapons on Janson's company. His selfless heroics left him severely wounded but saved the hill from falling back into German hands.

On that overcast day in 2013, as light filtered through the verdant canopy, our guide transported us back to the grit and guts of 1918. After the battle, Janson emerged as one of America's first Medal of Honor recipients during the Great War. Shearer told us Janson later became "a Body Bearer, selected by General Pershing to carry home the remains of the Unknown Soldier."

His statement immediately piqued my curiosity. I wondered: who were the other men Pershing selected to serve as Body Bearers, and what feats of courage did they perform to earn this honor?

All the books I have written have serendipitously found me.

Though their stories have remained nearly unknown for a hundred years, Pershing's Body Bearers were some of the most decorated, intrepid enlisted men who fought in World War I. They uniquely span

America's service branches and specialties, uncovering an untold story within a forgotten story: Army, Navy, Marines, Infantry, Cavalry, Field Artillery, Coast Artillery (Heavy Artillery), and Combat Engineers.[2] Their ranks included a cowboy who relived the charge of the light brigade, an American Indian who heroically led the way by breaching mountains of barbed wire and captured scores of German prisoners, a salty New Englander who dueled a U-boat for hours in a fierce gunfight, a tough Bostonian who sacrificed his body to save his ship, artillerists who bombed and shelled their way to victory, and an indomitable hero blinded by gas who destroyed five machine-gun nests, killing one German soldier with a mighty swing from his pickaxe.

The Unknowns is a timeless tale of heroism, of heeding the calls of duty and brotherhood. It is replete with the tragedy of callous decisions and lives needlessly sacrificed. It is an account of shedding obsolete tactics and of the arrival of novel technology—the birth of a modern US military. It marks the start of America's emergence as the dominant world power in the twentieth century.

The Unknowns captures the Body Bearers' untold stories chronologically through the war, telling the larger story of America's involvement in the Great War, all of them ultimately culminating in the story of the Unknown Soldier.

We will never know the identity of the first man chosen to lie in America's Tomb of the Unknown Soldier. But we do know that he fought and died by the side of these heroes who laid him to rest. The Tomb is a powerful monument, an expression of closure and healing.

Their story is his story.

Their saga is the narrative of all Americans' sacrifices in war.

Their epic exemplifies who we are as Americans. The conflict that consumed them continues to affect our lives to the present day.

PROLOGUE

On October 24, 1921, light filtered through the small panes of glass ensconced in the imposing stone edifice of the *hôtel de ville* (city hall) in Châlons, France, illuminating four caskets, each draped with an American flag. Reflexively, Sergeant Edward F. Younger took measured steps, in pace with the mournful dirge of Chopin's Funeral March permeating the town square. The pungent scent of the white roses he carried mingled with the perfume of thousands of petals strewn across the floor, wafting in the air as the American infantryman slowly trod beneath the tearful eyes of dozens of French and American officials.

The archetypal doughboy, Younger no longer resembled the enthusiastic, inexperienced young man he had been before enlisting. Like most of his fellow soldiers, he bore the visible scars of numerous battles— as well as invisible scars seared in his mind. As a member of the elite 2nd Division (Regular) who had participated in several crucial battles in the Great War, Younger was familiar with the dread of anticipating combat, the anxiety of going over the top in the trenches, and the agony of watching his best friends die, felled by bullet, mortar, bayonet, or gas.

Nevertheless, nothing had prepared him for this moment.

Younger's mind raced as he repeatedly circled the four coffins. He was ordered to select one of them to be the Unknown Soldier, but how could he choose? Could one of the bodies lying here belong to someone he had known? Had one of them taken a bullet that would otherwise have struck him?[1]

Unsure of how to proceed, the young soldier prayed silently while he continued to pace. As if summoned by some invisible force, he homed in on one of the flag-swathed caskets. "I know this man," he thought. His arms seemed to move of their own accord, placing the roses he held atop the coffin.[2]

November 10, 1921, Washington, DC

With flawless precision, a testament to their expert horsemanship and endless days of drilling in the saddle, a regiment of cavalrymen wheeled their mounts to form two lines flanking the entrance to the US Capitol. The sharp ring of cold steel echoed off the pavement and marble buildings as they drew their blades in unison.

While drizzly rain dripped from their hats and soaked into their dress uniforms, eight men slowly lifted a flag-draped coffin off the caisson. The Unknown Soldier had come home to American soil at last, and it was their duty and honor to see him through the last steps of his trek. Sergeant Samuel Woodfill of the US Army infantry, Sergeant Harry Taylor of the Cavalry, Sergeant Thomas D. Saunders of the Combat Engineers, Sergeant Louis Razga of the Coast Artillery, Staff Sergeant James W. Dell of the Field Artillery, Chief Torpedoman James Delaney of the US Navy, Chief Water Tender Charles Leo O'Connor of the US Navy, and Gunnery Sergeant Ernest August Janson of the US Marine Corps elevated the body of the Unknown Soldier to shoulder height and marched beneath the upraised cavalry sabers and up the long flight of granite steps.[3]

Beneath the day's fading light, spilling from windows high above, they gingerly placed the body upon the catafalque in the Rotunda. Here on the same platform where President Lincoln had lain after his assassination, the Unknown Soldier would lie in state before the final journey to his eternal resting place in Arlington National Cemetery.

Within minutes, some of the most powerful men in the country joined the Body Bearers to pay their respects to this exemplar of America's fallen heroes. The president, vice president, speaker of the House, chief justice, secretary of war, and secretary of the Navy all laid flowers around the platform. But in the minds of the military men who formed an honor guard around the body, surely the most important visitor that night was the last.

In solemn silence, General John J. "Black Jack" Pershing strode across the Rotunda in his dress uniform. Having witnessed firsthand the terrible carnage of World War I, he understood the price of victory in a way that the other dignitaries could only begin to imagine. He tenderly laid a large wreath of pink chrysanthemums in tribute to the Unknown Soldier, who had fought and died at his command. Then the general stepped back and drew himself up to his full height before snapping a sharp military salute.

Pershing, the Body Bearers, and the Unknown Soldier had come full circle. They had left America's shores years earlier, prepared to sacrifice yet not fully comprehending the true cost of war. One had paid the ultimate price, but each had come home forever changed by battles won and friends lost.

For all of them, the odyssey had commenced with a fateful voyage across the Atlantic through waters prowled by one of the Great War's most lethal killing machines: the U-boat.

DRAMATIS PERSONAE

General John J. "Black Jack" Pershing: Commander of the American Expeditionary Forces who made the final selection of the Body Bearers

Sergeant Edward F. Younger: Chicago native and veteran doughboy infantryman who selected the Unknown Soldier

BODY BEARERS

Chief Gunner's Mate James Delaney: Tough Irish-American from Boston in command of a naval gun crew on board the SS *Campana*

Gunnery Sergeant Ernest A. Janson: Marine who fought outside Belleau Wood on Hill 142 and one of the American Expeditionary Forces' first Medal of Honor recipients

Color Sergeant James W. Dell: Member of the US Army Field Artillery decorated for valor outside Soissons, France

Corporal Thomas D. Saunders: American Indian US Army combat engineer who breached enemy wire obstacles before the main Allied attacks

Chief Water Tender Charles Leo O'Connor: US Navy sailor who sacrificed his body to save his ship

First Sergeant Harry Taylor: Cowboy who served with the 91st Division headquarters troop (mounted cavalry) and charged in an epic assault in the Meuse-Argonne

Sergeant Samuel Woodfill: US Army regular and Medal of Honor recipient considered by Pershing to be one of the greatest soldiers of the American Expeditionary Forces

First Sergeant Louis Razga: Member of US Army Coast Artillery Corps who commanded a battery of heavy artillery and was gassed in the final days of the war

Supporting Witnesses

Kapitänleutnant Victor Dieckmann: U-boat ace and English-speaking captain of *U-61*

Major George Wallis Hamilton: Commander of the 49th Company, which fought in nearly every major engagement during the American Expeditionary Forces' time in France

Captain John William Thomason, Jr.: Texan whose pen-and-ink sketches and vivid prose brilliantly captured the 49th Company's war

Corporal Elton Mackin: A messenger runner, one of the most difficult positions on the WWI battlefield, who had an unparalleled view of the 5th Marines' war in France

Lieutenant Farley Granger: Commander of the platoon that survived its own charge of the light brigade in the Meuse-Argonne

Colonel John Henry "Gatling Gun" Parker: Early American pioneer of machine guns and recipient of four Distinguished Service Crosses for his courage on the battlefield

Sergeant Alvin Cullum York: Honorary participant in the Tomb of the Unknown Soldier procession and recipient of the Medal of Honor

Major Charles White Whittlesey: Commanding officer of the "Lost Battalion," participant in the Tomb of the Unknown Soldier procession, and recipient of the Medal of Honor

Major General John Archer Lejeune: Eventual division commander of the 2nd Division (Regular) and commandant of the US Marine Corps who was present at the Unknown Soldier ceremony

Lieutenant Colonel George S. Patton: Pioneer and a key commander in the nascent American tank forces in WWI

Sergeant Stubby: Brindle-patterned bull terrier Army mascot and combat veteran of many battles, who was twice wounded and the only American canine promoted to sergeant during WWI

I

AMERICA GOES TO WAR 1917

Chapter 1

Getting Over There

Each of the Body Bearers for the Unknown Soldier had a deep and personal connection to a chain of events triggered in the summer of 1914. War began with the Austrian declaration of war on Serbia in response to the assassination of Archduke Franz Ferdinand. The incident escalated into a conflagration that enveloped all the world's major military powers. The nations of Europe and Asia chose sides: the British Empire, France, the Russian Empire, Belgium, Japan, Portugal, and Romania stood with Serbia, forming the Allied or Entente Powers, which Italy joined in 1915. Opposing them were the Central Powers: Germany, Bulgaria, Austria-Hungary, and the Ottoman Empire, which included Turkey and most of the Middle East.

In August 1914, on the Western Front, the formidable German war machine invaded Belgium. Initially, the Germans rolled through Belgium, Luxembourg, and northern France, making it all the way to the Marne River about thirty miles northeast of Paris. But the Allies rallied, even pressing available taxicabs into service to bring the troops to the front; their efforts pushed the Germans back to the line of the Aisne River. There both sides dug in, constructing belts of trenches that stretched five hundred miles from the English Channel to the Swiss border. The defensive lines consisted of trenches, bunkers, barbed wire, and blockhouses. Life in the trenches was horrific; the water-filled, muddy earthworks were infested with rats and lice. Each side defended its line with thick belts of barbed wire intermixed with machine guns. When attacking, men went over the top, crossed no-man's-land, and cut through multiple strands and coils of barbed wire. If they survived the bursts of machine-gun fire and barrages of artillery fire and breached the wire, they savagely fought hand to hand inside the enemy trench with bayonets, clubs, pistols, and trench knives. The trenches provided some cover from lethal new technology like high-explosive artillery shells, machine guns, and later poison gas, tanks, and airpower. When combined, these new weapons could slay tens of thousands in a single battle. As the Great War progressed, both sides learned and adapted, improving their tactics and weaponry—killing ever-increasing numbers of combatants. With their bodies mutilated beyond recognition, many of these unknown casualties would never be identified.

Battles on the Western Front took on an epic scale never seen before. Instead of days, battles would linger weeks or even months. The world watched in horror as more than a million men died in the Battle of Verdun, which lasted almost the entirety of 1916. Then another million-plus lives were lost in 1916 on the Western Front at the Battle of the Somme, with the British reporting nineteen thousand dead in just the first day, July 1. Despite the colossal expenditure of human life, neither side gained much ground.

On the Eastern Front, near the present-day city of Olsztyn, Poland, German forces in late August 1914 annihilated the Russian Second Army in the Battle of Tannenberg, killing or wounding seventy-eight thousand Russian troops and capturing ninety-two thousand prisoners, while losing only between ten thousand and fifteen thousand of their own men. Following the debacle of Tannenberg, Russian General Alexander Samsonov committed suicide in disgrace.

Subsequent battles on the Eastern Front during the next two years destroyed large portions of the Russian First Army as well, leaving Germany in control of most of the territory throughout Serbia, Romania, Poland, Ukraine, and the Baltics. Russia reversed some of these losses in the summer of 1916 by defeating Austrian armies in the Brusilov Offensive in present-day Ukraine. However, within Russia, the earlier string of defeats fomented civil unrest, which culminated in the Russian Revolution of February 1917. Leftists deposed the czar and installed the socialist Aleksandr Kerensky as leader of the provisional government.

Despite defeating a combined French and British imperial force at Gallipoli, by 1917 the Ottomans were losing portions of their empire, including most of Palestine and the Arabian Peninsula, which was in revolt. And in Italy, the Italians were losing ground and suffered enormous casualties after several doomed offensives against the Austrians.

The war in the West had reached a stalemate. The trench lines of 1917 were nearly the same as they had been in 1914.

Against this backdrop, Germany began considering unrestricted submarine warfare in 1917. The Allies had set up a blockade of German ports and were starving the population. Hundreds of thousands perished.[1] The U-boat seemed an ideal way to strike back.

Although the United States hadn't officially entered the war, it was providing food and other supplies that allowed the British to continue fighting on the Western Front. German leaders reasoned that if they could halt that flow of supplies to Britain, this could break the stalemate in the trenches. But attacking the United States also carried great risk; if the Germans angered the Americans, they faced the very real threat that the United States—with its prodigious industrial capability and its population of ninety million—would fully enter the war.

Although the United States had been nominally neutral before entering the war, the truth was that it had begun participating in the conflict long before 1917. America served as the Allies' banker. Before committing troops to the conflict, the nation contributed colossal sums of money to the cause. American sources loaned $3.5 billion to the Allies. That would be the equivalent of $85.58 billion today, and it was enough to finance the entire defense budgets of Great Britain and France for several years. Before the war was over, the Allies would borrow $10.5 billion from the Americans.[2]

America was an economic powerhouse. Its gross domestic product was nearly twice that of Germany or Russia.[3] The Entente was highly motivated to get America into the war. "By April 1917 the British government's collateral in gold and securities had dwindled to $219 million to cover purchases of $75 million per week; the Chancellor of the Exchequer, Andrew Bonar Law, warn[ed] that he could finance only three more weeks of spending."[4]

The United States supplied the Allies with a vast amount of commodities and other matériel. Without American supplies, everything from foodstuffs to steel and oil, the Allies could not have held the Western Front.[5] The Americans also contributed large quantities of explosives, specifically trinitrotoluene, or TNT. Manufacturing TNT requires a source of toluol, which in 1917 usually came from coke ovens. Because the Germans destroyed most of the French coke ovens early in the war and Great Britain had limited supplies of toluol, the Allies were unable to churn out artillery shells as quickly as they would have liked. In response, the Americans ramped up production of toluol. In 1914, the country could produce seven hundred thousand pounds of toluol per month, and by 1917, it was cranking out six million pounds per month.*[6]

Despite this knowledge and participation, America had done almost nothing to prepare itself in terms of raising, training, and outfitting an army. The US Army and National Guard were minuscule by European standards, ranking alongside the armed forces of tiny powers like Belgium. Early on, public sentiment favored making peace between the warring parties, and President Wilson unsuccessfully tried to end the war through mediation. Both sides rejected his overtures.

Over time, the American public began to favor the Allies, thanks to an injection of British propaganda highlighting German atrocities. In May 1915, a German U-boat sank the British passenger ship *Lusitania*, leading to the loss of 128 American lives and planting seeds of resentment against Germany deep in the American psyche. When more Americans were lost with the sinking of the French liner *Sussex* a year later, Wilson threatened to break off diplomatic relations with Germany. To keep

---

* Manufacturing TNT also requires a source of nitrates, which are commonly used in fertilizer. The Americans diverted so many nitrates to the production of explosives that supplies for agriculture ran dangerously low; this shortage probably contributed to the Dust Bowl of the 1930s. Source: Grosvenor B. Clarkson, *Industrial America in the World War* (Boston: Houghton Mifflin Co., 1923), 233.

peace with the Americans, Kaiser Wilhelm II agreed to restrictions on submarine activity in the Atlantic, including providing warning to merchant ships before attacking. However, those restrictions put a huge damper on the effectiveness of Germany's fleet of U-boats. The Germans thought a return to surprise underwater attacks might end the stalemate, starve Britain out of the war, and give the Central Powers an advantage.

In early 1917, the fifty-eight-year-old kaiser, the last ruler of the German Empire and the Kingdom of Prussia, made a fateful decision: Germany would resume unrestricted submarine warfare on February 1.

The submarine had come a long way since 1775, when American David Bushnell built the first underwater vessel capable of independent operation. Large enough for just one man, *Turtle*, as it was known, was about ten feet long, three feet wide, and six feet high. For propulsion, it had a screw turned by a hand crank, and hand pumps brought water into the bilge tank, allowing it to dive. Although it was intended as a means for attaching explosives to British ships during the American Revolution, none of its attempted attacks were successful.

American engineers worked to refine the submarine, and in 1863, the Confederate States of America launched a submarine called *H. L. Hunley*. This vessel was about forty feet long and carried a crew of eight. Seven of those were necessary to turn the hand cranks for the propellers that moved the sub forward. In addition, it carried a spar torpedo, a bomb on the end of a long pole, to be used against enemy ships. During test runs, *Hunley* repeatedly sank, killing several crews, but the Confederates kept raising the ship, hoping to put it to use. On February 17, 1864, *Hunley* made its first attack—which would also be its last. It sank the steam-powered warship USS *Housatonic*, but failed to return to its base, probably having been damaged itself in the attack.

In 1896, Irish inventor John Philip Holland built the first modern submarine, the Holland Type VI. The vessel was the first to feature dual engines: gasoline for surface use and electric for underwater. Holland, who immigrated to America, did more than any other person to transform public perception of the submarine as a death trap for its crew. In 1898, a cartoonist published a drawing of Holland sticking his head out of a submarine hatch with the caption "What? Me worry?"

The US Navy purchased and commissioned Holland's ship in 1900, renaming it the USS *Holland*. Nearly fifty-four feet long, it carried a crew of six and could dive to a depth of seventy-five feet. *Holland*'s weaponry was much improved over that of earlier models; it had a reloadable torpedo tube as well as a deck gun. Although the vessel never saw action in war, it proved very useful for conducting experiments and training sailors, and what the US Navy learned from *Holland* helped it build its own fleet of underwater vessels. Britain's Royal Navy also commissioned ships based on Holland's designs, building up a fleet of seventy-four subs before the start of World War I.

At the same time, Germany was also working on the development of an *Unterseeboot*, or U-boat. The earliest German model, *Brandtaucher*, sank during testing in 1851. It wasn't until 1903 that the Friedrich Krupp Germaniawerft shipyard built *Forelle*, the first operational German submarine. It incorporated many of Holland's design ideas as well as concepts suggested by other inventors. The Russians purchased *Forelle* for use in the Russo-Japanese War, but soon the German Navy was commissioning U-boats for its own use. The Germans continued to refine their designs, adding a double hull, diesel engines, and dual torpedo tubes. However, German commanders initially discounted the possibilities offered by the new kind of vessel. The secretary of state for the Reichsmarineamt (Imperial Naval Office) said, "I refused to throw money away on submarines so long as they could only cruise in home waters."[7]

When the Great War began in August 1914, Germany had only twenty-six commissioned U-boats with fifteen more in production. In what became known as the "Ring of Steel," the British severed the German undersea cables on August 5 and began blockading the Central Powers, cutting off vital imports of food and supplies and attempting to starve the German population. The German Navy began to see how submarine warfare could be an effective response. That month, it sent out the first submarine war patrol in history—ten U-boats with enough range to reach the North Sea. However, the results of this first patrol were less than spectacular. The U-boats failed to sink any Allied ships, and the Germans lost two U-boats on the patrol.

Initially, the U-boats focused on attacking Allied warships. History was made on September 5, 1914, when the German *U-21* sank the cruiser HMS *Pathfinder*, the first combat victory for a modern submarine. About three weeks later, *U-9*, commanded by Captain-Lieutenant Otto Eduard Weddigen, sank three British cruisers, HMS *Aboukir*, HMS *Cressy*, and HMS *Hogue*, also known as the "Live Bait Squadron" because they were believed to be at extreme risk from German submarines owing to the age of the vessels and the inexperience of their crews. In the attack, 62 officers and 1,397 British sailors died.

In February 1915, the Germans altered their submarine warfare strategy. Instead of attacking only military vessels, they also began sinking Allied and neutral merchant ships that were carrying valuable goods to Germany's enemies. In general, before attacking they allowed the crews of these vessels to disembark, but that wasn't always the case. On May 7, 1915, *U-20* sank the passenger ship *Lusitania* with no advance notice. 1,198 people died, including 128 Americans.

The American people were outraged. Woodrow Wilson's government demanded that Germany end the practice of sneak attacks or else it would cut off diplomatic relations. Acquiescing under pressure, the kaiser halted unrestricted submarine warfare in May 1916 and withdrew his U-boats from the English Channel.

But Germany resumed unrestricted submarine warfare in early February 1917, destroying another ship named *Housatonic*, an American cargo ship carrying wheat from Galveston, Texas, to London, on February 3 without any warning. Just over a week later, the Germans followed up with an attack on schooner *Lyman M. Law*, sunk about twenty-five miles off the coast of Sardinia.

In addition to these submarine attacks, Americans also had other matters closer to home on their minds. Nearly a year earlier, in March 1916, Francisco "Pancho" Villa, a Mexican rebel, attacked the New Mexico town of Columbus, killing seventeen Americans. With permission from the Mexican government, President Wilson sent thousands of troops led by Brigadier General John J. Pershing to capture Pancho Villa and his men. Despite spending months in Mexican territory, Pershing failed to capture the slippery revolutionary, and his own presence led to increased tensions—and even a couple of skirmishes—between Mexican troops and the United States.

Hoping to exploit the diplomatic situation, the German foreign secretary, Arthur Zimmermann, sent a message to the German ambassador in Mexico City, Count von Eckhart, in January 1917. Zimmerman wanted Germany and Mexico to "make war together, make peace together," with the promise of "generous financial support and understanding on our part that Mexico is to reconquer the lost territory in Kansas, New Mexico, and Arizona."[8] British Naval Intelligence codebreakers intercepted the telegram and dropped the bombshell on Wilson in late February.

When President Wilson made the telegram public, the American people became outraged. The sensational news changed public opinion overnight. Wilson addressed Congress on February 26, asking for permission "to supply our merchant ships with defensive arms, should that become necessary, and with the means of using them, and to employ any instrumentalities or methods that may be necessary and adequate to protect our ships and our people in their legitimate pursuits on the seas."[9] The House of Representatives granted him the authority, but a filibuster by one senator killed the bill in the Senate. Overriding Congress, Wilson issued an executive order arming the merchant ships, moving the United States closer to war with Germany.

The return to unrestricted submarine warfare took a huge toll on transatlantic shipping. At the beginning of 1917, all of America's ships combined could carry a total of about 1 million tons of cargo across the Atlantic.[10] In February, German U-boats sank 536,000 tons of Allied shipping. In March, the Allies' total tonnage losses climbed to 603,000, and U-boats sent additional American ships to the bottom of the Atlantic.

The loss of American ships and their crews, the Zimmerman Telegram, and a variety of other factors converged to propel America into the Great War. On April 2, 1917, Wilson delivered his speech to Congress urging it to declare war: "The world must be made safe for democracy."[11] After four days of deliberation, Congress declared war on Germany.

The Americans and the Allies worked frantically to build more ships, but they could not keep pace with the rate of losses. Soon Germany was sinking two to three times as many ships as were launched worldwide every month. As a result, merchants couldn't find the ships they needed to carry their goods.

To counter the losses, American shipyards began building six times as many cargo ships as they had been previously. Employment in the shipbuilding industry skyrocketed from 45,000 to 380,000. Much of the work took place at Hog Island near Philadelphia. The largest of America's seven shipyards, the muddy site had enough capacity to work on fifty ships at once, with spaces for fifty more at its piers. On average, workers could complete a single vessel in eighty-seven days, plus thirty-five more days for finishing. At its maximum capacity, Hog Island could launch a new ship approximately every few days. Despite the Herculean effort, the United States produced a total of only 107 steel ships, 67 wooden ships, and 4 composite ships.[12]

To make up the shortfall, the US government commandeered all German vessels docked in American harbors just prior to the US declaration of war in April 1917, nearly one hundred ships,[13] including warships and mighty ocean liners. The Allies were still losing vessels faster than they could build them or seize them. Germany was winning the war in the Atlantic, led by intrepid officers like Kapitänleutnant Victor Dieckmann, who commanded *Unterseeboot 61*.

Chapter 2

The Kaiser's
Killing Machine

Dawn, August 6, 1917,
Bay of Biscay, Aboard U-Boat 61

Twenty-nine-year-old Kapitänleutnant Victor Dieckmann peered through his high-powered binoculars. Scanning a horizon pierced by the golden rays of dawn, he spied a solitary Allied steamer in the distance. The day was fair, and the seas were calm, despite a slight westerly breeze that swept across his face. Sensing the possibility of another kill, the U-boat captain immediately ordered the crew of *Unterseeboot 61 (U-61)* to dive. Dieckmann's men scrambled down the ladder in the conning tower and closed watertight hatches before the sub dove under the blue-gray waters of the Bay of Biscay.

Since April 1916, Dieckmann had sunk or damaged more than forty Allied ships, and he was rapidly closing in on ace status.* Laid down by the German firm AG Weser in June 1915, the 220-foot, 756-ton[1] *U-61*, one of twelve boats designated Type 57,† was a high-tech

---

* The top U-boat captains, or "aces," each sank more than fifty ships with a combined weight of 100,000 tons. By March 1918, Victor Dieckmann's crews had sunk forty-three ships (93,446 tons) and damaged twelve ships (28,738 tons).

† There were forty-one types of U-boats, divided into the following main classes: U-boats built for export, gasoline-powered U-boats (some of the earliest models), oceangoing diesel-powered torpedo-attack U-boats (like *U-61*), U-cruisers, and merchant U-boats, which were heavier U-boats initially designed as undersea merchant ships but later converted into military vessels with larger deck guns and more torpedoes. This last

killing machine for its time, and Dieckmann knew how to handle it well. Inside the vessel's cramped and dirty quarters, bathed in a red-yellow light while the submarine was submerged, Dieckmann pressed his eye against the rubber guard of the sub's periscope. He focused through the Zeiss eyepiece and rotated the device on its axis, placing the Allied steamer in his crosshairs.

The veteran commander initiated a series of orders familiar to all U-boat crews, first instructing his men to set the depth the torpedo would run below the surface of the ocean.

"Ready first torpedo-tube!" Dieckmann shouted the instructions belowdecks into the control room of the submarine, and each crew member repeated the orders.

U-61 had four torpedo tubes, two in the stern and two in the bow. The men loaded the torpedo into the first tube and flooded the compartment with water. "Torpedo-tube ready," the torpedo mate reported through a voice tube in the forward compartment.

Dieckmann was a born leader, and after months at sea, the crew trusted his instincts. They worked perfectly with the machine they crewed. "The ship is like a live creature" with "the blending together in a single harmonious body of the steel and nerves and spirit of a thousand inanimate things with the whole human element," one U-boat commander explained.

Dieckmann next was likely to have directed, "Stand by for firing the torpedo."

Tension arced across the entire crew of the boat, and they anticipated the next command.

"Fire!"[2]

A slight tremor shook the submarine as the torpedo exited the craft.

---

category included *Deutschland*, a commercial U-boat that even made what was thought to be a peaceful appearance in America in 1916, but was also surreptitiously involved in a sabotage plot. Smaller craft included U-coastal torpedo attack boats that operated in the Baltic Sea, along with UC-coastal minelayers that disgorged deadly mines in and around the waters of German territory, and UE-ocean minelayers, which were large oceangoing vessels that could lay up to forty-two mines in foreign waters.

Dieckmann's boat carried six precious torpedoes, or "eels."[3] With such a limited number of torpedoes aboard for long war patrols, Dieckmann had to make every one count—with each hopefully sinking an Allied warship before the crew returned to a friendly port for resupply and refuel. One or two torpedoes were kept in reserve for the journey home in the event of an encounter with an enemy warship.

German World War I torpedoes were fickle. *U-61* was armed with G6 "gyroscopic" torpedoes. They were nineteen feet long, and the warheads contained 362 pounds of a TNT-hexanite mixture. Weighing as much as an automobile of the day, torpedoes were expensive and prone to mechanical breakdown: warheads failed to detonate, propulsion mechanisms didn't work, and torpedoes sometimes veered off course—wildly. One eel fired from a U-boat at an enemy vessel circled back and nearly sank the submarine that had launched it.

Aiming these deadly weapons was an art. The captain had to perform a myriad of calculations: determining the distance, speed, and course of the enemy ship as well as the depth the torpedo should travel below the surface. Dieckmann had to aim for where he thought the steamer would be twenty or so seconds after he gave the order to fire.

Clasping a stopwatch, the helmsman next to Dieckmann knew how many seconds it would take for the torpedo to reach its target based on the captain's firing calculations. The crew listened for the explosion indicating contact with the Allied vessel. The torpedo ran for about 1,800 yards, leaving a broad white streak of bubbles on the surface of the water from the compressed gas that powered the eel. Much to the crew's dismay, the torpedo struck the ocean floor instead of the intended target.

Like a fisherman allowing his catch to run out line, Dieckmann waited while the steamer drew away at a 260-degree angle. He then ordered his crew to surface so that they could finish off the Allied ship with the sub's deck guns.

WWI submarines utilized different power sources depending on whether or not they were submerged. When subs were on the surface, they could use their high-power diesel engines to close in on prey rapidly. However, these engines were noisy, required oxygen, and created toxic exhaust fumes, rendering them unsuitable for use underwater. Instead, they had nearly silent, but painfully slow, electric motors powered by massive batteries rechargeable on the surface when the U-boat ran on its diesel engines. Battery power allowed the submarine to travel at only half of its full speed, about 8 knots at best. Underwater, the U-boat possessed a maximum range of less than a hundred nautical miles.

Prior to surfacing, Dieckmann ordered his men to disengage battery power and recouple the diesel engines. Positioning his vessel with the rising sun behind him to decrease its visibility to the Allied steamer, Dieckmann then ordered his crew to close with the ship at full power. The twin diesel 1,800-horsepower engines of *U-61* churned out a robust 14.7 knots, while the Allied ship could manage only around 10 knots.[4]

Steering on a zigzag course to avoid torpedoes, the steamer desperately tried to escape. Surfaced, with ammunition loaded, Dieckmann's sub aimed and opened fire with its 105 mm deck gun, quickly sending three rounds toward the tanker *Campana*, and Body Bearer James Delaney.

CHAPTER 3

JAMES DELANEY
AND THE SS CAMPANA

Dawn, August 6, 1917,
Bay of Biscay, Aboard the SS Campana

Chief Gunner's Mate James Delaney and his crew were on watch in the SS *Campana*'s wheelhouse when they heard artillery shells whistling over their heads, barely missing the ship. The lookout in the crow's nest yelled that a submarine was off the starboard quarter, 7,500 yards to the stern. A general alarm sounded, and Delaney's crew raced to man the ship's armament: two 3-inch guns bolted to the stern of the ship. Their adrenaline surging, Delaney's crew plunged into their first combat.[1]

One day prior, *Campana*, a Standard Oil steamer, had left the deep-water commercial port of La Pallice, France, bound for Huelva, Spain. It had discharged its cargo of oil in France and had taken on ballast to provide stability for the journey to Huelva.

Delaney, a thirty-two-year-old from Boston, Massachusetts, commanded a thirteen-man crew of naval guards assigned to *Campana*. Separate from the ship's crew, the guards were on board solely to protect the ship from attack, and while on board, they answered to Delaney. Blue-eyed with dark brown hair and a ruddy complexion, Delaney stood nearly five feet eleven and weighed 160 pounds. A true salty man of the sea, Delaney was inked with numerous tattoos, including a list of ships on which he had served, a rooster, an Indian maiden's head, the words

"Rock of Ages," hands across the sea, and a crucifix. Having enlisted as soon as he turned eighteen, he had been a sailor his entire adult life. His service in the Navy would span both world wars.[2]

In March 1917, after Germany readopted the policy of unrestricted submarine warfare, President Woodrow Wilson signed regulations that would arm American merchant ships to deal with this menace. Within a week, two US merchant vessels, *Manchuria* and *St. Louis*, sailed with armed guards on board.

To govern the conduct of those armed guards, the Navy drew up a set of rules and regulations that would "enable the Armed Guard to give real protection to the ship, while still adhering strictly to the standards of International Law as understood by this country."[3] Often viewed as too restrictive, the regulations came under considerable criticism. Prior to America's declaration of war on Germany, they did not allow the armed guards to "take any offensive action unless first attacked" or unless a German submarine approached within four thousand yards of the merchant vessel. They were also not permitted to continue firing on a sub that was "retiring or attempting to retire. . . , unless it may be reasonably presumed to be maneuvering for renewal of attack."[4] Merchant shipping lines paid for the armament and supplied quarters, pay, and food, and the Navy furnished the trained personnel assigned to the ships.

The code of conduct for the men leading these crews was also very rigorous: "You must be the leader of your men. Good manners, coolness, and self-control are the first attributes of an officer. You must so control your men as to gain their respect and confidence. Remember it is expected of you to lead, and then to follow, whatever duty demands, even if death be the result. Be firm; be strict; be fair. Develop the teamwork of your command. . . . Never forget that good men with poor ships are better than poor men with good ships."[5]

The Navy expected commanders to exercise strict control over the gun crews. "Your success will depend very much on the discipline you maintain in your command. Instruct your men so they will see the necessity of observing the rules and regulations you prescribe. Make them realize the safety of the ship as well as their own lives depends upon the strictest possible performance of duty. . . . A recent report received by the department told of the complete failure of the Armed Guard to handle the situation created by the sudden appearance of a submarine. The men had been slouchy in their appearance, careless in their attention to orders, inattentive on lookout, and generally slack during the voyage. When the test of action came, they failed for lack of discipline."[6]

After the US Congress declared war on April 6, 1917, the Armed Guard program expanded, "as rapidly as the supply of guns would permit, to include all vessels traversing the so-called war zone."[7] Later, when U-boats began showing up near the shores of the United States, coastal vessels in the Atlantic also began carrying armed guards.

Delaney ran a tight ship. He instilled a strong sense of duty and discipline in his crew—discipline that would be put to the ultimate test as round after round sailed over *Campana*, barely missing the ship.

The captain of the steamer ordered his ship to its full speed of 10 knots, maintaining the undulating course to make it more difficult for the submarine to strike.

A desperate chase ensued.

Delaney and his men went to work. Raising the stern gun to maximum elevation to give its shells a chance of hitting the sub at such a long distance, Delaney ordered his men to commence "rapid fire."[8] Small plumes of ivory, frothy water rose close to the sub—near misses from Delaney's guns. The sub kept its distance, staying more than six miles from *Campana*, the maximum range of the steamer's guns.

"The chase continued. . . . The submarine firing continually at intervals of about forty seconds, and *Campana* replying with stern gun firing about one shell to two from the submarine." As the sub pursued, *Campana's* crew passed ammunition to the gun crew, who loaded the 3-inch deck gun and "fired 110 rounds of ammunition, continuous firing."[9]

More than an hour into the battle, the recoil and concussion generated by the artillery had taken a toll on Delaney's men, whose "eyes were badly swollen and whose ears were running blood."[10] Even after switching crews, "their eyes became swollen."[11]

Delaney then ordered his men to stop for a few minutes to recalculate the range of the U-boat. *Campana* slowed, and the submarine followed suit to remain outside the range of the Allied steamer's guns. One of Delaney's guards recalled, "[Shells were] bursting in the air above the ship, while our shells falling way short of the submarine."[12]

The cat-and-mouse chase persisted, as Dieckmann wisely kept his distance from the American guns. A single hit or even a splinter of shrapnel from Delaney's guns that pierced *U-61*'s hull could take away Dieckmann's ability to submerge, robbing him of the "equivalent of Samson's hair."[13]

Suddenly, one engine on *U-61* "dropped out of commission." But the loss of the engine didn't faze the veteran sub commander, who had been in scores of engagements with surface ships and had always come out on top. "With one engine full power and the other on battery at half speed, [we] closed the range," Dieckmann recorded.

Following a brief pause, the U-boat commander again opened fire. Dieckmann ordered "economical expenditure of ammunition," hoping to score a fortuitous hit below the waterline to disable or sink *Campana*. A little more than an hour after the commencement of battle, the German commander "scored the first hit" on his prey.

The commander reduced speed, buying time for his engineers to get the sub's second engine back online. He patiently waited for the opportunity to present itself to "close quickly to 60 hm. [about 6,500 yards] and attempt to finish him off with a sudden attack using both guns."

Even at the maximum range of their weapons, *Campana*'s guns were coming very close to hitting the U-boat. The American shells "whistle by close over us," recalled Dieckmann. "Enemy is now firing very stubbornly. Both shells of his fall close together and near the submarine." But the sub commander was able to avoid the potential

deadly impact by "stopping and using hard rudder" to change the sub's
direction.[14]

Throughout the entire engagement, Delaney remained unflinchingly at
his post, even as Dieckmann's shells began hitting their mark.

"After two hours, the submarine gun got the range, and shells fell
close to the stern. Four hits were made, one in the number one hold,
one in the number four hold, and one in the mid-ship on starboard side,
and one through the engineer's storeroom, which caused a fire. This
was extinguished by the ship's crew after causing leaks in the auxiliary
steam line."[15]

These leaks had a debilitating effect on *Campana*'s speed, and Captain Alfred Oliver wanted to abandon ship. Oliver, a New Yorker and
civilian sea captain of many voyages, recognized the hopelessness of the
situation and wisely wanted to sacrifice the steamer rather than his men.

Delaney and the third officer originally protested; however, by 9:40
in the morning, *Campana* had expended nearly all its ammunition and
was down to just ten shells of the 180 originally on board. The boat's
first officer, Andrew L. Mellgard, direly recalled, "It was then clearly
evident that we were completely outranged by the submarine, who by
now was making frequent hits."[16]

As the morning wore on, Delaney, seeing how close *U-61*'s shells
landed and how far they were outranged, finally relented. He gave the
order to abandon ship "in order to avoid useless loss of life."[17]

Delaney's gunners ceased fire. *Campana*'s crew sounded a whistle
and sent up code flags to indicate their intention to abandon ship. They
also sent a radio message: "Leaving ship."[18] But before they entered the
lifeboats, they placed all their papers, machine guns, ammunition, and
anything else that might be of value to the Germans in weighted bags
and threw them into the sea.

Still under fire, Delaney's men and the steamer crew loaded up
onto the lifeboats and lowered themselves down to the water. Despite
the ship's clear signals, "until 10:00, the submarine kept steaming toward

Campana and continued firing rapidly, shells striking the ship and falling all about the lifeboats."

Dieckmann continued attacking the steamer in the event that it was a decoy vessel or "Q ship."* As a ruse, the Allies would sometimes abandon ship in an attempt to lure an unsuspecting U-boat closer. Once the submarine was within range, the Q ship would reveal hidden guns and attack the German vessel. Dieckmann was not taking any chances with *Campana* and continued firing until all four lifeboats pulled a quarter mile from the ship and "lay to."

The submarine then moved toward the lifeboats at full speed and "nearly rammed the boats," but stopped alongside them with its large deck gun trained on the armed guard. Eight of the submarine's crew pointed their revolvers at the men on the lifeboats. Dieckmann shouted in nearly perfect English, "Captain of the ship come alongside and come aboard."

Captain Oliver obeyed Dieckmann's order and climbed aboard the U-boat. Dieckmann called out, "Lieutenant of the gunners." No one replied, and Oliver told Dieckmann that there was none aboard. Dieckmann retorted, "Man in charge of the gunners."

Delaney did not respond, but several of the guards reported that no one was in charge.

"All gunners, hands up!" Guns to their heads, the bluejackets obeyed.[19]

Dieckmann turned to the other three boats and inquired if there were any Englishmen aboard. Many Germans harbored a burning hatred for the British given their encounters at sea and the impacts of the Allied embargo on the German people. Heavily reliant on imported foodstuffs, millions of Germans starved because of the blockade, resulting in hundreds of thousands of civilian deaths. The population dined on ersatz food such as war bread containing sawdust and turnips. The U-boats represented Germany's chance to strike back at the draconian blockade.

---

* The name "Q ship" referred to Queenstown (now Cobh), Ireland, where the British constructed the vessels.

Toward the Americans, the Germans felt friendlier, despite the fact that the United States had officially entered World War I on April 6, 1917.

Hearing that there were no British among them, and realizing *Campana* was crewed by Americans, Dieckmann added, "I am sorry that America has entered the war and hate to fight Americans because I have always liked them, but I must do my duty. They are good sports and always play the game well. I hate the French and more especially the English."[20]

Next, the sub commander ordered the captain of the vessel, Delaney, and four other members of the armed guard onto the submarine, where they met Dieckmann's barrage of pointed questions: "Who fires the gun? Who points the gun? Who finds the range? Who gives the order to fire?"

Delaney and his crew coyly answered, "Anybody."

Unamused, Dieckmann conversed in German with his lieutenant and directed his attention toward the business of sinking *Campana*. "The Germans got into our boat and were towed towards the ship. They were pulled alongside by our gunners and went aboard." Dieckmann and his men began searching the steamer for confidential publications and instruments. Finding none, because the crew had dumped them overboard, the Germans began ransacking the vessel for copper and brass fittings and provisions, "principally canned goods, clothing, and bedding." After several weeks at sea and having expended all their fresh food, the U-boat crew were hungry and craved real food. Pillaging Allied ships to augment their supplies was standard operating procedure.

Interestingly enough, "they asked if we had any soap as it was the one thing they needed the most. And on being told that we had, made another trip for it."[21] According to one crew member of *Campana*, "All officers' rooms and crews' quarters were ransacked and robbed of everything of value."[22] The Germans even stole the meager supplies from one of the lifeboats.

The Germans attempted to take *Campana*'s deck guns and even rigged a block and tackle to load them onto the submarine. But removing the guns proved difficult, so they settled for taking the breach block and sights from both guns. They then placed mines in the forward hold of the ship and departed for the submarine.

At 12:00 Greenwich Mean Time, the mines were fired, and *Campana* disappeared under the waves an hour later. "During the interval of one hour, the *Campana* settled gradually, the first 55 minutes, but very rapidly during the last five minutes, disappearing in a final dive bow-first."[23]

With Delaney and the other Americans on board, Dieckmann ordered the men belowdecks. Next, the U-boat captain and his crew put away their revolvers and lined up on the deck of *U-61*, standing at military attention. They saluted *Campana*'s crew and the surviving members of Delaney's guard in the lifeboats. Dieckmann respected the resistance that *Campana* put up, noting in his diary, "After brave resistance, [*Campana*] surrendered after a three-hour battle and three heavy hits, of which one was in the engine room, because, so thought her Captain, men's lives were more valuable than ships."[24]

One of the survivors also noted that their captors provided parting advice to the sailors in the lifeboats. "The Germans talked very nice to us when we shoved away from the submarine," recalled one *Campana* crew member. "They warned us not to get on a French or English ship that was going to our rescue, that they were going to [sink] her."[25]

Around six o'clock in the evening, the French gunboat *Audacieuse* discovered the lifeboats and brought the men back to port. But for Delaney, Captain Oliver, and the four other members of the guard captured by the Germans and now on board *U-61*, the war was just beginning.

CHAPTER 4

Q SHIPS AND DEPTH CHARGES: *DAS BOOT*

As the six Americans descended belowdecks into the bowels of *U-61*, Delaney and the four other members of the armed guard became the first American naval personnel captured by Germany in the Great War.* They would experience firsthand the gripping life-and-death experience below the waves in one of the kaiser's iron coffins. Delaney's time aboard the sub began with the first of many interrogations.

After learning that Delaney was in charge of the gun crew, Kapitän-leutnant Dieckmann asked, "Where was your ship bound?"

"New York," Delaney replied.

Unconvinced, and knowing their true destination, Dieckmann countered that the ship was actually headed for Spain.

"I told him that I knew nothing about it as I had nothing to do with the navigation of the ship," Delaney later recalled.[1]

At that point, the sub commander dismissed the American gunner to the small compartment he would share with Captain Oliver. The other captives from the armed guard, Seaman Second Class William A. Miller of Chicago; Seaman Second Class Fred S. Jacobs of Pittsburgh; Boatswain's Mate Second Class Ray Roop of Boyne City, Michigan; and Gunner's Mate Third Class Charles Levan Kline of Reading, Pennsylvania, were also housed two to a compartment. They

---

* Germany captured about four thousand American fighting men during the course of the war.

would spend nearly all their time over the coming days in these tiny, cramped quarters.

A German U-boat comprised several major sections. One German sub commander described the vessel as being "like a large creeping cat, with back arched and bristling whiskers. The eye is represented by the periscope, the brain by the conning-tower, the heart by the control room."[2] The sub's hull made up the legs and the body of the cat. Thirty-six men occupied the sub's pressure hull, a large cylinder running from stem to stern on the boat. The bow and stern each contained a torpedo room. An engine room housed powerful diesel engines for when the boat operated on the surface, and electric battery cells engaged when the U-boat operated underwater. If damaged, these cells would release deadly chlorine gas and acid that could cause horrific chemical burns.

Pipes, tubes, valves, gauges, and dials were crammed throughout the U-boat, most of them terminating in the control room, where the crew would maneuver and guide the vessel. The submariners used a dizzying array of valves and levers in the control room to manipulate the rudder and hydroplane to pilot the ship. As in a surface ship, the rudder controlled the sub's direction right or left. The hydroplane lay at right angles to the rudder and directed the U-boat up or down when it was moving forward.

Somewhere within these cramped quarters, the men had to live. A mess and kitchen were jammed into the space, and collapsible bunks filled every nook and cranny.

Much of the boat's space, however, was occupied by giant tanks on either side of the inner hull. When the sub was diving, seawater filled the tanks; a series of pumps emptied the tanks when the sub surfaced. In general, the U-boat commanders preferred to maintain their vessels at neutral buoyancy. With the level of water in the ballast tanks perfectly balanced, the sub would neither sink nor rise, providing them the option of quickly flooding or emptying the tanks in an emergency situation.

Before setting out on a war patrol, the crews packed the boats to the gills with fresh food, which quickly spoiled. U-boat scavenging missions could be comical. On one patrol, a U-boat popped up in the midst of several French fishing boats. After listening to Allied propaganda,[3] the fishermen expected to be massacred at once but "laughed and cheered"[4] when they found out the U-boat crew wanted only fresh fish. After commandeering their daily catch, the German submariners jokingly gave the fishermen a bogus paper IOU from the French government as payment. Submerged for the evening, the U-boat crew feasted on the fresh catch fried and slathered in butter. In another incident, fed up with canned goods, a German sub crew landed on an uninhabited island and went ashore with rifles and hunted wild goats; this resulted in a "magnificent feast of roast goat."[5]

The food on board *U-61* was spartan. Delaney explained that the crew "mostly figure[d] on getting food from captured ships." For breakfast, the prisoners received coffee and some brown bread. The biggest meal of the day came at noon; the food was "hot and consisted of stew, macaroni, prunes, figs, etc." The typical evening meal consisted of nothing more than coffee. Despite the meager rations, the prisoners felt that the German crew treated them fairly. The Germans had little food themselves but "gave us everything they could to eat," Delaney remembered.[6]

During a long journey, the diesel fuel carried on the vessel seemed to seep into everything on board, including the food. Temperatures on the submarine regularly rose to more than a hundred degrees Fahrenheit, leading to an oily condensation known as "U-boat sweat." It made everything damp and provided the perfect conditions for colonies of mold to grow. One U-boat captain wrote, "The sweat which collects on the deck during the long journeys under water, just as in a dripping stone cavern, was falling on my head and into my food, and the film of oil . . . was thus deposited on my pea-soup."[7]

The quarters of a U-boat were a cramped, hellish space that reeked of sweat, mildew, and diesel fumes. The crew members wore a variety of leather outfits and nonconventional uniforms that typically did not allow their skin to breathe. Thirty-six souls crewed *U-61*, and the boat had just one toilet and no shower. Water use was rationed, and the reek of perspiration permeated everything. The toilet added to the unpleasant smell. The men could flush the lavatory only when the submarine was near the surface, or else the pressure would cause the toilet water, and everything in it, to blow back over the inexperienced crewman who had tried to flush. Delaney, Oliver, and the others were now additional bodies aboard the tiny boat, adding to the heat and stench.

Over the next week, Dieckmann would carry on several conversations with Delaney. At times he seemed simply to be making small talk, but at others he was obviously probing for details about American readiness for war. Around 4:30 p.m. on the day the Americans were captured, Dieckmann sent for Delaney.

Initially, the conversation centered on the battle they had recently fought. "He wanted to know if I would allow him to congratulate me on the long battle I had put up," Delaney recalled. He added, "The Captain told me that he believed that up until that date our fight was the longest and hardest fought battle that any submarine had."[8]

Both Dieckmann and his first lieutenant spoke fluent English, and for some time the American and the two Germans swapped stories as if they were merely sailors meeting in a bar. Like Delaney, the first lieutenant had spent time guarding a merchant ship, so he understood the nature of the job.

As the conversation continued, the men began a play-by-play dissection of the recent engagement. Delaney asked the captain how many rounds of ammunition he had fired at *Campana*. "The Captain would not tell me, but the First Lieutenant told me that he fired about 400 rounds or more," Delaney recalled. In addition, the lieutenant revealed that the sub had fired two torpedoes. *U-61* carried six torpedoes in total and had fired most of them on prior engagements.

"Who does the spotting of your shells?" Dieckmann asked next.[9]

"All the gun crew in the American Navy are taught to spot their own shells," Delaney replied.[10]

"How long have you been in the Navy?"[11]

Delaney lied: "About one year."[12]

At this point, Dieckmann boasted about how easy it was to sink Allied ships. In response, Delaney said, "I told him I could hardly believe it, and he said that he would prove it before we arrived in Germany, which would be in about nine days."

"What do the people in the United States think about going into the war?" Dieckmann wanted to know.[13]

"Everybody is up and ready."[14]

In reality, many Americans were not enthusiastic about the war. It had to be sold to the American public, and the man who did the job was George Creel.

Seven days after America's entry into WWI, President Wilson created the Committee on Public Information, a US government propaganda agency to release news on the war, censor news stories, and develop propaganda abroad. Creel led the committee, which later came to be known as the Creel Committee.

Street-smart with a hardscrabble past, Creel was the son of an alcoholic father and a mother who provided for the family by operating a boardinghouse. He ran away from home at the age of fifteen and worked at a series of county fairs. He received little formal education, but his mother had instilled in him a love of literature and writing. He had been a flamboyant supporter of Wilson's election campaign, and he brought all his substantial charisma to promoting the war effort. He became an investigative journalist and later even a police commissioner. Creel zealously and intensely sold the war to the American public. He recruited prominent journalists to join his Division of News, which put out more than six thousand press releases that provided fodder for more than twenty thousand newspaper articles. Creel also recruited movie stars like Mary Pickford, Douglas Fairbanks, and Charlie Chaplin to travel across the country and sell war bonds. His enthusiasm for the war effort inspired songwriters like Irving Berlin and George M. Cohan, whose morale-boosting hits helped drum up even more support for the American military.

Through the committee's Four Minute Men division, seventy-five thousand civilian volunteers spoke in public forums, often movie theaters, on topics such as victory gardens, the draft, and war rationing to bolster support for the war. To deal with the public's limited attention span, the volunteers limited their pep talks to four minutes—roughly the time it took to change a movie reel in 1917.

Creel was equally enthusiastic in his work to quash any criticism of himself or President Wilson. Pundits and commentators accused him of censorship, but they could do little to affect the flow of information. Creel controlled the news, and that allowed him to play a huge role in changing the minds of the American people about the war.

In the event that Creel's efforts failed, the Sedition and Espionage Acts clamped down with an iron fist on Americans' free speech. They fostered a climate of intolerance and self-censure. The Espionage Act, passed in 1917, prohibited support of enemies of the United States or interference with US military recruitment and operations.* During WWI, the courts applied it to prosecute the filmmaker behind the Revolutionary War movie *The Spirit of '76*, which they feared might generate distrust for the British. The Sedition Act of 1918 amended the Espionage Act and outright prohibited "any disloyal, profane, scurrilous, or abusive language about the form of government of the United States . . . or the flag of the United States, or the uniform of the Army or Navy." It was repealed in 1921.

The laws and the climate that they created also spawned the American Protective League (APL). Although officially a private organization, it was an amateur auxiliary of the Justice Department. By the end of the war, the APL claimed to have more than a quarter million volunteers, who snooped and spied on their fellow citizens. In reality, it was a giant vigilante force that often terrorized people unjustly and harmed, rather than helped, American law enforcement

---

* Still on the books and enforced to this day, it has been used to charge numerous socialists, communists, anarchists, whistleblowers, Jehovah's Witnesses, and even Edward Snowden.

organizations. The APL stifled debate and promoted an early-twentieth-century version of political correctness, spawned under the progressive Wilson administration.

After interrogating Delaney about American public opinion, Dieckmann switched topics and wanted details on the location of the American fleet.

"You better not go looking for them!" Delaney said defiantly.[15]

It was the final straw; Dieckmann had grown weary of the interrogation with Delaney. "He told me not to be so sarcastic and sent me below."[16]

It didn't take long before Dieckmann had an opportunity to make good on his promise to show Delaney how easy it was to sink a ship. At six in the evening, the sub's forward gun fired three times, and one of the sailors called out, "One more ship!"[17]

This prey was not as easy to take down as Dieckmann had hoped. The boat, disguised as a Spanish ship, launched three small lifeboats after spotting the Germans, in order to give the illusion that the crew had abandoned ship. However, when the sub came within two hundred yards, "she dropped her sides and let go three salvos." Ironically, they had encountered one of the Allies' decoy vessels, or Q ships, the very thing Dieckmann had feared when engaging *Campana*.

From the beginning of the war, the Allies had immense difficulty dealing with a U-boat's ability to submerge and launch sneak attacks. The earliest Allied ships attempted to shoot surfaced submarines, but the U-boats were able to submerge quickly, and this made them difficult to hit. Another tactic involved ramming a submarine at high speed with the bow of an Allied warship. But prior to the development of the depth charge, the Allies' best tactic for defeating submarines involved Q ships. These were nonmilitary vessels that the Allies outfitted with hidden armament.

One of the first Q ships was the HMS *Pargust*. Concealed behind fake lifeboats and compartments were swiveling twelve-pound guns. A four-inch gun covered by a dummy lifeboat was also mounted on the poop deck. When the vessel was under attack, hatches on the sides of the ship popped open to reveal the weaponry. The vessel also had two fourteen-inch torpedo tubes and a complement of active machine guns.

Upon sighting a U-boat, the *Pargust* crew set in motion a series of choreographed actions. Part of the crew would board lifeboats, feigning that they were abandoning the ship. The rest of the men remained on board. When the U-boat came close enough, they threw open the hatches, overturned the lifeboats, revealed the hidden weaponry, and turned their blazing guns on the unsuspecting submarine.

Almost immediately after realizing that they had encountered one of these deadly Q ships, Dieckmann ordered an emergency dive and took his vessel down to a depth of about two hundred feet. "The submarine seemed to stand on her bow end, everything capsized, and she submerged," Delaney recalled. "A little water came down the hatches."[18]

The esprit de corps of the crew and their trust in their captain and boat were affirmed by the efficiency with which they were able to execute the dive that saved their lives. Seconds separated life from death. A well-trained crew could get their boat under the waves in ninety seconds. Older boats, seen as death traps, could take as long as three minutes. Every second on the surface after a sighting by an Allied ship was more time for the decoy ship to fire at the U-boat or ram it, which was nearly certain to sink the sub. Another U-boat captain in a similar situation waxed poetic about the feeling the crew had of symbiosis between man and machine: "Brave, dear, true boat, how we learn to love you at such times." He added that he "would like to embrace you, as if you were a human being, for your intelligence and obedience, and for forgetting all your whims and becoming unselfish when all is dependent on you. We all trust you, all we men on board, just as we also trust each other, united as we are in common danger and in common success."[19]

Delaney, his fellow Americans, and the crew heard the shrill buzzing sounds of propellers from the Q ship over their heads. Seconds later powerful explosions rocked the boat from stem to stern. Depth charges or "ash cans," as the Americans called them, were the latest development in anti-submarine warfare tactics. Invented a few months earlier, the barrel-sized bomb contained several hundred pounds of high explosive, fitted with a timer that could be set for a desired depth for the charge to detonate. A direct hit from a depth charge could crack the hull of a U-boat in half. A near miss might damage the craft by springing leaks in the U-boat's seams, forcing rivets out of their fittings and potentially disabling the submarine. The Allied boat peppered *U-61* with numerous depth charges. According to Delaney, the German crew "was scared and they told us that our allies were trying to drown us."[20]

Although the depth charges didn't appear to have damaged *U-61*, the development of the depth charge had an immediate impact on U-boat operations, sending many crews to their death. One U-boat captain mused, "It was an evil invention and one destined to become part of our daily experience."[21]

Dieckmann fired a torpedo at the decoy ship, but it missed. Rather than be drawn into another lengthy battle, the German captain, who was running low on torpedoes, decided to remain submerged as the Allies, eventually thinking they had sunk the U-boat, left the area.[22] The Q ship then reported sinking *U-61*, and the US Navy followed suit by issuing a press release reporting the deaths of Delaney, his captured gunners, and Captain Oliver. A grim headline in *The New York Times* read, "American Gunners Lost on Submarine."[23]

Delaney, very much alive along with the other Americans, found out firsthand that one of the most perilous aspects of a U-boat war patrol involved sleeping at night in a surfaced U-boat. The chance of an accidental collision with an Allied or friendly vessel in the dark was significant if the sub remained on the surface. Many commanders would submerge to the safety of the depths. First the crew inspected the boat for leaks in the hull or valves. If everything checked out, "All tight!" would be repeated by the crew, followed by Dieckmann's issuing the order, "All hands rest!" The tension on the submarine was palpable; the men were constantly on their guard, nerves frayed. Resting on the ocean floor offered unparalleled solace. One captain opined, "An evening's rest on the bottom! No other evening's rest can be compared with it. An evening's rest after so much excitement and such a day's work. Can anyone realize how much we enjoyed it? We did not worry about the fact that we were not in harbor and that a mountain of water lay overhead; we felt as safe and snug as if we were in the most secure place in the world." The captain went on to describe the esprit de corps and élan of his crew, which were similar to the spirit Delaney and his fellow Americans undoubtedly witnessed in Dieckmann's crew: "The crew passed by us on their way forward from the eight spaces, the stern compartment, and the engine room. Pale faces smeared with oil and dirt, but with eyes beaming at me with pride and happiness as they went by, in a manner that rejoiced my heart."[24]

After an uneventful night of rest, the German sub crew would get another chance to prove their abilities the very next night, August 7, around the same time in the evening.

With the weather getting rough, *U-61*'s crew spotted an Italian ship *Trento*. After capturing its captain and sending him below with the Americans, the Germans set about destroying the vessel. "They were all night trying to sink her with bombs," Delaney said.[25]

Their difficulties in scuttling the ship resulted in an unexpected reprieve for the American prisoners. With the sub remaining at the surface, the Germans allowed Delaney and the others to come out on deck for a breath of fresh air and a smoke.

Continuing the friendly rapport he had initiated with Delaney, Dieckmann called for the gunner again. He offered the American a unique opportunity: the chance to look through the periscope at a British cruiser that had just come into range. Delaney took him up on the offer, but much to the chagrin of the German crew, Dieckmann again declined to fight. With so little armament left in its stores, the U-boat would let this prize go by. According to Delaney, "The sailors were damning the Americans for making them lose all their [precious] torpedoes."[26]

Dieckmann and Delaney resumed their conversation with Dieckmann remarking that he was "not in the habit of taking prisoners." Although the sub had sunk several vessels, prisoners were just troublesome, plus they required food that could otherwise go to the sub's crew.

"Why did you take us then?" Delaney asked.[27]

Dieckmann's reply was that he had used up so much ammunition in the fight with the American ship that he needed "proof of the battle."[28]

"Doesn't the kaiser believe his men?" the American asked cheekily.[29]

The commander cut him off in no uncertain terms: "You must not say that!" He immediately sent Delaney down below to his quarters.[30]

But the discussion wasn't over yet. The next day, Dieckmann again brought Delaney out of his quarters and asked "what the people in the United States thought about President Wilson and the war."[31]

"Everybody thinks President Wilson is a fine man, or he would not be president of the United States," Delaney replied.[32]

"The people of the United States will find out different later on," Dieckmann asserted.[33]

Delaney couldn't let that comment go by. "Germany will find out later on that she will have to take her hat off to us."[34]

Dieckmann took the reply with fairly good humor. "He said the Americans are noted for independence and that [Delaney and his men] were good types of Americans." With that exchange, the conversations between the two men ceased for the remainder of the trip back to port.[35]

Very soon, the sub commander would have more pressing matters on his mind than interrogating Delaney. About a week into the journey, the vessel passed through a minefield.

The captain ordered *U-61*'s crew to submerge, and it would remain underwater for the next nine and a half hours.

Navigating the minefield was incredibly tricky, even with the captain and crew knowing the location of the mines. If the vessel struck a mine, "it would roll along midships or aft and blow up." To avoid this dire possibility, the sub stayed as low as possible, but that put it in danger of crashing into the ocean floor, something it did with alarming frequency. "Every little while the submarine hit bottom and then would come up to a higher level," Delaney recalled.[36]

Those weren't the only close calls. "Three times a mine anchor cable scraped the side of the submarine." Delaney noted that each time the crew's faces grew pale as they waited to find out whether the ship would explode.[37]

Eventually, the sub passed out of the danger zone, and on August 15, it headed into port in Heligoland, an archipelago in the North Sea. As it made for the harbor, *U-61* docked next to a destroyer headed for Germany.

Before disembarking, the Americans got their first bath and shave since boarding the sub. "The submarine crew were very good to us and let us take their razors and shaving outfits."[38] Clean and shaven, the Americans posed for pictures topside on the sub. While none of them knew it at the time, it was a picture capturing thirty-six men who would soon be buried in an unknown watery grave. Seven months later, *U-61* sank in a depth charge attack in St. George's Channel on March 26, 1918. All hands were lost.

Dieckmann shook Delaney's hand before the Germans transferred him and his fellow Americans to another vessel, a destroyer that made its way to the northern German port at Wilhelmshaven, a boomtown that flourished as the kaiser's navy grew. One of the largest stations for U-boats, the young city swarmed with tens of thousands of sailors and the merchants, hoteliers, entertainers, prostitutes, and restaurateurs who catered to returning U-boat crews. The submariners knew that every trip ashore could be their last. They were determined to live life to the fullest, and Wilhelmshaven catered to their every need. They thronged the town's casino, restaurants, bars, and dance halls and helped give the port city a never-ending party atmosphere.

Unlike their captors, the Americans were arriving not as heroes but as the first American prisoners of war inside Germany. Another round of questioning ensued on board the destroyer, but the German lieutenant in charge of the interrogation was less than thrilled with the responses Delaney gave him. "He told me that I was insulting," Delaney recalled. "I would not give any information. He asked how long I was in the service, and I told him one year. He said I talked as if I had not been in very long."[39]

Fed up with Delaney, the lieutenant moved on to questioning Delaney's gunners, Miller and Jacobs, both of whom could speak German. Like Delaney, Miller offered belligerent answers.

"Where is the US fleet?" the lieutenant asked.[40]

"It's at home, and you better not go after it," Miller replied.[41]

"Tell the truth or you will be hung."[42]

"Well, you'd better start right in," Miller suggested, "You have all the information that you are going to get from me."[43]

That evening the Germans transferred the men to another vessel. This time, all the prisoners from *Campana* were housed together in a room on the third deck, which "looked like an old magazine."[44] And once again, Delaney was questioned, this time by a lieutenant "who looked very much like a Scotchman and spoke very good English."

"How long have you been in the service?" the lieutenant asked.[45]

"One year."[46]

"How long do you have to be in the American Navy to become a chief petty officer?"[47]

"Six months."[48]

To soften up Delaney, the lieutenant offered him a cigarette, which he declined, thinking it "might be doped." The German looked insulted. Then Delaney "told him the place we were imprisoned in was not fit for the worst criminal and that although we were prisoners we wanted decent treatment."[49]

"What do you think about the Jutland battle?" the lieutenant asked.[50]

"I'm an American," Delaney responded. "I don't know anything about Jutland except that the Germans got a good licking."[51]

In actuality, the Battle of Jutland had been closer to a draw with both the Germans and the British claiming victory. Between May 31 and June 1, 1916, 151 German ships and 99 British ships met in the North Sea off the coast of the Jutland Peninsula near Denmark. It was the largest surface battle of World War I, with the British losing 6,784 men and 111,000 tons, compared with Germany's losses of 3,058 men and 62,000 tons. The tactics and outcome of the battle remain a source of controversy to this day.

Not amused by Delaney's answer, the lieutenant told the gunner not to be so sarcastic, but the admonition had little effect. At this point, the questions surrounded the rise of the American Expeditionary Forces (AEF). "He asked me about doubling the Army and Navy," Delaney recalled. "I told him that I did not know anything about it, that I left before they started to do this."[52]

The interrogation marked the beginning of a long journey of captivity inside Germany for Body Bearer James Delaney and his compatriots.

As Delaney's captors pressed him for details, General John J. Pershing, the man selected to lead the AEF and tasked with "more than doubling the army," was making his own journey.

II

BUILDUP
1917–1918

CHAPTER 5

PERSHING AND THE AEF

General John J. "Black Jack" Pershing pulled his overcoat tight against his body in an attempt to ward off the cold as he walked the deck of the ship that was just leaving New York Harbor. Known for his ramrod-straight posture, the six-foot-tall, sandy-haired general appeared far younger than his fifty-six years. He peered back over his shoulder to what should have been the New York skyline; however, nothing met his gaze but the endless, impenetrable gray fog.

It was the afternoon of May 28, 1917, and the general had just boarded *Baltic*, the White Star liner that had been the world's largest ship until 1905, when even larger White Star vessels, such as *Titanic*, eclipsed it. For the next ten days,[1] the ship would be home to Pershing and the select group of men who would help him lead the American Expeditionary Forces (AEF) in France.* Their ranks included Pershing's friend and chief of staff James Harbord, future 5th Marine commander Logan Feland, future quartermaster general A. W. Brewster, and future generals Hugh Drum, Fox Connor, John Hines, and George Patton, who would have a pioneering role in the yet-to-be-formed American tank corps. For this inner circle, the voyage was no luxury cruise. Their packed schedules included two hours of daily French lessons, briefings from British officers, and appointments for health checkups, which included typhoid shots and lectures about the dangers of venereal disease. The men spent every spare minute in endless planning sessions, preparing to join their Allies and lead America's forces into battle. Throughout the

* A popular quip at the time was that "AEF" stood for "After England Failed."

journey, *Baltic* managed to avoid the German U-boats and their highly effective captains. In the spring of 1917, the United States faced the colossal task of mobilizing for war and building a huge army.

The Americans and Germans entered a desperate race. Could the Americans field an army before the Germans won the war on the Western Front? One general directly told Pershing after his arrival, "I hope you have not arrived too late."[2]

The task of creating an enormous independent American Army seemed insurmountable. Even Great Britain, with its long military history and experience in raising large forces, required fifteen months to assemble an infantry division for battle. For the Allies, America's ability to mobilize its troops posthaste would be a matter of life or death. Germany appeared to be on the verge of winning the war outright; the Allies' only hope for preventing the Germans from conquering Europe rested on the Americans delivering large numbers of troops to the field.

Entire American industries, such as railroads, were nationalized and placed under federal control. Washington set up an alphabet soup of agencies to manage the war; the government expanded greatly and dominated all aspects of the economy. Artillery would play a key role in the conflict, but the United States had only hundreds of artillery pieces, most of them 75 mm field guns. And the Americans had limited capacity to manufacture more. Instead, while they waited for their own production to catch up, they turned to the Allies, which by this time had a well-established artillery industry. The Americans generally traded raw materials and commodities in exchange for Allied artillery and, later, tanks.

America's primary focus was building an army. In 1917 the United States' peacetime Regular Army and National Guard numbered about 214,000 men,[3] less than even Belgium's army. But plans for the AEF called for sending millions of men to Europe. Pershing had to convert mobs of untrained Americans into a modern army. Training enlisted men would be relatively easy; building a trained and competent officer corps and infrastructure to support them would be far more difficult.

After arriving in France on June 14, 1917, Pershing had to create entire organizations from whole cloth. His handpicked team went to work and established supply chains, warehouses, assembly areas, training grounds, workshops, ordnance depots, hospitals, and a general staff college in France to train officers. They also needed to develop intelligence, tactics, and training regimens. Pershing's knack for picking the right men for the job enabled him to pull off a modern miracle in logistics and organization. In a relatively short period of time, America forged the American Expeditionary Forces.

The AEF's troops would come to be known as "doughboys." The etymology of the word is not entirely clear; however, it was likely first used during the Mexican-American War, perhaps because the dust that covered the men's uniforms looked like unbaked dough or the buttons on their uniforms resembled flour cakes called "doughboys." Or it might have been a derisive term, a description of field rations or a reference to the doughnuts that Salvation Army volunteers furnished for soldiers in the field.

Just as the origin of the name remains a mystery, this forgotten generation is also unknown to many Americans. Corroded statues of doughboys adorn small towns across the United States, but most passersby remain oblivious to the sacrifice they represent. Who was this generation? What inspired them? How did they fight? Most Americans either do not know or harbor misconceptions about the horrors of war the doughboys experienced. If they have any concept of the war at all, they envision the trenches and masses of men going over the top to their deaths.

But the story is far more complex than that.

In part, it is the saga of an extraordinary metamorphosis. While the American military included a small core of professionals, most of the doughboys were raw conscripts fighting the most seasoned army in the world. War is transformational; however, in this case the evolution of the unseasoned doughboys at the war's inception into the dauntless men they became is especially striking. The stories of the Unknown Soldier's Body Bearers reveal their generation's story of war.

* * *

One man in particular was responsible for the dramatic rise of the AEF: General John J. Pershing. Few general officers in America were more qualified to build the AEF than Pershing. But in early 1917, the War Department and President Wilson set their sights on another man: Major General "Fighting" Fred Funston. Five feet five and 125 pounds, the Medal of Honor recipient for his actions in the Philippines had bragged, "I personally strung up thirty-five Filipinos without a trial."[4] Funston, however, dropped dead of a heart attack in February, after which Pershing threw his hat in the ring.

Born September 13, 1860, on a farm in Laclede, Missouri, to a prominent local businessman who supported the Union during the Civil War by serving as a civilian merchant for the infantry, Pershing could recall Confederate soldiers looting his father's store when young Jack was nearly three years old. The memory of that raid and firsthand accounts of Civil War veterans left an indelible impression on Pershing and propelled him toward military service. One of six siblings, he attended a prestigious local high school and took a job teaching African American children for two years before enrolling in the North Missouri Normal School, which later became Truman State University. Dissatisfied with the academic opportunities in rural Missouri, Pershing applied to the United States Military Academy at West Point.

Arriving a few months before the term started, Pershing studied under a former Confederate officer renowned for preparing students for the entry exam. Pershing passed the test and distinguished himself immediately among the academy cadets. Over the next four years, he rose to first captain, the highest possible rank for West Point cadets. Duty-bound, resolute, steadfast, and unwavering, Pershing possessed presence and exuded authority—he was a natural leader. But as one cadet remarked, "Pershing was never the kind of guy you walked up to and greeted with a slap on the back and a crude remark."[5] In 1886, at the age of twenty-six, he accepted his first commission as a second lieutenant in the US Army.

At the time, the United States was embroiled in conflicts with Native Americans, and Pershing saw his first action fighting against the Apache and Lakota Sioux. Assigned to the 6th Cavalry, the future general served in the New Mexico Territory, California, Arizona, and North Dakota fighting against members of the "Ghost Dancer Movement"— Indians who believed that if they performed ritual dances they would be immune to bullets. These actions earned him a reputation for bravery and superior marksmanship. Pershing was a crack pistol and rifle shot, one of the best in the US Army. As a result of his experiences, Pershing came to believe ardently in the importance of rifle marksmanship to overcome the enemy—a tenet he carried into the Great War.

In 1891, he returned to his first career—teaching. He took the post of professor of military science and tactics at the University of Nebraska–Lincoln, which he held for four years while also attending law school. In his free time, he formed a prizewinning drill company, the forerunner to the Pershing Rifles fraternal organization for military drill.

Following his graduation from law school, Pershing accepted the assignment that would later earn him his nickname. Now a first lieutenant, he took command of a troop in the 10th Cavalry, one of the so-called Buffalo Soldier regiments that consisted entirely of African Americans led by white officers.[6] For two years, Pershing and his men patrolled the western regions of the country.

Having proven himself in the field, in 1897 Pershing again returned to teaching, this time at West Point. A strict disciplinarian, Pershing became unpopular with the cadets, who took to calling him "Nigger Jack"[7] behind his back, in reference to his service with the 10th. Over the years, the offensive nickname softened to "Black Jack," which was the version reported by the press. For his part, Pershing remained committed to the African American troops he commanded throughout his career, often advocating on their behalf, and his nickname would follow him for the rest of his life. He also never shook off his reputation for sternness. One of the officers who served under him would later explain, "Pershing inspired confidence but not affection. He won followers, but not personal worshipers, plain in word, sane, and direct in action."[8]

However, Pershing did inspire affection among one group—the young officer always had many female admirers.

When the Spanish-American War began in 1898, Pershing's brief career at West Point ended, and he returned to the Buffalo Soldiers of the 10th Cavalry, this time as the regimental quartermaster. He fought valiantly in Cuba, remaining "cool as a bowl of cracked ice"[9] while under the fiercest fire.

Following the Spanish-American War, Pershing headed to the Philippines after the archipelago became an American possession. The United States first crushed an insurgency led by Emilio Aguinaldo, who wanted Filipino independence, and then had to deal with the Moros, who generally were Muslim in the mostly Catholic Philippines. Assigned to the southern island of Mindanao where the Moro insurgency raged, Pershing built relationships with the various tribes and factions and tried to understand their cultures, languages, and rituals—he was using the fundamental principles of counterinsurgency before the term was even coined. Pershing's duty was not all hearts and minds—he had to contend with real threats, including *juramentados*, the nineteenth-century equivalent of suicide bombers who took an oath to kill as many infidels as possible before succumbing. He fought in multiple skirmishes and battles and received more than one citation for bravery. In the jungles and mountains of Mindanao, the *kris*, the Moros' ancestral blade that could sever a man in two with a single blow, met the .45 pistol. The powerful rounds of the .45 stopped many raging *juramentados* dead in their tracks. Black Jack listened to his subordinates and learned from his mistakes. He also forged alliances with some factions of Moros. These approaches would serve him well in the messy coalition warfare in France. Pershing's ruthless side also emerged. He wrote to his mother, "I have many very strong personal friends among the Moros. Some of them will do anything for me. If I should say: 'Go and kill this man or that,' the next day they would appear in camp with his head."[10]

Aware of Pershing's service record and proven abilities, President Theodore Roosevelt personally petitioned the US Army to promote him to colonel, but the Army declined, citing its policy of promotion based on seniority rather than merit.

Captain Pershing returned to Washington, DC, and made a decision that would have an immense impact on his life and military career. In 1905, he married Helen Frances "Frankie" Warren, the daughter of a powerful senator from Wyoming who chaired the US Military Appropriations Committee. That same year, Roosevelt, still irritated by the Army's refusal to promote Pershing to colonel, asked Congress to authorize a diplomatic posting for the forty-five-year-old officer. This time, Roosevelt got his way. Pershing headed to Tokyo, where he served as an observer in the Russo-Japanese War. When Pershing returned to the United States in the fall, Roosevelt nominated him for a post of brigadier general, which Congress approved, even though it allowed Black Jack to jump up three ranks and skip ahead of 862 other officers with more seniority.[11]

After a brief posting in the Balkans, Pershing returned to the Philippines as military governor of Moro Province. He brought his family, which now included four children. Once again, Pershing immersed himself in the culture, as he had to deal with a bewildering number of factions and tribes. Black Jack broke up his men and sent them into small outposts to live with the population. He continued to distinguish himself in battle, receiving a nomination for the Medal of Honor, which Pershing requested not be granted as he had only been doing his duty. Throughout this time, Pershing's relationship with his men followed the pattern established in his early career and tenure at West Point. They hated him for his strict discipline and cool demeanor, but they loved him for his unparalleled ability to lead. One veteran who said he "hated his guts" and called Pershing an "S.O.B." also noted, "But as a soldier, the ones then and the ones now couldn't polish his boots."[12]

In 1913, tensions between the United States and Mexico were inflamed. To handle the situation, the Army sent Pershing first to the Presidio in San Francisco and then to Fort Bliss in Texas. But before Pershing's family could join him at Fort Bliss, tragedy struck. A fire broke out in the Presidio, and his wife perished of smoke inhalation, along with their three daughters, Helen (age eight), Anne (seven), and Mary (three). Only his son Warren, then six years old, survived. Despite the catastrophe in his personal life, Pershing continued to execute his duty, organizing and leading the expedition into Mexico that attempted to capture Pancho Villa. He took ten thousand men deep into Mexican territory, but the expedition failed to apprehend the revolutionary. Yet it gave Pershing valuable experience that he would carry with him into World War I.

In the years before America entered the war, Pershing pursued a relationship with Anne Wilson "Nita" Patton, the younger sister of George Patton, Pershing's protégé. The two became engaged briefly, but the distance imposed by the war—and Pershing's wartime romances—ultimately doomed their love affair. Pershing later met a beautiful young painter, Micheline Resco, with whom he fell madly in love. He secretly set her up in an apartment in Paris.

In the second week of May 1917, President Wilson selected Pershing as the supreme commander of the AEF; Secretary of War Newton Baker conveyed this message to Pershing. Although Baker, the former mayor of Cleveland, was a pacifist devoid of military experience whose curiosity had never even been piqued by toy soldiers when he was a child, he nevertheless turned out to be an outstanding secretary of war, mainly because of his skillful delegation of authority. To Pershing, Baker verbally communicated a few simple orders, including that he select his own staff and leave for Europe as soon as possible. The final order: come home. Black Jack also received written orders from the president through Newton. The most salient: to form and fight as an independent American army. "The forces of the United States are a separate and distinct component of the combined forces, the identity of which must be preserved. This fundamental rule is subject to such minor exceptions in particular circumstances as your judgment may approve. The decision as to when your command, or any of its parts, is ready for action is confided to you, and you will exercise full discretion in determining the manner of cooperation."[13]

* * *

In the spring of 1917, the Allies went on the offensive with disastrous consequences. The British, fighting near the French city of Arras, initially made some territorial gains; however, the Germans' defensive tactics mauled the attackers. Ultimately, the British suffered more than 160,000 casualties. During the same period, the French launched the Nivelle Offensive, attacking in several other locations, including St. Quentin, the Chemin des Dames, and Champagne. It was named after General Robert Georges Nivelle, an ardent follower of the "cult of the offensive," which blindly urged the attack regardless of cost or circumstances. Supremely confident of success, Nivelle took his wine cellar to the field along with his favorite subordinates, including General Charles "the Butcher" Mangin, whose nickname stemmed from treating his men like statistical cannon fodder. Many on the French and British general staffs tried to stop the offensive they saw as hopeless, but Nivelle prevailed. The Nivelle Offensive rolled forward. Charging to their deaths, waves of infantry made frontal assaults against some of the most formidable defenses on the Western Front. The German defenses, part of what was known as the Hindenburg Line, lay on top of a high wooded ridge hollowed out with caves and tunnels.

Constructed during the winter of 1916–1917, the Hindenburg Line was a gargantuan belt of defensive fortifications spanning most of the Western Front. Germany had a manpower shortage, and the strategically constructed line helped alleviate that problem. The forward positions consisted of fortified concrete bunkers and blockhouses armed with machine guns and arranged in a checkerboard pattern. Behind those forward defenses, additional true defensive lines and German reserves, often beyond the range of Allied artillery, formed a defense in depth. Mazes of barbed wire surrounded the concrete bunkers, forming part of an elastic defense that funneled attackers into a miles-deep kill zone where they could be pummeled by German machine guns, gas, and artillery. As their defenses gored the attacking force, the Germans would mount a counterattack at vulnerable inflection points to hurl the Allies back.

Estimates vary, but French casualties may have neared two hundred and seventy thousand, including tens of thousands killed. Despite the failure, Nivelle refused to step down until General Philippe Pétain was named commander in chief. The Allies were exhausted.

Meanwhile, revolution had broken out in Russia in 1917. The political changes ultimately disintegrated much of the Russian Army, culminating in the collapse of the entire Eastern Front. Defeat now seemed a real possibility for the Allies.

As the year progressed, the Allies attempted some limited assaults on the Western Front without any greater success. Worse, the mounting losses and the Nivelle Offensive debacle had led to significant morale problems, particularly for the French; as many as twenty-seven thousand French soldiers mutinied during 1917. Rather than continue to sacrifice their troops for minimal gains, the Allies halted their offensives. Instead of attacking, they now defended their positions; but despite this, losses continued to rise. The Allies were desperately trying to hang on until America arrived in force.

Racing against time, Pershing and his staff spent the summer of 1917 building the infrastructure essential for an independent American Army. Thinking months into the future, they planned to fight in the Lorraine region, where links to the deepwater ports and French rail network would provide a source of supply. After arriving in Europe, American units would assemble and continue to train in proximity to where they planned to go into action: the Lorraine town of St. Mihiel, where a bulge in the front lines created a prominent salient.

Colonel James Guthrie Harbord, the fifty-one-year-old veteran of the Spanish-American War who had tracked Pancho Villa with Pershing and now served as the general's chief of staff, provided a snapshot of Pershing's character: "He thinks very clearly and directly; goes to his conclusions directly when matters call for decision. He can talk straighter to people when calling them down than anyone I have seen. . . . He has naturally a good disposition and a keen sense of humor. He loses his temper occasionally, and stupidity and vagueness irritate him. . . . He develops great fondness for people whom he likes and is indulgent toward their faults, but at the same time is relentless when convinced of inefficiency. Personal loyalty to friends is strong with him, I should say, but does not blind him to the truth."[14]

Drawing on all his prior experience from the Indian Wars to his military governorship in the Philippines, Pershing developed and expertly managed a sprawling organization. He set high standards and demanded success. One general officer recalled, "Pershing intends to build an army and he wants only results. He will crush anyone who gets in his way and ruin anyone who disappoints him."[15]

In May 1917, America resorted to a compulsory draft for the millions of men necessary to build, train, and supply Pershing's army. Men from ages twenty-one to thirty-one registered. Eventually, age limits changed to eighteen years old (seventeen with parental consent) to as old as forty. Plans for the draft submitted to Secretary of War Newton Baker called for four million Americans to be formed into an army, most of them through the draft. The bulk of the draftees would serve in what became known as the National Army (a temporary force intended to serve only during the war). The National Guard formed another group of men, and the professionals of the Regular Army comprised a third.[16] The lines of distinction among the groups sometimes became blurred, as some Regular Army officers were assigned to the National Army and some draftees were assigned to fill in the depleted ranks of the Regular Army and National Guard. Hundreds of thousands of Americans, including all the Body Bearers, did not wait to be drafted and volunteered for service.

Those volunteers included an unusually high number of African Americans. A little more than fifty years after the end of the Civil War, American society was still highly segregated, and African Americans faced rampant discrimination and hostility. Many viewed war service as an opportunity to prove their worth and perhaps gain better treatment for their entire race.

The Army, while highly inequitable, at least let African Americans fight. In this way, it was more progressive than the Navy or Coast Guard, where blacks could serve only in low-skilled roles. The Army had four all-black regiments, which were primarily led by white officers. After America entered the war, it took just one week to fill the ranks of these regiments completely, and the War Department started turning away African American volunteers. About 350,000 African Americans served in WWI.[17]

The black draftees and volunteers continued to serve in segregated units, and few African Americans saw combat in the Great War. Most served in labor battalions and support, although the War Department did create two black, segregated combat divisions—the 92nd and 93rd (provisional, not completely staffed)—in 1917 in response to the black community's demand that African American soldiers be allowed to fight. Several units, notably, the 369th Infantry Regiment, otherwise known as the "Harlem Hellfighters," served heroically under French command. More than 170 of the 369th's members received the French Legion of Merit. Another regiment, the 371st, served under the French Red Hand Division.* The Army made one other significant change during the war: it began training black men to serve as officers in all-black units. Despite this adjustment, black men who served as both enlisted personnel and officers faced harsh, racist treatment from their brothers in the military. African Americans would not be integrated within the American military for another generation.

---

* While assigned to the Red Hand, Corporal Freddie Stowers led an assault on a German trench, where "interlocking bands of machine-gun fire and mortar fire caus[ed] well over fifty percent casualties. Faced with incredible enemy resistance, Corporal Stowers took charge, setting such a courageous example of personal bravery and leadership that he inspired his men to follow him in the attack." Wounded twice and suffering from a loss of blood, Stowers crawled forward "urging his men to continue the attack on the second trench line." Motivated by his actions, the Americans captured the German position as Freddie bled out and died on the hill. He received the Distinguished Service Cross and was recommended for the Medal of Honor shortly after the war. Seven decades later, the Army reviewed Freddie Stowers's citation and elevated the award to the Medal of Honor. President George W. Bush presented the decoration to Stowers's two surviving sisters. (Quotation comes from Stowers's Medal of Honor Citation.)

* * *

To receive the influx of men and transform them into warriors, camps and cantonments sprang up around the United States. Initially, uniforms and weapons were scarce, and many men drilled in civilian clothes with brooms and wooden weapons filling in for the real thing.

At full strength, American divisions consisted of about 27,000 enlisted men and 1,000 officers—around twice the size of Allied or German divisions. The Americans organized their military into "square" divisions, so named because they consisted of four infantry regiments, which resembled a square on an organizational chart. Those four regiments could be grouped together into two brigades. The regiments were further subdivided into three battalions, each of which included four companies of around 250 men each. In addition to these infantry units, the division possessed its own artillery brigade and a regiment of engineers and supply and communication units.

To the Europeans, who had military traditions that reached back centuries, the idea that these untested and, in their view, inexperienced, troops could defeat an enemy that had stymied them for years seemed an impossibility. When he arrived in France, Pershing ascertained that the Allies distrusted his capabilities and the capabilities of his men. The British and French commanders wanted to integrate the Americans within their own forces, filtering individual soldiers into their own regiments as replacements for their losses—so that the Americans would amount to cannon fodder. However, Wilson had insisted that the American Army fight as a distinct unit—a directive that Pershing staunchly obeyed. In addition, the British and French each desired ultimate control over the armies, resulting in an internal power struggle, a running battle that Pershing would fight for nearly the entire war.

Black Jack correctly believed that his million- or two-million-man force, once in the field, could ultimately make the difference that would break through the stalemate of the war. Cynically, the Allies didn't want the Americans claiming credit for winning the war with their large independent army.[18]

Pershing's peers included three men: Marshal Ferdinand Jean Marie Foch, General Henri Philippe Benoni Joseph Pétain, and Field Marshal Douglas Haig. France's Foch was an aggressive strategist. This professor of military science, like his colleague Nivelle, had an almost reckless adherence to the cult of the offensive. His words highlight his tenacity and willingness to attack: "My center is yielding. My right is retreating. Situation excellent. I am attacking."[19] Bold but "chair-borne," Foch never slept in the field with his men. Renowned for his punctuality with meals and other habits, the marshal always went to bed deep behind the lines in his command post at the same time, even during raging battles. After the German offensives in 1918, the Allies determined they needed unified command and named Foch commander in chief of the Allied Armies.

Foch's right hand, the commander in chief of the French Army, Pétain, was a more conservative strategist, earning the name "Lion of Verdun" for his defense of the strategic town.

Also involved in the military planning was Haig, who commanded British forces in France. Cut from the same cloth as Foch, Haig became known as the "Butcher of the Somme" for his epic and costly offensives that killed hundreds of thousands of his countrymen.

Pershing got along well with Pétain, and they shared similar traits. They were nearly the same age, strong willed, and ambitious. In one of their first meetings, Pétain explained the urgency of the situation and how close the war teetered on the edge of defeat, saying, "I hope it is not too late."[20] He added, "The Allies will not acquire numerical superiority until the American Army is in position to send a considerable number of divisions into the lines. Until then we must avoid ruinous losses and maintain a waiting attitude."[21]

Complicating the relationship among these leaders, some of the Allies viewed Pershing as an intellectual who had attained his position through political connections. His education and law degree set him apart from his British and French counterparts, who lacked experience considering or dealing with issues beyond their narrow military focus.

But Pershing had the full backing of President Wilson, while the British and French leaders stood on much shakier ground with their political leaders. Pershing was also remarkably stubborn and possessed a knack for getting his own way. When his rivals schemed to minimize the importance of his position, they often found that he had outmaneuvered them. His years of experience in the Philippines had schooled Black Jack in the art of coalition warfare, something no American general had needed to master since George Washington.

Remarkably quickly, Pershing and his staff built an army that would shape the course of the war and modern warfare.

CHAPTER 6

ERNEST AUGUST JANSON:
FIRST TO FIGHT

With his rifle in hand and brown campaign hat pressed down firmly on his head, Body Bearer Gunnery Sergeant Ernest August Janson strode down the gangplank of the USS *DeKalb* to set foot in France. It was June 26, 1917. As members of the 49th Company of the 1st Battalion 5th Regiment Marines, Janson and his fellow Marines were attached to the hastily assembled 1st Division (Regular), the earliest American ground troops deployed to France. Their gear stuffed into knapsacks and slung across their shoulders, the men of 1/5 disembarked from the ship that had briefly served as home and took what for most were their first steps on French soil.

DeKalb had departed the United States just twelve days earlier. Like many of the vessels operated by the US Navy, it had originally been a German ship that the United States impounded. When America entered the Great War, the Navy repurposed the cruiser formerly known as *Prinz Eitel Friedrich* as a troop transport capable of hauling more than a thousand men across the Atlantic. Traveling in convoy with several other vessels, including the USS *Henderson* and USS *Hancock*, *DeKalb* was attacked but managed to avoid torpedoes fired from a German U-boat and safely deposit the Marines she was carrying in the port city of Saint-Nazaire.

To keep the convoy's route secret from the Germans, the Allies had safely guarded the location where the first troops would unload; however, the arrival of thousands of Americans was impossible to hide from the local population. As the men formed into their ranks on shore, a crowd of residents gathered to watch and cheer. Built on some of the swampiest ground in France, the bustling seaport, located about 270 miles southwest of Paris, was home to thriving fishing and shipbuilding industries, as well as a number of legal brothels. Pershing immediately designated the brothels off-limits. The troops would spend about three weeks in Saint-Nazaire before boarding the trains that would take them about 420 miles northeast to the tiny farming village of Naix-aux-Forges, located in the Meuse department of France.

Born August 17, 1878, in New York City, Janson was nearing his fortieth birthday in the summer of 1918; this made him an old man in the eyes of the men he led. He had originally enlisted in the US Army under his real name, Ernest Janson, and served for ten years before going absent without leave, a criminal offense. He later had a change of heart and reenlisted in the Marine Corps. To avoid detection, he altered his name to Charles Hoffman before joining the Marines.[1] His ruse worked, and Janson was a model Marine. His service records state that he was an expert rifleman and a sharpshooter.[2] He had received a promotion to sergeant in 1914 and served aboard US Navy ships during the lead-up to America's involvement in the Great War. In the first weeks of May 1917, Janson and many of his fellow Marines, who had served as members of the Marine Guard on board the USS *New Hampshire*, formed in the 49th Company, 250 men strong, at Norfolk, Virginia.

The 49th had a colorful and diverse start. Dubbed the "foreign legion,"[3] the company gained a reputation as a dumping ground for ADIs (aliens who had declared their intention of becoming US citizens) and crews from foreign ships interned by the United States. Some of these crews made their way into the Corps and into the 49th, "where the best were kept, and each one made good."[4]

Captain George Wallis Hamilton commanded the 49th. An outstanding officer, Hamilton led by example. He enjoyed the love and respect of his men, who fondly called him "skipper." Born on July 5, 1892, to an upper-middle-class family, including a father who was a correspondent for *The Washington Post*—Hamilton was twenty-one when he joined the Marines in 1913. He had briefly attended Georgetown University, where he played football, before dropping out and getting a job at a nearby bank. Disliking banking, he took and passed the Marine Corps officer exam. During training, Hamilton excelled in marksmanship and won numerous rifle competitions, which would serve him well in battle. Like Janson, he had been assigned to a variety of navy ships and *New Hampshire* before heading to France.

Hamilton, Janson, and the older noncommissioned officers (NCOs) trained the company, and at the end of May, the 49th became part of the 1st Battalion of the 5th Marine Regiment commanded by Major Julius S. Turrill, a forty-two-year-old mustachioed veteran from Shelburne, Vermont.* Known as the "Fighting Fifth," the regiment consisted of three battalions: 1/5, 2/5, and 3/5.

The history of the US Marine Corps begins prior to the establishment of the United States as an independent nation. On November 10, 1775, the Second Continental Congress approved the creation of two battalions of Continental Marines; the modern Marine Corps still proudly celebrates this date as its official birthday. The unit acted as shipboard fighters for the fledgling Continental Navy. In February 1776, the Marines embarked upon their first mission—an attack on a British fort in Nassau in the Bahamas. Marines also joined Washington's army and battled the British at Princeton and would progress to play a decisive role in many of the key naval battles of the Revolution. After the war ended, Congress disbanded the Continental Marines and sent the men home, only to reestablish the US Marine Corps in 1798.

From that time to the present, the US Marine Corps earned a reputation as an elite force that could turn the tide of battle in both

---

* Three companies—the 49th (B Company), the 66th (C Company), and the 67th (D Company)—composed of Marines largely serving as ships' guards formed the 1st Battalion. This book follows Janson's 49th as a through line because it was involved in nearly all the major engagements of 1918.

small and large conflicts. Whenever America required a cohesive, tough-as-nails, highly mobile amphibious force, Marines answered the call. They fought pirates in the First Barbary War, stood firm against the British in the War of 1812, led expeditions in the Caribbean and South America, battled the Indians in the Seminole Wars, assaulted the Halls of Montezuma in the Mexican-American War, escorted Commodore Perry to Japan, assisted in the overthrow of the Kingdom of Hawaii, played key roles in the Spanish-American War and the Philippine-American War, and took part in dozens of other nineteenth-century operations in China, Japan, Korea, Mexico, Uruguay, Haiti, Samoa, Panama, Cuba, and many other countries.

Despite its long and storied history, the Marines remained a relatively small branch of the US military prior to World War I. Since 1834 the Marines have been a component of the Department of the Navy. On the day the United States entered the Great War, the Corps had 419 officers and around 13,000 men.[5] Within a month, Congress approved expanding that latter number to 31,000.

In early 1917, the Marine Corps launched a recruiting campaign under the slogan "First to Fight." In response to the large number of young men who responded to the call, the Corps became extremely selective about those it would accept. To become a Marine, a man had to be between the ages of eighteen and thirty-six, and "not less than five feet five inches, nor more than six feet two inches in height; weigh not less than 130 pounds." In addition, the Corps wanted a man of "steady and regular habits; unmarried, with no one wholly dependent upon him for support; of good health, strong constitution, well formed, sound as to senses and limbs and not addicted to the use of intoxicants or drugs."[6] Few men met the stiff requirements. For example, in the month of April 1917, 14,607 men applied to the Corps; of those, only 2,864 were accepted for enlistment. The medical officer rejected the vast majority, 11,673, as unfit for service.[7]

Not only were the new officers and enlisted men imposing physical specimens, but many were highly educated as well, having attended institutions such as Yale, Harvard, Cornell, the University of Wisconsin, Virginia Military Institute, and the University of Minnesota. One Marine officer noted, "Sixty percent of the entire regiment—mark this—sixty percent of them were college men. Two-thirds of one entire company came straight from the University of Minnesota."[8] As one combat-decorated officer reflected, "If we had the opportunity to pick men individually from the United States, I doubt whether we could have much better. There were as fine a bunch of upstanding American athletes as you can meet, and they had brains as well as brawn."[9]

Most of new recruits headed to Parris Island, or P.I., while a smaller number trained at Mare Island north of San Francisco. Before the war was over, 46,202 men would pass through Parris, while 11,901 received their initial instruction at Mare.[10] Parris Island was a swampy piece of sand off the South Carolina coast, most notable for its enormous population of mosquitoes and omnipresent sand. In the summer of 1917, the recruits resided in canvas tents and slept on bedding infested with vermin. One raw recruit recalled, "I thought they had landed us on an island for the insane; but later I was told it was the old quarantine camp."[11] As newcomers arrived by barge, those who had been there a while greeted them, yelling, "S.O.L., shit out of luck."[12]

Not only was the environment unforgiving; formidable drill instructors (DIs) barked orders at the recruits in endless, profanity-laced tirades. The young college boys and other men soon discovered that nothing they did was good enough to please these grizzled veterans. In the words of one recruit, the instructors were "old Marines, the tall, straight, mustached professionals who dressed their pride in gaudy blue uniforms, decorated their bodies with salty tattoos, fed their thirst with chewing tobacco, frequently dipped snuff, assuaged fatigue with whiskey, cursed with the metric vigor of Kipling, drilled their troops night and day, held frequent and demanding inspections, and knew everything there was to know about the Springfield 03 rifle."[13] The drill instilled unwavering discipline.

The men endured an extraordinarily intense eight-week regi-men of training and work detail; some would argue it was even more difficult than that endured by the legendary French Foreign Legion. As soon as the recruits arrived, they began marching, practicing formations, and learning to handle their rifles. Calisthenics drills often required them to hold their eight-pound weapons over their heads in the hot sun until their arms trembled and their muscles cramped with fatigue. They spent a full two weeks on the rifle range, where many qualified as expert marksmen. The honor bestowed a small financial reward as well as bragging rights; expert riflemen earned an extra five dollars per month. The Marines' exceptional rifle abilities were—and remain to this day—a point of pride. In 1917 this prowess astounded their European allies.

Their two-month stay on Parris Island transformed the men, fortifying them for battle and building mental toughness that lasted a lifetime. One Marine eloquently wrote, "The first day at camp, I was afraid that I was going to die. The next two weeks my sole fear was that I wasn't going to die. And after, I knew that I'd never die because I'd become so hard that nothing could kill me."[14] Enduring the excruciating ordeal left the Marines feeling confident in their abilities and infused them with the grit and determination they would need to prevail on the battlefield. The DIs also imbued the men with the proud history of the Corps. One recruit explained, "The island should not be visualized as an island of total gloom and grim torture, but as a place where sissies and boys are made into men. A place where people on leaving have few regrets, but admire, respect, and appreciate the products of its labor. The island is a workshop and not a playground for pleasure-seeking playboys. [It is] a tough school that turns out tough graduates."[15]

Having survived P.I., the men next headed to Quantico, Virginia, for more training. In the same way that sand was omnipresent on Parris Island, mud pervaded Quantico. Because of the haste to set up facilities to train thousands of new Marines, the grounds took on the appearance of a mining camp. A legion of construction workers chopped down the forest and in its place erected a collection of ramshackle wooden huts that provided minimal protection from the elements. When it rained, the paths between the huts became a soupy morass, sometimes concealing the multitude of stumps and other hazards that caused the men to trip and fall as they navigated the camp. The sludge sometimes grew so thick that trucks could not get through and instead sat mired in the mud.

The Marines assigned fifty men to each of the huts, which often had cracks in the walls that allowed sunlight, wind, rain, and occasionally snow to enter. The men who slept there did not even receive blankets, and some resorted to using mattresses to cover themselves while they slept.

The training proved to be as harsh as the accommodations. Before the sun rose, the trainees would begin their day with calisthenics, rifle drill, and a run in formation—all before breakfast. As the war progressed, French and British soldiers provided instruction in trench warfare, and the Marines practiced digging fortifications, slowly transforming Quantico into a piece of the Western Front. They also learned to fight with bayonets and throw grenades safely. They even endured simulated gas attacks in preparation for what they would encounter in Europe. The whole experience aimed to forge the mental toughness that the Marines would need as they faced one of the most determined and battle-hardened armies in the world. The shared misery and brutal training fostered fellowship, brotherhood, and esprit de corps, vulcanized in the crucible of battle.

The Marine Corps can lay claim to having fired the first American shot of WWI after the United States declared war. Hours after President Wilson signed the congressional war resolution on April 6, 1917, a contingent of Marines and US Navy personnel headed toward the German cruiser SMS *Cormoran* in Guam, with orders to take the crew prisoner and commandeer the ship. The vessel had sought refuge in a harbor on the island in 1914 while fleeing British warships and had not been allowed to leave. For nearly three years, the *Cormoran*'s crew and Americans had lived in harmony.

Hoping for a peaceful resolution to the situation, a US Navy officer boarded the ship and handed the captain an official letter demanding that he surrender the vessel. The captain responded, "I am willing to turn over the officers and crew of the *Cormoran* to your charge, but I cannot turn over the ship."[16]

The naval officer replied, "Then I have to inform you, sir, that when your answer is received, you will be treated as an enemy, and your vessel as an enemy vessel."[17] He then saluted and requested permission to disembark.

As he jumped onto a nearby barge, men throughout the ship shouted, "*Cormoran! Cormoran!*" A band played, and Germans started throwing boxes and life preservers into the water. The crew dove into the ocean, and the captain departed on a motor launch. Shortly afterward, "there came the dull heavy shock of muffled underwater explosion. Red flames with little smoke shot up around the bridge of *Cormoran*; pieces of debris rose, arched, fell; the bridge and region of the captain's cabin popped up, crumpled, collapsed."[18] Hundreds of heads bobbed in the water. "A strong true deep voice"[19] began singing "Deutschland Über Alles"; the rest of the men joined in.

The Germans eventually lost a total of seven crewmen from the sinking. The captain and a portion of his crew made their way to shore. After docking, the captain, continuing in the spirit of not handing over anything useful to the Americans, ordered the engine on the launch demolished. A German engineer on the launch picked up a large sledgehammer. Anticlimactically, "a Marine sentry seeing the pantomime, and sizing up the situation, snapped his gun to his shoulder, sighted on the engineer, but as he fired, the muzzle of the gun was thrown violently by a Marine officer who stood near, and the shot went harmlessly overhead."[20]

The Marines almost did not have the opportunity to fire another shot in the war. Wilson had campaigned for president on the slogan "He Kept Us Out of War" and was reluctant to send American troops to France until the country could form a substantial American army.

The Army general staff believed sending troops piecemeal into battle would result in slaughter—but this is exactly what the Allies wanted, amalgamation of American forces into their exhausted armies. The two sides reached an initial compromise that avoided amalgamation: a US Army division, the 1st, formed from Regular Army regiments and volunteers, would immediately ship out for France to provide support for the beleaguered Allied forces. The remainder of the AEF would not ship out until later and would fight as an independent army. However, the battle over amalgamation would rage throughout the entire war.

While the Army stood up the 1st Expeditionary Division,* the commandant of the US Marine Corps, Major General George Barnett, maneuvered behind the scenes to get his Marines into the fight. Because of a rivalry that persists to this day, Barnett knew the Army would demur and perhaps even refuse to have a Marine brigade contained within an Army division. Barnett worked with his superior, Secretary of the Navy Josephus Daniels, to appeal directly to Secretary of War Baker. Army Chief of Staff Tasker H. Bliss gave way. The Navy supplied the vessels to transport the Leathernecks to France, and the Fighting 5th Regiment became one of the first US military units to arrive in Europe.

After their brief stay in Saint-Nazaire, Ernest Janson and the 49th boarded "forty men and eight horses" train cars and traveled inland to Naix-Aux-Forges, where the 1st Battalion 5th Marines trained intensively under the Chasseurs Alpins, or Alpine Hunters, nicknamed the "Blue Devils," an elite French unit renowned for its skills in climbing, cross-country skiing, and mountain warfare. "The tedious grind of preparation was on,"[21] but the Marines and *chasseurs* found "that they had much in common and through the remainder of the war, Alpine Chasseurs and the US Marines were devoted brothers-in-arms," recalled the Marine responsible for writing the battalion history.[22] The French

---

* The 1st Expeditionary Division was later designated the 1st Division (Regular).

troops passed on valuable skills acquired during the Great War, including trench construction, machine-gun assembly and operation, automatic-rifle marksmanship, grenade use (throwing in the French manner, a high-arcing toss), night attacks, and small-unit combat formations that had proved effective for trench warfare. By the time Pershing and Pétain arrived for inspection on August 17, Janson and the others had made significant progress and were nearly ready for battle. Turning out for inspection along with the rest of the troops was a "black and tan crippled dog known as 'Parade Rest,'"[23] who had been adopted by the 49th as a mascot.

The men trained for gas attacks and bayonet use but mainly endured endless miles of painful, ball-busting forced marches in full equipment. One Marine remembered, "Cold wet and hungry we marched, hour after hour, each man bearing a pack weighing about forty-five pounds consisting of two blankets, a supply of underclothes, a pair of trousers, 100 rounds of ammunition on our belts, emergency rations of hardtack, and 'monkey meat' [a canned beef reviled by most troops]."[24] The forced marches continued. "Erect, determined, undaunted, the tramp, tramp of our hobnail shoes brought us nearer and nearer to the front."[25]

On September 23, 1917, the 1st Battalion 5th Marines again loaded up on French trains, this time headed for the village of Breuvannes, about fifty miles south of Naix-aux-Forges. They set up a regimental headquarters position and continued drilling.

While the 5th trained, Commandant Barnett pressed to get more Marines into the action. In July, the Corps activated the 6th Regiment, a unit composed almost entirely of newcomers, many of them college graduates. After a concentrated training period in Quantico, the 6th began shipping over to France in September 1917 along with the 6th Marine Machine Gun Battalion. On October 23, 1917, the newly arrived Marine units had officially joined the 5th Regiment to form the 4th Marine Brigade, which became part of the 2nd Division (Regular).[26] This division also included soldiers in the US Army 3rd Brigade (9th and 23rd Regiments) as well as the 2nd Brigade (12th, 15th, and 17th Field Artillery Regiments) and 2nd Engineer Regiment, among other units.

Several of these units included men who would become Body Bearers and would fight in significant battles throughout the course of the war. US Army Major General Omar Bundy arrived in November to take command of the 2nd Division, which continued its training throughout the winter of 1917–1918.

Ernest Janson and his fellow Marines arrived in France wearing their distinctive forest green wool M1917 uniforms. "At the time, the Marines were said to be the best-dressed soldiers in France."[27] The four-pocket tunics bore the Marine Eagle, Globe, and Anchor (EGA) buttons and disks that fitted on the collar of the uniform. Older Marines, veterans of fighting in Haiti and other small wars, also had summer cotton khaki uniforms. The US Army, on the other hand, had its own wool uniform for the enlisted men. Once the Marines' beloved forest greens wore out in the field, they were forced to use the Army supply chain and wear the Army's uniforms. Many enterprising Marines saved their Marine Corps buttons emblazoned with the EGA and sewed them on their Army uniforms.

Officers purchased their uniforms from clothiers such as Brooks Brothers or had them hand-tailored in France. The uniform had a narrow braid sewn around each cuff and rank insignia on each shoulder strap. They were expensive and difficult to replace in battle.

Generally, the uniforms' wool was coarse and itchy to wear. Even worse, it did not breathe—the men sweltered in their uniforms on hot summer days. As a result, they sometimes shed the tunics and wore button-down shirts. Wet wool retained water and did not dry quickly. The damp uniforms became the perfect breeding ground for lice, fleas, and other bloodsucking vermin that the doughboys called "cooties."

The men wore chunky, heavy, stiff hobnailed boots with small metal horseshoes on the soles. Doughboys attempted to waterproof them with grease. Universally, the men condemned their footwear as ill-fitting and uncomfortable. Above the boot, men typically wore puttees, strips of wool tightly wrapped around the lower legs to provide support and protection. British troops serving in India in the late nineteenth century adopted the leg wear, and puttees had become a standard part of uniforms across Europe and Asia prior to the Great War.

For weapons, the doughboys typically carried a rifle fitted with a sixteen-inch bayonet. For both the US Army and the USMC, the standard rifle was the well-made bolt-action Springfield M1903. It fired a .30-06 round from a five-round magazine; an experienced rifleman could fire fifteen aimed rounds per minute. The Army and Marine Corps never had enough of these excellent weapons, and American forces supplemented them with the M1917 Enfield manufactured by Winchester and Remington.

Officers and senior NCOs carried pistols: the M1911 Colt automatic pistol or the Smith and Wesson M1917 revolver. Both close-quarter weapons fired the powerful .45 cartridge, renowned for its stopping power and ability to kill opponents at short range, as it effectively demonstrated in the Philippines against the Moros.

Web gear, such as a cartridge belt, and canteen, mess kit, gas mask, blanket, knapsack, and bandoliers of ammunition, further weighed down the doughboys. To stop low-velocity shell fragments, the men wore steel, dishpan-shaped helmets based on the British Brodie. Like much of the soldiers' other gear, these helmets were also named M1917 for the year of manufacture. The helmet's thin steel could generally stop only a bullet that was already largely spent. To differentiate themselves from those in the army, some Marines punched a small hole in their helmets and proudly affixed the Eagle, Globe, and Anchor. After the war, US Army soldiers and Marines typically painted the fronts of their helmets with their shoulder sleeve insignia or patch—the Indian Head in different shapes and colors based on battalion and regiment.[28]

Even as weapons technology advanced, the men also required weapons for fighting hand to hand in the trenches. Doughboys armed themselves with a variety of simple, brutal, deadly weapons designed to bludgeon and kill; clubs, maces, and trench knives topped the list. The M1917 trench knife featured a menacing, triangular stiletto blade with a knuckle guard that could be used to throw a brass-knuckle-like punch.

Some Marines, typically medical corpsmen, also carried a broad blade known as a bolo knife. Inspired by knives carried by insurgents in the Philippines at the turn of the twentieth century, the blade doubled as a machete, and the men used it for chopping and clearing brush.

Trench warfare also renewed interest in the hand grenade. To clear bunkers and trenches, Americans employed a variety of French, British, and American grenades. Activating the explosive required a doughboy to grip the spoon attached to the striker, which in turn was connected to the mechanical fuse, while pulling a cotter pin. He then tossed or threw the grenade in a high arc to land in a shell hole or bunker. Once the grenade was airborne, the safety spoon flew off and the striker ignited a five-second fuse. The grenade detonated, and if the wielder was not careful, on foe and friend alike. A rifle grenade, a standard rifle fitted with a cylindrical cup discharger, could expand the range of grenades up to about six hundred yards. When a doughboy fired a round, the gas produced thrust the grenade into the air.

Much of the fighting in the Great War occurred in and around the complex maze of trenches constructed by both sides. Often the trenches began as little more than foxholes, but over time the armies dug them deeper and connected them. In some cases, they reinforced the trenches and bunkers with concrete. These defensive positions sheltered the men from new technological horrors, such as machine guns, and also provided some protection against high-explosive artillery barrages. On the other hand, they also limited the mobility of the ground forces, leading to long-term standoffs during which neither side could gain ground. The trenches also placed soldiers from the two sides in relatively close proximity to each other, at times close enough to carry on a conversation.

The exact layout varied from place to place, but in general, the Allies constructed three parallel lines of trenches. However, these lines did not follow a straight path but instead zigzagged from side to side to prevent a clear line of sight for any enemy riflemen who made their way into the trenches. The front line looked out over no-man's-land, the space in between the opposing armies. To prevent enemy soldiers from making their way across, huge coils of barbed wire snaked through no-man's-land, and the armies set up machine-gun positions with interlocking fields of fire, creating a kill zone. The second support trench offered a fallback position yards behind the front line, and the third reserve trench provided a staging and supply area as far as two miles to the rear. Connecting the three lines was a series of perpendicular communication trenches that allowed men, ammunition, food, and supplies to move from the rear to the front.

The German Army on the Western Front pioneered a revolutionary form of defense in depth to sap the strength of the attacker and often lured the Allies into traps. German soldiers would lie in wait until Allied troops, exhausted after crossing no-man's-land, entered German frontline trenches manned by minimal numbers of machine guns and troops. The defenders then blasted the attacking force with gas and high-explosive shells. After thinning down the offensive force, the Germans pounced, delivering a devastating counterattack and often destroying the attackers. Ernest Janson and his fellow Marines, as well as most of the other Body Bearers, would somehow have to adapt to and overcome this brutal nature of modern war on the Western Front.

Pershing believed that continuing to fight from the trenches would simply prolong the stalemate of the war. Confirming his opinions, the Americans who had begun to move into the frontline trenches were reporting minimal fortifications on the German side. If the Americans could break through, he concluded, agile forces could overcome German resistance. He believed that maneuverability and tactical mobility, both of which were impossible when men were fighting within a trench, would ultimately lead to victory, particularly if supported by accurate rifle fire and bayonet charges. Before the war, this concept, dubbed "open warfare," was nebulous and ill-defined. Most manuals, such as *Infantry Drill Regulations* and *Field Service Regulations*, did not expound upon it in detail. Even Pershing did not officially promulgate or properly explain open warfare. Instead, he left it up to individual commanders to interpret the concept; determining what worked was generally painful.

However, Pershing's stratagy of open warfare had an underlying problem: firepower. Fatally, the doctrine considered artillery, tanks, and machine guns as ancillary to the infantrymen; it held that accurate rifle fire laid down by the infantry combined with American élan could overcome any obstacle. Among the Allies, combined arms warfare was becoming accepted strategy—a fact that Pershing did not fully appreciate. Pershing's beliefs were a dated product of his experience fighting American Indians and Moros. Yet his determination to escape the trenches made sense, and in the crucible of war, American innovation prevailed. Individual American soldiers and Marines adopted new techniques, learned from the Allies, and developed their own tactics to survive.

In the labyrinthine trenches on the Western Front, technology favored the defender. Artillery, poison gas, and especially the "beastly little weapon," the machine gun, killed on an industrial scale. In 1917, the United States had a paltry 430 heavy machine guns.[29] Two or three men manned each of the weapons.

However, American doctrine focused on rifle fire, musketry, and even outdated notions of utilizing the infantry in glorious bayonet charges. Prevailing US strategy before the war considered machine guns "emergency weapons" to be used for short durations.

Not everyone agreed. Among the most vocal advocates for greater machine-gun use was Captain John H. "Gatling Gun" Parker. A bear of a man standing more than six feet three and resembling Buffalo Bill, Parker earned his nickname "Gatling Gun" after deploying hand-cranked Gatling guns, Civil War–era technology, to provide suppressing fire at the Battle of San Juan and Kettle Hills during the Spanish-American War. He also innovated other tactics that helped the Americans achieve critical victories. Rough Rider Teddy Roosevelt extolled him: "I think Parker deserved rather more credit than any other man in the entire campaign. He had the rare good judgment and foresight to see the possibilities of the machine-guns."[30] Roosevelt went on to identify one of Parker's hallmarks—leading from the front. "By his own exertions, got it to the front and proved that it could do invaluable work on the field of battle."[31] Parker advocated better and more improved guns, new tactics to deploy them, and "a model unit of machine guns"—a precursor to a machine-gun company. Tradition-bound officers scorned him for his innovation, labeling him a "a pestiferous, immodest ass."[32]

During World War I, machine guns directly and immediately supported the troops in their area of operation. The alternative was to call in an artillery strike, which took time. Plus, artillery tended to be inaccurate and practically unable to hit moving targets. Unlike rifle fire, machine-gun fire produces a line of bullets similar to a powerful stream of water from a fire hose. A rifleman hits targets whereas a machine gun covers an entire area. Machine guns fired from a flank could inflict heavy casualties. A British lecturer at the US Army War College explained that six German machine guns arrayed on the flanks hit British troops with devastating enfilading fire, inflicting twelve thousand casualties and stopping cold two British divisions attacking at Passchendaele, Belgium.[33]

Machine gunners generally operated independently; this made them unique on the WWI battlefield, where most units operated in large groups. Crews remained in reserve or moved in front of main defensive positions so they could hit an attacker with flanking fire. The weapons played a crucial role in taking ground and holding it, defending against enemy counterattacks.

In the hands of an experienced crew, most machine guns could deliver a rate of fire of more than three hundred rounds per minute. Rates of equivalency varied—some estimates had a single machine gun performing the job of 120 riflemen, while another study rated a gun equivalent to 60 riflemen. In any case, a single machine gun delivered tremendous firepower.*[34]

The Maschinengewehr 08, or MG 08, was the Imperial German Army's workhorse machine gun during WWI. Largely adapted from American Hiram S. Maxim's original 1884 Maxim gun, the MG 08 could fire up to four hundred or five hundred rounds per minute, depending on the model. A crew of three fed the lethal weapon 250-round canvas belts. The gun sat on a heavy tripod, or sled, and boasted a mind-boggling effective range of about two thousand yards, with a maximum range of 2.2 miles. To protect their gunners, the Germans equipped many of them with steel trench armor, and they could also attach a thick metal brow plate to the front of their helmets.

---

* The Marines had several machine-gun units. The 6th Machine Gun Battalion comprised multiple companies; each company had crews manning sixteen superb Lewis guns. The Marines also possessed independent machine-gun companies, such as the 73rd Machine Gun Company and the 8th Machine Gun Company. After arriving in France, the Marines equipped each company with sixteen French Hotchkiss machine guns, and the gunners' lighter and more maneuverable Lewis guns went to Marine aviators operating in France.

Ponderous and equipped with a heavy tripod, the Hotchkiss fired the 8 mm Lebel cartridge—very accurate at one thousand yards and able to reach three thousand yards. A three-man crew fed twenty-five or thirty cartridge strips into the weapon. Unlike the Maxim, the Hotchkiss was air-cooled, and the barrels tended to overheat, requiring the crews to cease firing temporarily. However, an experienced crew could replace a barrel in a minute.

A great deal went into properly training a machine-gun crew. Math played a huge role in a machine gunner's proficiency: understanding range and angles separated the men from the boys. Gunners employed formulas to compute wind and other atmospherics, as well as elevation. Battle-tested machine gunners, drawing on their experience, could intuitively adjust their weapons.

In addition, handheld machine guns had just come onto the scene. Within rifle platoons, the French issued the Marines with the Chauchat (pronounced "sho sho" by some doughboys), a French machine gun with a half-moon-shaped clip of bullets initially chambered for the French 8 mm Lebel round. The Americans modified the weapon to fire the standard .30-6. An open clip revealed how many bullets remained, but it also allowed the entrance of dirt and grime from the battlefield, causing the gun to jam frequently. Despite its flaws, the weapon was ahead of its time, and with modifications and improvements, it played an important role in increasing the firepower of the individual doughboy.

*   *   *

Throughout the fall of 1917, both sides remained locked in a desperate race against time. While Janson and the 49th trained for war, the Allies suffered a series of damaging setbacks. First, the Austrians, with the help of several German divisions, dealt a crushing blow to the Italians at Caporetto in October and November 1917, threatening Italy's ability to stay in the war. In the Middle East, the Turks had defeated the British at Gallipoli more than a year earlier, but an insurgency in Arabia fanned by British Lieutenant Colonel T. E. Lawrence threatened the southern portion of the Ottoman Empire.

Following the October Revolution, the Germans also facilitated the return of Vladimir Lenin, who traveled back from Switzerland to Petrograd, also known as St. Petersburg. On October 26, 1917, Lenin signed the Decree on Peace, which called on the warring parties to begin peace negotiations. After that, Russia effectively withdrew from the war, and in March 1918, the Treaty of Brest-Litovsk established formal peace between the Soviets and the Central Powers and ceded much of Eastern Europe to the Germans. The series of events sowed the seeds for the rise of communism and a regime responsible for the deaths of tens of millions, as well as the eventual emergence of the Soviet Union as a world power. As a result, Germany was now fighting a one-front rather than a two-front war, and hundreds of thousands of fresh troops moved from east to west. With the infusion of all these fresh battle-hardened troops, Germany now had superiority in numbers on the Western Front for the first time. The Germans hoped to deliver a knockout blow to the Allies before the American Army could be fully mobilized.

To break the deadlock in the trenches, each major power innovated. The Allies developed the tank, among other weapons. The Germans also turned to technology, such as flamethrowers and gas, but their most significant breakthrough came from harnessing artillery and their human capital in the form of stormtroopers, or *Stosstruppen*.

Stosstruppen tactics originated from multiple sources, but one man had a larger role than others. A lowly thirty-eight-year-old captain named Willy Rohr, who had spent years as a lieutenant, developed many of the basic infantry tenets of "fire and maneuver," techniques that later became the basis of all modern small-unit tactics.

In March 1915, the German War Ministry ordered the formation of the Assault Detachment from men in the pioneer, or combat engineer, units. Rohr replaced waves of charging soldiers with squads of stormtroopers. Through experimentation, Rohr coordinated the use of machine guns, flamethrowers, and trench mortars (*Minenwerfer*) to suppress or paralyze an adversary, preventing the enemy from firing back as his Stosstruppen took out trench positions using hand grenades. The Assault Detachment tested steel body armor and was the first unit to try out the *Stahlhelm*, or steel helmet. Rohr found that the body armor cut down on mobility and speed, but he retained the iconic helmet that would distinctively identify German soldiers in both world wars.*

Instead of hitting a fortified position head-on, Rohr's Stosstruppen espied Allied weak spots on the line. Here, specially trained men equipped with the best weapons and utilizing their brains, initiative, and grit would infiltrate a position and continue to rear areas. The attack commenced with a short artillery preparation aimed at softening up the enemy. Next, the artillery would begin a creeping barrage, paving the way for the elite troops armed with flamethrowers, light machine guns, grenades, and satchel charges to penetrate behind enemy lines.

The Stosstruppen rushed forward in squads using whatever cover they could find and then laid down suppressing fire to keep their opponents' heads down and hamper them from firing back. Meanwhile, other groups of troopers charged forward, flanking the enemy. Junior NCOs could exercise their own initiative and issue orders based on the fluidity of battle. The shock troops would seek out command posts and artillery installations and knock them out of commission. With the enemy confused and weakened, the main infantry would follow behind,

---

* Later, modern US helmets adopted a similar shape.

aiming to destroy the bulk of the forces before reserves eliminated any remaining resistance.

Rohr's tactics were a sea change from earlier techniques that involved waves of cannon fodder that machine guns and artillery easily destroyed. Equally novel, instead of following rigid orders, each squad could think on its own and innovate based on the changing conditions—something practically unheard of in early-twentieth-century battle.

Stosstruppen trained differently from the typical German grunt. A day of training included live-fire exercises, clearing obstacles, breaching barbed wire, coordinating with flamethrowers, and moving forward in a barrage. To keep themselves in shape, they engaged in running, soccer, gymnastics, and a sport with a martial twist: grenade throwing.[35]

Rohr's tactics worked, and the Assault Detachment morphed into a battalion. With success came promotion and the ear of Germany's most powerful men, including the kaiser. Eventually, entire armies applied his ideas on a grand scale. In particular, General Oskar von Hutier and his artillery chief, Lieutenant Colonel Georg Bruchmül-ler, wielded them on the Eastern Front at the Latvian port of Riga in September 1917. Hutier utilized infiltration tactics, such as bombardment, assault, and encirclement, to great effect.* Quartermaster General Erich Friedrich Wilhelm Ludendorff considered Bruchmüller, nicknamed "Breakthrough," to be one of the most important men in the Imperial German Army. "His great knowledge and capacity, his devotion to his profession and his artillery, and his military enthusiasm marked him out as one of the most prominent soldiers of this war."[36] The brilliant artillerist devised a complex series of barrages that shifted between frontline and rear targets, such as the enemy artillery. To preserve the element of surprise, Bruchmüller based his targeting on mathematical calculations and did not use registration rounds to preregister the artillery, which telegraphed an imminent attack. His

---

*Modern writers often refer to these tactics as "Hutier tactics," but no contemporary written German accounts during World War I, not even Ludendorff's, used that term.

artillery bombardments lasted hours instead of days. The Germans stunned their enemies with a mixture of gas and high-explosive shells, followed by accurate, creeping barrages.

At Riga, elite assault units using the element of surprise hit weak spots in the Russian lines, and the Stosstruppen pressed forward, deeply penetrating the enemy defense before encircling and defeating the Russians. Hutier's and Bruchmüller's victory made a deep impression on Ludendorff. Following this victory, scores of divisions transferred after Russia was knocked out of the war. Ludendorff also sent Hutier and Bruchmüller west, but instead of heading for France, they first went to the Italian front, where the Austrians had been battling in a grinding war of attrition in the peaks of the Dolomites for two years. Moving with them were a few infantry divisions and the *Alpenkorps* (elite mountain troops). Hutier and Bruchmüller were about to break the front wide open at Caporetto.

At Caporetto on October 24, 1917, Bruchmüller coordinated artillery and used an insidious cocktail of high-explosive and gas shells. Shells marked with a blue cross contained "mask breakers" such as chloropicrin, which caused violent fits of sneezing that prompted Allied fighters to remove their gas masks, making them more susceptible to other pulmonary agents. Shells marked with a green cross contained phosgene or diphosgene gas that attacked the lungs. The Germans smothered the Italian trenches with the deadly combination of blue-cross and green-cross shells. They knew the Italians could wear their gas masks for only two hours before the gas seeped into them and they had to rip them off. The deadly combination slew entire units.

Using infiltration tactics, the Germans broke through three lines of resistance. The Italians fell back in disarray. At Caporetto, Erwin Rommel, a young junior officer commanding a company of *Alpenkorps*, made a name for himself, earning the Pour le Mérite, Germany's highest award, by forcing the surrender of thousands of Italians. In all, the Italians suffered 305,000 casualties, including 265,000 captured. The Austrian-German offensive drove them nearly to Venice.

The new tactics produced astonishing results. With the infusion of troops from the East, Quartermaster General Ludendorff had the ability to combine the tactics, gas, aircraft, and artillery together into a large-scale offensive in a bid to end the war before the growing American army could put victory out of reach. Ludendorff calculated the American Army would not pose a problem until the summer of 1918, when its sheer numbers would begin to tip the scales toward the Allies.

As 1917 came to a close, the war was going badly for the Allies. In three deadly years of fighting, the French and British alone had lost three million men—the Entente desperately needed American help to stave off defeat. But would the Americans arrive in large enough numbers in time?

Ludendorff was born to Prussian merchants in 1865. He attended a prestigious cadet school, where he consistently distinguished himself and was placed in a class with young men two years his senior. A stern workaholic, Ludendorff was a loner who deliberately avoided close friendships. Even his wife said, "Anyone who knows Ludendorff knows that he has not a spark of humor."[37] When the war began, Ludendorff became chief of staff in East Prussia under Hindenburg. Ludendorff won major battles at Tannenberg and Masurian Lakes, victories that propelled him to a position of power. Although Hindenburg was nominally in charge of the Central Powers forces, Ludendorff demanded and received an equal say in decision-making. He also inserted himself into politics, causing some historians to liken him to a dictator.

Chief of the General Staff Paul Ludwig Hans Anton von Beneckendorff und von Hindenburg was descended from Prussian nobility. He lived a privileged life and enthusiastically followed the family tradition of infantry service. When the Austro-Prussian war began in 1866, the six-feet-five, nineteen-year-old Hindenburg sent a letter to his parents: "I rejoice in this bright-colored future. For the soldier war is the normal state of things. . . . If I fall, it is the most honorable and beautiful death."[38] After a bullet grazed his skull in battle, he simply wrapped his head in a towel and carried on. Hindenburg advanced rapidly through the military ranks, rising to command of the Fourth Army. In 1911, he retired, but the army recalled him when the Great War began, placing him in charge of the Eighth Army, with Ludendorff as his second in command. Hindenburg's philosophy was that "the commander in the field should only lay down the broad lines, leaving the details to his subordinates,"[39] a concept that suited Ludendorff's personality precisely. The two men enjoyed an uncommonly good working relationship, together leading the German forces.

After touring the Western Front in the fall of 1917, Ludendorff announced his decision regarding where and when he would attack: St. Quentin east of the old Somme battlefield to drive the British out of the war, and then turn on the French before the Americans could arrive in overwhelming numbers. Ludendorff tapped Hutier and Bruchmüller to lead the "Peace Offensive," employing the infiltration and artillery tactics the team had honed at Riga and Caporetto. Their strategies became the basis of a new treatise called "The Attack in Position Warfare."[40] The best men and officers headed to Germany to engage in a crash course in stormtrooper tactics and equipment. In an immense undertaking, Ludendorff planned to convert forty-two of his divisions into assault units—a full quarter of the German infantry becoming stormtroopers—and outfitted them with the finest armaments available, including the superb Bergmann MP18 submachine gun, which gave them a firepower edge.

In a marvel of modern warfare, the Germans completed the training and reequipping of the assault divisions and secretly moved hundreds of thousands of troops right under the noses of the British. Germany's elite, most experienced combat veterans brimmed with confidence. They prepared to win the war with an offensive code-named Operation Michael. On the morning of the attack, they achieved surprise and, fortuitously, gained the cloak of an impenetrable fog. However, the campaign had a major weakness: it lacked strategic objectives and a grander vision. When Crown Prince Rupprecht, a skillful and experienced army commander, and a Bavarian, not a Prussian, requested more details, Ludendorff responded, "We will punch a hole. For the rest, we shall see. That's what we did in Russia."[41]

On Thursday morning, March 21, 1918, sixty-four hundred guns near St. Quentin and the Somme River opened up using Bruchmüller's deadly crescendo of high-explosive and blue-cross and green-cross shells—smashing into front and rear areas of the British lines and smothering them with clouds of noxious gas and deadly high explosives. Through the dense mist, tens of thousands of stormtroopers armed with sharpened shovels, light machine guns, trench mortars, and flamethrowers penetrated British lines, nearly destroying much of the Fifth and Third Armies. Foolishly, the British had deployed most of their troops in frontline positions, and once the Germans infiltrated the lines, they were able to advance almost forty miles—a true breakthrough and a first on the Western Front.

The war hung in the balance.

Ludendorff had predicted that the massive sixty-nine-division German juggernaut would blow a hole in the British lines. But as Prince Rupprecht had foreshadowed, objectives mattered. The crucial rail and road hub at Amiens, on which the Allies relied to connect and reinforce their armies, lay within striking distance. If the Allies were to lose this crucial city, the British Army would be separated from the French. The course of the war could have changed if the Germans had attacked there in force, but Ludendorff unwisely sent his army in multiple directions, instead of focusing on Amiens. Ludendorff squandered crucial hours before eventually redirecting his effort toward the city, which should have been the key objective all along.

The Germans also had a recurring problem with pursuit capability. Highly mobile behind their own lines, employing the rail network, the Germans for various reasons were not able to pursue very quickly upon breaching the Allied lines. The troops were exhausted from days of unrelenting combat, and although the Germans were known for their discipline, many men took time away from fighting to loot captured Allied supplies. In addition, German trucks, equipped with steel wheels because of a lack of rubber, did not perform well in mud. Finally, while

Operation Michael nearly destroyed the British, it also handed Ludendorff a forty-mile salient of largely useless territory that he had to defend.

The crisis had one silver lining for the Allies: it forced them to create a unified command structure. The Supreme War Council named Marshal Foch commander in chief with authority to coordinate the Allied armies. No longer did each Allied army operate independently.

Ludendorff followed up Michael in Flanders in April 1918 with another hammer blow on the British: Operation Georgette. The Germans smashed the Portuguese, nearly annihilating an entire division that held a portion of the British line. The Allies feared the Germans would advance to the channel ports of Dunkirk, Calais, and Boulogne and force a British defeat. In fact, the German assault nearly pushed the British into the channel. German forces came within six miles of the crucial town of Hazebrouck; if it fell, Dunkirk would follow, resulting in the annihilation of the British Army. The dire situation inspired British Field Marshal Sir Douglas Haig to issue his famous "backs to the wall" order, urging his men to fight on to the end.[42] Repeatedly rallying as they withdrew toward the French coast, the British and French displayed stiff resistance, but it cost them dearly: the British lost one hundred and fifty thousand dead and missing, and the French about sixty thousand.[43] Operations Michael and Georgette mauled and exhausted entire German divisions, as well, and Germany lost many of its finest trained and experienced Stosstruppen.

In the midst of the unfolding crisis, Pershing offered up the AEF, then consisting of only a few divisions: the 1st, Janson's 2nd, the 26th, and the 42nd—each at various stages of training and readiness—hardly an army. The Allies immediately accepted. General Pétain funneled the Americans into quiet sectors to replace other Allied troops, allowing the French to send reinforcements into the Somme to aid the British. The 4th Brigade of the 2nd Division went to Lemmes in the Toulon sector, near the highly contested city of Verdun. Here, Janson, the 49th, and other units within the 4th Brigade rotated to forward fighting positions in the trenches—where they received their baptism in the flames of combat.

CHAPTER 7

TRENCH WARFARE

"You stick there until hell freezes over and then skate on the ice," barked Colonel John "Gatling Gun" Parker, regimental commander of the 102nd Infantry Regiment of the 26th Division. He was replying to one of his subordinates who had desperately beseeched Parker to allow him to withdraw.

For the past thirty-six hours, the Germans had rained high-explosive shells on a section of trench line occupied by Parker's men outside the small town of Seicheprey, located near Verdun and a bulge in the Allied lines near St. Mihiel. About twenty-five hundred handpicked men the Americans later dubbed "Hindenburg's Traveling Circus,"[*1] descended upon C and D Companies on April 20, 1918. Since the Americans' arrival in France, the Germans had targeted the doughboys in a series of raids, hoping to crush their morale.

Fortified with a triple shot of rum in a blazing hot cup of tea, the Stosstruppen surged forward. Paul Coelestin Ettighoffer, a member of the Traveling Circus, recalled:

> "Los! [let's go]" We move over the light planks and the soggy ground between the lines, become swallowed up by the mist.
>
> The well-known terrain and the sense of superiority in the face of an inexperienced enemy gives us strength. And the prospect of looting and bringing in many fine things is compelling.

* The German units included *Sturmbataillon* 14, *Stosstruppen* of Res I.R. 258 and Res. I.R. 259.

We are the picked troops of our division, *Landsknechte*, knowing [our] trade for many years. . . .

The *Stosstrupps* to our left and right can't be seen anymore. Our only direction indicator is the crashing of the artillery ahead of us, towards which our *Stellmacher* leads us. Suddenly two clumps of bushes appear from the fog. . . . Our course is correct, between both copses our *Stosstrupp* enters the hostile line. Final *Minenwerfer* [mortars] are exploding barely 50m ahead, followed by the rolling barrage, jumping over to the enemy's communication and reserve lines. Now we are spotted and a burst of machine-gun fire is sent over.[2]

The Germans infiltrated Parker's forward trenches and started methodically destroying scores of dugouts, often with the Americans inside. Confusion reigned as the German bombardment severed telephone wires and communication among the various units. Employing satchel charges, the Germans wreaked havoc by blowing pillboxes, and flamethrowers incinerated Americans.

"Finally they [Parker's men] become alive, commands in English are shouted, hand grenades are thrown. A stubborn resistance, which neither the exhausted French nor English would be able to put up any longer, is checking our advance," recalled the seasoned German trooper.[3]

The Americans fought back violently with clubs, pistols, grenades, and anything else they could find. With orders to stand their ground, many of Parker's men, isolated in small pockets, battled on. Even Stubby, the 102nd's brindle-patterned bull terrier mascot, fought ferociously despite being wounded in the foreleg by a German grenade.

Ettighoffer continued:

We take full cover to get a better view. Ahead lies a strong dugout, pouring out defenders constantly. It looks nasty for us, but finally the *Stellmacher* [our commander] has fixed his plan. We are divided into three groups and attack simultaneously from three sides. [In the assault] *Unteroffizier* [Sergeant] Roos gets a fatal shot in the head.

The enemy gives ground at last, fighting back desperately. Nothing but dead or wounded he leaves behind, all of them big, athletic physiques in wonderful uniforms and rubber boots.* A party which begins to yield during close combat is lost, and we begin to feel superiority. . . . The Americans withdraw to the next cluster of dugouts. We follow closely, sloshing through mud, passing by tins, woolen blankets, and various booty. But there is no time to touch anything. The main resistance is yet to come.

The stormtroopers operated in a carefully choreographed manner putting their skills, training, and courage to full use. One stormtrooper noted, "This kind of fighting seems made for the German with his feeling for discipline and order, analogous, one might say, to the musical coordination of an orchestra."[4]

Shells and mines are crossing our heads frighteningly low. We believe the enemy to have escaped, when suddenly, just around a trench shoulder, we face them nose to nose. Strong, healthy men, the flat steel helmets worn obliquely over angular, beardless faces. There they stand, preparing two machine guns.

"Hands up, you bloody fools," the *Stellmacher* shouts at them, bringing up his dagger to a nearby officer's throat.

The officer haltingly lifts his hands, but his men turn around a machine gun and start firing. We throw our stick grenades. Fountains of mud splash around, covering both adversaries over and over, leaving us almost unrecognizable. Stones, clumps of dirt and splinters fly in all directions. Again we push forward and suddenly those big buggers [Americans] start to grin merrily, offering hands, remarking, "This damned bloody war is now finished for us!"[5]

---

* The Germans prized the Americans' rubber boots, ideal foot protection in the muddy trenches of the Western Front.

As a stormtrooper, Ettighoffer felt an extreme sense of pride in his unit and experience. The Germans schooled the Americans in the art of war and infiltration tactics, leading Ettighoffer to remark, "Real sportsmen against us *Landsknechte*!"*[6]

Following infiltration tactics, the Traveling Circus bypassed strongpoints, occupied Seicheprey, and entered rear areas, including a field kitchen. The action grew so desperate that an American cook threw a pot of boiling water at a German flamethrower operator, while another took out two stormtroopers with a meat cleaver.[7] Compounding the situation, the damaged American communication made it impossible to coordinate an answering barrage. Moreover, German counterbattery fire disabled many of the American guns.

Colonel John "Gatling Gun" Parker entered the trenches and himself manned one of the machine guns that had been silenced after the Germans killed its crew. Only weeks earlier, Parker had been instructing at a machine-gun school in France dubbed the "Suicide Club,"[8] until Pershing, through his chief of staff, Brigadier General James Harbord, tapped Parker to assume command of the 102nd Infantry Regiment. Harbord related, "Someone needs to put a soul into this outfit, you are the man he believes best fitted to do it."[9]

While Parker rallied his men, the Germans continued sowing chaos: blowing up scores of bunkers and cellars, as well as destroying two bridges, ammunition depots, and a tunnel system. It was over in forty minutes; the Germans withdrew according to plan. As the Traveling Circus fell back, they temporarily held the frontline American trenches in case of a counterattack. It never materialized.

Despite a direct order from Parker, a company commander in the fog of war refused to launch the counterattack. For this insubordination, the US Army court-martialed the officer and later ejected him from the service.

---

* *Landsknechte* were formidable German mercenary soldiers of the sixteenth century, a group of men the Stosstruppen idolized.

The German raid proved deadly, resulting in about 650 Americans killed, wounded, gassed, or missing. In addition, the Germans bagged more than a hundred prisoners.

Pershing was livid over the Americans' defeat. Parker's heroics aside, the Allies seriously questioned the Americans' fighting capability. German newspapers gloated that the Stosstruppen had taught the Americans a lesson and echoed Ettighoffer's words that war was not a game. While Allied newspapers claimed the 102nd stopped a German attack from penetrating Allied lines, this ignored the fact that the Germans intended only to raid, capture prisoners, and reap destruction. The Germans wanted to embarrass the Americans—which they did very effectively.

Despite the drubbing, Allied papers lionized Stubby, who received a wound stripe. After the raid, the intrepid canine continued to serve with the regiment throughout the remainder of the war, warning the men of gas attacks, locating wounded soldiers in no-man's-land, and alerting soldiers to incoming shells. The regiment officially promoted him to sergeant for his service.*

But Parker's men demonstrated something that alarmed the Germans: inexperienced American troops would fight tenaciously, even to the death. A German report after the raid noted, "The American is most courageous individually and resists desperately to the last with pistol, knife, and hand grenade; he is a considerable, cunning, and ruthless adversary in close-quarters combat. . . . His extraordinarily fatal losses are a result of his defiant behavior. Many dugout garrisons, refusing to surrender, had to be blasted by the *Stosstrupps*. . . . In several cases only *Flammenwerfer* (flamethrowers) could break the opposition. This enemy can only be beaten by reckless action."[10]

For his courage, Parker received the Distinguished Service Cross. Astonishingly, it would be the first of four he received during WWI.

---

* Even Pershing joined in and presented Stubby with a gold medal following the war. The bull terrier later led parades and became Georgetown's official mascot. After he died in his sleep in 1926, he was stuffed and shipped to the Smithsonian.

*   *   *

Hundreds of Stosstruppen, possibly men from Hindenburg's Traveling Circus, targeted the 2nd Division's 9th Regiment at Maizey in northeastern France. After pummeling the sector with a barrage, the Germans employed a ruse. Disguising themselves as *poilus* (a term for French soldiers), they gained entry to the frontline trenches. After overpowering the Americans, pioneers breached the wire, allowing about four hundred Stosstruppen to stream through and hit the Americans. The stormtroopers killed and wounded scores of men and captured more than a dozen prisoners.

Following the assault, each side raided the other's position several more times, including one attack involving the 49th Company. During the raid, Captain Hamilton made a surprising discovery. Dashing across no-man's-land, Hamilton and another soldier were among the first to approach the enemy trenches. A star shell fired by the artillery momentarily lit up the night sky, allowing them to see each other's faces.

"It's Burwell!" Hamilton gasped, recognizing his brother.

"George!" Burwell exclaimed in response.

For a brief moment, they clasped hands before returning to the grisly task at hand.

According to a report in *The Washington Post*, when the assault was over, the two brothers, now both captains, found each other again. Before the United States declared war on Germany, George Hamilton had enlisted in the Marines, while his brother Burwell had chosen to join the Army. "Although in the same sector, neither brother was aware of the presence of the other. They had not seen each other since the United States entered the war, and neither knew that the other was even in France."[11]

But the German and American raids—and the drama and terror they generated—proved the exception rather than the rule. Artillery caused the Marines' first casualties. Shells hit the entrenchments, and razor-sharp shrapnel, traveling hundreds of feet per second, sliced men in half and severed limbs. But sheer monotony, replete with large helpings of rain and mud, dominated trench life. In addition, Janson and the 49th contended with thousands of ticks, lice, and other vermin the men nicknamed "cooties" or "arithmetic bugs." One Marine explained, "They added to our troubles and subtracted from our pleasures and divided our attention and multiplied like hell."[12] Most of the vermin feasted on human blood and caused a great deal of irritation as they burrowed into their human hosts' uniforms and bodies. Rats the size of small cats roamed in the trenches feasting on human corpses and propagating rapidly. "My bunkmate and I used to plug every hole we could find in our dugout. They still got in and crawled all over our blankets at night. I was never bitten. Some men were, but I don't believe anyone was seriously ill from it. I guess we were as tough as the rats."[13]

In early May, the company was transferred away from the front. Leaving the grime, water, and vermin of the trenches, the 49th and the rest of the 4th Brigade Marines trained in Pershing's nebulous maneuver warfare. The men drilled in large formations and expected their marksmanship to eject the Germans from behind concrete bunkers, fortifications, and machine guns. The tactics and training were outdated and, in hindsight, naïve. Mental toughness and training helped them adapt, but the Marines and other Americans would painfully learn from the initial slaughter before innovating their own way of war.

After Brigadier General Charles A. Doyen, commander of the 4th Marine Brigade, failed a mandatory physical and returned to the United States, where he died several months later from influenza, Brigadier General James Harbord moved over to command. The Marines, who had no say in the matter, could not have been too pleased when Pershing assigned Harbord, a US Army general, to command a Marine brigade. Nevertheless, it turned out to be a good match. Harbord, brilliant at managing supply, logistics, and the other building blocks of an army, now had his first field command in the AEF. Imposing, pompous, impressive, and a bit of a showman, he always wore a French Adrian helmet rather than the dishpan-shaped Brodie or M1917. Despite his flashy personality, he fought for his men. Eventually the Marines considered him one of their own and gave Harbord an EGA emblem, a great honor the general treasured for the rest of his life.

Shortly after Harbord's appointment, the AEF finally attacked. On May 28, 1918, the 28th Infantry Regiment of the 1st Division assaulted the small town of Cantigny, near the salient created by Operation Michael. The battle's stated objective was to capture and hold the town, but the unstated goal was mainly to give the French and English confidence in the AEF's ability to fight. Leaving nothing to chance, the French generously reinforced the attack with artillery, flamethrowers, and tanks. With overwhelming firepower, the 28th Infantry seized the town and withstood several determined German counterattacks. The 2nd Division planned to relieve the 1st Division at Cantigny, but orders countermanding travel to Cantigny arrived in the afternoon of May 30.

Pershing directed the 2nd to mount up in French camions (trucks) and speed toward the Chemin des Dames region of France, where the Germans launched an offensive aimed at capturing Paris. Here men like Body Bearer Gunnery Sergeant Ernest A. Janson and the US Marine Corps would shape history.

III

DEFENDING PARIS
1918

CHAPTER 8

BELLEAU WOOD

Body Bearer Ernest Janson sat on a hard wooden seat in the back of a camion. The solid rubber wheels of the French truck seemed to hit every bump in the road and failed to provide any shock absorption. His spine jerked from side to side. The truck drivers raced one another, each hoping to be first to the front, exacerbating the rough ride. Every minute counted; the French Army was melting away at the close of May 1918, as the German Army rumbled southwest toward Paris, a mere forty miles away.

Even worse than the jolting was the dust. Great billows of grayish grit swirled behind each camion, lingering in the air and coating the men's hair, skin, and clothing, morphing them into walking ghosts. Tiny spurts of dust erupted through the cracks in the truck's floorboards as the camion bounced across the heavily rutted roads.

Racked by coughing fits, some of the men in the 5th Regiment decided to don their gas masks. The headgear filtered the dust; however, the gear blocked most of the air as well. Feeling smothered in the back of the stifling truck bed, most of the men soon removed their masks and resigned themselves to a miserable ride.

As Janson and Captain George Wallis Hamilton, commanding officer of the 49th Company, tried without success to brace themselves against the constant lurching of the camion, they gazed into the faces of refugees fleeing from the invading German forces. Caked in the ever-present dust, crowds of men, women, and children clogged the roads, the expressions on their faces bearing testimony to their exhaustion and terror.

Eventually, the number of refugees dwindled, only to be replaced by the equally demoralizing sight of French troops racing to retreat from their German foes. Horse-drawn artillery galloped by, followed by small groups of infantry and engineers, all of them having abandoned hope. *"Fini la guerre!"*[1] ("The war is finished!") they shouted to the passing Americans.

The men rode in silence. Gone were the jokes and laughter. One Marine described how the chaotic journey transformed boys into men: "Their mouths were set with grim sternness, their skin seemed drawn tightly over their high cheek bones, and their eyes did not sparkle with mischief any more. It was as if the emotional strain of witnessing so much misery had suddenly turned carefree youths into mature men."[2]

Janson and the Marines and soldiers in the camions felt swept up into something far larger then themselves and on the edge of an inflection point. Officers told them they could save Paris—and they believed it. These privates, corporals, and sergeants might make the difference between victory and defeat.

In late May 1918, the German Army had launched Operation Blücher (named for the Prussian commander at the battle of Waterloo) against the Allies at the Chemin des Dames, a heavily fortified east-west ridge and roadway northeast of Paris, where French General Robert Nivelle had launched his bloody offensive that nearly broke the French Army months earlier. Blücher, which included thirty-six divisions, many recently released from the Eastern Front after Russia's withdrawal from the war, began as an elaborate feint to draw Allied reserves away from the true objective. The Germans employed their proven infiltration tactics, and the country's artillery expert, Lieutenant General Georg Bruchmüller, organized a symphony of death, launching nearly three million gas and high-explosive shells that pulverized the Allied line. Past experience had taught the Germans that whenever an attack placed Paris in peril, the French would react and send significant reinforcements to protect the capital.

However, Blücher was an unexpected success. General Max von Boehn's Seventh Army furiously gouged a huge gap in the Allied line manned by ten understrength Allied divisions that had previously been refitting in a "quiet sector." The French and English lost sixty thousand men as casualties and POWs, not to mention thousands of machine guns and 650 pieces of artillery. German forces seized a bridgehead on the Marne, a feat that they had not accomplished since 1914.

Rewarding success, Ludendorff chose to continue the offensive, though they had not seized the key city of Reims; the prize of Paris and a potential negotiated peace was irresistible. Unrecognized by the Allies at the time was the fact that the Germans were overrunning their supply and communication lines. Blücher's failure to take Reims meant supplies, fresh troops, and ammunition traversed a single captured French rail line running through the city of Soissons, hindering the Germans' progress.

Nevertheless, the enormous German attack rolled forward. The French sent fresh troops straight into battle as they arrived. But these reserves became "overwhelmed by numbers, and they evaporated immediately like drops of rain on a white-hot iron."[3] The French, demoralized, largely fought like a beaten army.

To cauterize the desperate situation, Pershing, responding to desperate pleas from the Allies, ordered the 2nd Division (about 28,000 strong) rushed to the front. The 2nd included the 4th Marine Brigade with its approximately 9,400 officers and men. Janson and the Marines rode in the backs of the French trucks all night to plug the holes in the lines. Also racing toward the front was the 3rd Division; its lead unit, the 7th Machine-Gun Battalion, a motorized machine-gun unit, sped into the town of Château-Thierry, where it made a stand to slow the Germans. French engineers blew the bridges over the Marne behind them, leaving a railroad bridge standing for the Americans to cross.[4] But with the bulk of Château-Thierry in German hands, the thrust of the offensive shifted about seven miles west toward a series of small French towns and a centuries-old hunting preserve, a rugged ground called Bois de Belleau.

Like a swirling flood bursting through a levee, the German juggernaut advanced.

For the Allies, the situation on the ground was desperate. Reeling from the attack, General Jean Marie Joseph Degoutte, commanding the French Sixth Army, issued multiple deployment directives to the 2nd Division in a frantic attempt to halt the enemy. But the French Army was nearing collapse, and the demoralized troops were fleeing in panic. Confusion and frustration reigned in French headquarters as the officers scrambled to regain control. Recognizing the gravity of the situation, British General Henry Wilson wrote, "Tomorrow will be a critical day. If [Crown Prince] Rupprecht now attacks south from Montdidier to Noyon and takes Compiegne, the French Army is beaten."[5] Panic was setting in within the French ranks, and plans to abandon Paris were under way. General Haig even dusted off procedures for evacuating the British forces from France to England.[6]

When the 2nd Division staff arrived at French Sixth Army headquarters, the Germans had captured most of Château-Thierry, an important road junction and city on the Marne River, and Hill 204, which sat astride the Paris-Metz road that led to the French capital. General Degoutte aimed to commit American regiments to the front as soon as they arrived. However, he doubted that the Americans could hold and pressed Colonel Preston Brown, the 2nd Division chief of staff, about their abilities. Brown laconically responded, "General, these are American regulars. In 150 years, they have never been beaten. They will hold."[7] Brown also convinced the French general that committing the 2nd piecemeal, as the French had been doing with their own reinforcements, would be a disaster. Brown argued that the American riflemen carried only 150 rounds each, and he flatly refused to send his units into battle without artillery and machine-gun support. Brown also talked Degoutte into allowing the division to build a secondary line behind the French. These crucial decisions would have an impact on the course of the battle, potentially even the war, in the days to come.

As the 2nd Division's 4th Brigade (5th and 6th Marines) and 3rd Brigade (9th and 23rd US Army Regiments) marched into position, German artillery rained down upon them, and the French troops raced west past the Marines. In the unfolding melee, French General Victor-Constant Michel told Brigadier General James Harbord, commanding officer of the 4th Brigade, "Hold the line at all hazards."[8] Harbord told his Marines, "[Take] all necessary steps . . . to hold our present positions at all costs."[9] Harbord had his work cut out for him as an army general commanding Marines, leading a brigade of men he had just met, and dealing with a crisis.

After dismounting from their camions, Janson and the other 1st Battalion, 5th Marines marched about six miles to face off against the main German drive that had just routed the French. By the following evening, the Marines had accomplished their mission and had established a twelve-mile defensive line from Triangle Farm across to the French town of Lucy-le-Bocage and another French farm known as Les Mares.

Disregarding French advice to dig trenches farther in the rear, General Harbord ordered the Marines to "hold where they stand."[10] German artillery hit the Marine lines. In the meantime, the French launched a counterattack, which failed miserably. This breakdown, coupled with the earlier missteps, compounded the morale problems within the French Army. All the French troops next to Lloyd Williams's 51st Company retreated, leaving a gap in the front. A fleeing French officer confronted Captain Williams of the 2nd Battalion, 5th Marines and urged his men to fall back. Williams coolly responded, "Retreat, Hell! We just got here!" In his official report, the Marine captain communicated a sanitized version of the conversation: "The French Major gave Captain Corbin written orders to fall back—I have countermanded the order."[11] Later, while critically injured and suffering from the effects of gas, Williams pleaded with the corpsman trying to evacuate him, "Don't bother with me. Take care of my good men."[12] A German artillery shell killed the officer before he could be removed from the field.

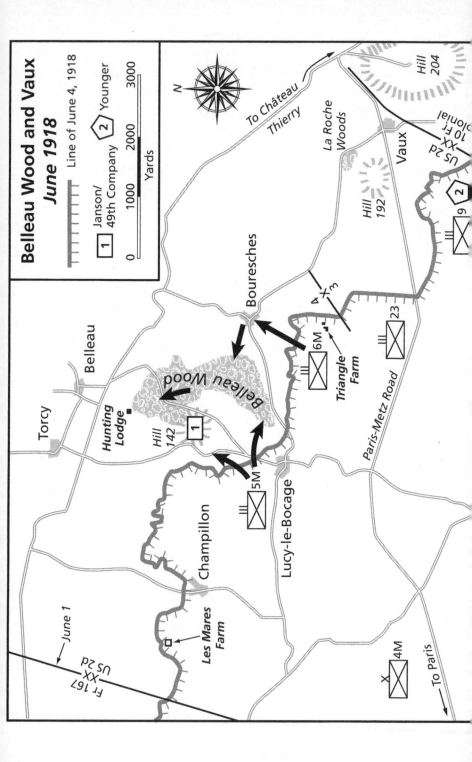

Belleau Wood and Vaux
June 1918

Janson/ [1] 49th Company
[2] Younger

Line of June 4, 1918

Yards
0   1000   2000   3000

N

To Château Thierry

Hill 204

La Roche Woods

US 2d / 10 Fr Colonial

Vaux

Hill 192

Belleau

Bo. X 4 / X 3

Boursches

Torcy

Hunting Lodge

Belleau Wood

Hill 142

[1]

6M

Triangle Farm

23

Champillon

5M

Paris-Metz Road

Lucy-le-Bocage

June 1

Fr 167 / US 2d

Les Mares Farm

4M

To Paris

The Marines dug shallow fighting holes with their bayonets and lay in wait for the inevitable ground attack.

After pushing aside the French assault, the Germans moved forward in force on the afternoon of June 3.* With bayonets fixed, the enemy infantry waded through waist-high wheat heading west toward Paris. Cool in the face of attack, the Marines waited at Les Mares Farm until the Germans were only three hundred yards away before opening up with deadly accurate rifle fire that mowed down the approaching men. Every Marine is a rifleman, and that truth had a devastating effect. Many of the men on the ground that day were crack shots, having qualified on targets in rigorous training as Expert Riflemen, Sharpshooters, or Marksmen. The deadly rifle fire tore the heart out of the advance; after the first and second lines of Germans crumpled into the wheat, the remaining troops broke ranks and ran back to their lines.

On Thursday, June 6, the Marines and Germans swapped roles. Ernest Janson, the 49th Company, and the 4th Brigade went on the offensive. Extraordinary valor and tragedy culminated in what would prove to be the bloodiest day in the 143-year history of the US Marine Corps up to that point.

---

* The combat-effective German divisions in the offensive were severely reduced. They had sustained heavy casualties from fighting in Operations Michael and Georgette and also suffered many killed and wounded from Operation Blücher. By mid-June, many German divisions were shells of their former selves, reduced to about fifteen hundred men. But at the time, no one on the Allied side had an inkling of how depleted Germany's divisions were. The French Army had lost over a dozen divisions to Blücher. Backstopping the Allied line was the fresh 2nd Division, considered almost a super-division because it was twice the size of a French division and multiple times the size of the exhausted German divisions.

CHAPTER 9

HILL 142

"Fix bayonets!"

The piercing shriek of Marine whistles and guttural bellows of "Follow me!" trailed the order as men of Gunnery Sergeant Ernest Janson's 49th Company emerged from the woods. Dawn turned gray, and light bathed the flowing fields of wheat that lay in front of the men. "Dewy poppies, red as blood"[1] were sprinkled randomly through the waist-deep wheat.

The Marines advanced in Civil War–style formations.* As they gazed to their right and left, they viewed a panorama largely untouched by the Great War: sinuous hills of grain, clumps of trees, and a lush, verdant forest that served as a hunting preserve prior to the war. The dense kidney-shaped woods known as Bois de Belleau occupied roughly one square mile of land. Two deep ravines cut through the trees, and massive boulders, some the size of a small building, littered the ground, making Belleau Wood a natural fortress. A ridge 142 meters high, and therefore dubbed Hill 142, sprawled to the west.

An angry red sun emerged just above the horizon in the cloudless blue sky behind the men's backs. Many turned their heads, some for the last time, to glimpse the blazing sunrise.[2] At that instant, German shells and machine-gun bullets ripped through the golden farmland, striking flesh and bone.

---

* To attack Hill 142, the platoons formed into assault waves. Only two companies advanced. The Marines planned to advance with five—including machine gunners—but the other three companies had not entered the line at 3:45 a.m. for the start of the assault.

As men began toppling like dominos, Marine officers screamed, "Battle-sight! Fire at will!"[3] Their voices broke through the din of the battle and anguished cries of wounded and dying men.

Only two companies from 1/5, the 49th and 67th, had arrived at the jumping-off point prior to 3:45 as instructed. The battalion commander of 1/5, Major Julius Turrill, who had received the order to attack Hill 142 only hours earlier, had earmarked five companies, or nearly one thousand men, for the assault. Short and stocky, Turrill had served in the Philippines, Cuba, and Guam, as well as on various ships. Unbeknownst to the attackers, the Marines faced a battalion from the German 460th Regiment and a battalion of the 273rd Regiment (both understrength), including several machine-gun companies. The hill lay on the boundary between the two German divisions. Fortunately for Janson and the 49th, the enemy had not dug in, and a command dispute prevented the two Boche units from tying together for maximum defense. Nevertheless, the Germans vastly outnumbered the two Marine companies.

The 49th's commanding officer, Captain Hamilton, led the Marines toward Hill 142. A rugged former football captain, exceptional athlete, and fighting Marine officer, Hamilton never asked his men to do anything he would not do personally. Before the charge, he realized the men "were up against something unusual, and ran along the whole line to get each man (almost individually) on his feet to rush the wood."[4]

Armed with Springfield rifles, Hamilton and Janson fired into the woods at field-gray German gunners wearing camouflaged *Stahlhelms* on their heads. While Janson, Hamilton, and most of the Marines carried the M1903 rifles, other men armed with the fully automatic Chauchat machine gun fired from the hip, laying down a heavy spray of lead as they surged toward the German gunners.

Its height in meters led to 142's designation as a hill, but in reality, the slope was more of a ridge that jutted from north to south in front of the Bois de Belleau. Patches of woods and wheat fields and ravines bracketed the mound, which dominated the battlefield. Both sides coveted 142's high ground and would fight to the death to possess it.

Although many of their brother Marines lay dead or wounded in the grain, Janson, Hamilton, and other men in the 49th emerged unscathed. They descended on the Germans, quickly hurling grenades, plunging the blued steel of their sixteen-inch bayonets into the bodies of the enemy, and dispatching others with small arms fire. Later, Hamilton had vague recollections of "snatching an Iron Cross off the first officer . . . and of shooting wildly at several rapidly retreating Boches." He added, "I carried a rifle on the whole trip and used it to good advantage."[5]

The 67th did not fare so well. Lieutenant Orlando C. Crowther, its leader, and 1st Sergeant "Beau" Hunter both died from wounds inflicted by Maxim nests concealed in a ravine. Hamilton and Janson reorganized what was left of the shattered platoons in the 49th and 67th. Then they had to do it all over again: yet another open wheat field lay in front of the murderous fire of several companies of German machine gunners defending Hill 142.

Once again, the Marines burst from cover and waded through waist-high wheat. Hill 142 loomed ahead, crested with pine trees that ominously appeared black as they reached skyward against the background of the blue sky.[6] Colored tracer rounds from the Maxims whizzed by the Marines, and German rifle and machine-gun fire cut through the front ranks. Most of the men dove to the ground, prone, hoping the fragile stalks would obscure the gunners' line of sight.

A Marine officer barked, "Can't walk up to these babies. No—won't be enough of us left to get on with the war. Pass the word: crawl forward, keeping touch with the man on your right! Fire where you can."[7] Within minutes, the officer went down—a dozen Maxim bullets having ripped through his chest.

Another squad of Janson's men aimed to take out a Maxim crew. A corporal from the group got beyond the gun and tried to flank it. Attempting to coordinate their actions, one man yelled, "Get far enough past that flank gun, now, close as you can, and rush it—we'll keep it busy."[8] After maneuvering into position, the corporal shot up and, with a yell, attacked the gun. Keeping their promise, his brothers backed him and charged the gun. One member of the 49th remembered the grisly result after two gunners turned their weapons on the charging Marines: "[Their Maxims] cut the squad down like a grass-hook levels a clump of weeds. . . . They lay there for days, eight Marines in a dozen yards, face down on their rifles."[9]

Some Marines, repeatedly wounded, forged ahead. One small group of men from the 49th lay in wheat in front of the muzzle of a German machine gun. Bullets zipped by and "clipped the stalks around their ears and riddled their combat packs—firing high by a matter of inches and the mercy of God."[10]

One member of the 49th explained: "A man can stand just so much of that. Life presently ceases to be desirable; the only desirable thing is to kill that gunner, kill him with your hands!" He added, "One fellow seized the spitting muzzle and up-ended it on the gunner; he lost a hand in the matter. Bayonets flashed in, and a rifle butt rose and fell."[11]

Janson's and Hamilton's Marines improvised their tactics on the fly. Small groups of determined men surmounted the seemingly impossible with their iron will, taking out one nest after another as they rolled up the hill. Later Hamilton noted, "It was only because we rushed the positions that we were able to take them, as there were too many guns to take in any other way."[12]

The Marines had the enemy on the run. They took out several more nests; the Germans seemed to melt away. With resistance waning, Hamilton pulled out his map case and scanned the area for an unimproved road that appeared on the map. With only a platoon of men, including Janson, Hamilton set out for the road, moving over the nose of Hill 142 in the process. Unbeknownst to them, that road led to the German-held village of Torcy.

On the road, the men found themselves in a cleared area scattered with woodpiles. Hidden behind the piles, several Maxims started firing upon them. A stream of bullets struck one Marine. "The man's head was gone from the eyes up; his helmet slid stickily back over his combat pack and lay on the ground."[13] A Marine picked up the man's Chauchat and pulled the trigger back, unloading an entire half-moon-shaped magazine into three oncoming Germans, who appeared to "wilt."[14]

Hamilton pushed ahead with an automatic rifle team that had attacked to the left to take out one of the machine-gun nests in the mounds of wood. "What saved me I don't know—the Maxims on both sides cut at us unmercifully—but although I lost heavily here [the 49th lost several officers and enlisted men], I came out unscathed."[15]

During the melee, a corporal and two Marines wandered down the road into the town of Torcy. As they approached the first house, another squad of Germans pelted the Americans with heavy fire, wounding one and sending the Marines scurrying into a large shell hole where they attempted to hold out. The corporal sent one Marine back to gather reinforcements. Fighting in their own miniature Alamo, the pair of men held back the enemy until two Germans infiltrated their position. The Germans never returned, nor did the Americans. The two intrepid Marines were never seen again, and the 49th registered its first men missing in action; shortly thereafter, the disposition of their bodies was declared "unknown." Nine years would pass before a French farmer would discover the bodies of the unsung Americans and two Germans, along with their equipment and weapons, in the bottom of the fighting hole.[16]

Back on the road, Hamilton and his small platoon continued to encounter heavy fire, and he realized, "*I had gone too far—that the nose of the hill I had come over was our objective.*"[17]

Hamilton had to get back to the hill with his men and dig in. "It was a case of every man for himself. I crawled back through a drainage ditch filled with cold water and shiny reeds. Machine-gun bullets were just grazing my back and our own artillery was dropping close."[18]

Miraculously, Hamilton and Janson returned to the hill and started reorganizing what remained of the two shredded companies. Platoons with an original strength of around sixty men had withered to a pitiful handful of men led by a corporal. Most of his officers were dead. Reinforcements had not arrived. Moving from one position to another, Hamilton ordered his men to dig in and set up strongpoints and outposts. The Marines scoured the hill for working German machine guns and belts of ammo. Making the most of his meager force, Hamilton sent out a few men as scouts to keep an eye on his flanks.

Then the heavy thud and thunder of German artillery shook the hill. Hamilton and Janson knew the shelling signaled one thing.

The German counterattack on Hill 142 had begun.

The deafening blasts of grenades dashed Hamilton's feverish efforts to bolster the Marine's anemic defenses on Hill 142. A rock hurled by the explosion struck Hamilton behind the ear, temporarily stunning him. But through the din of battle, dense fog, and mass confusion generated in the melee, Hamilton heard a bloodcurdling scream emanating from the direction of Gunnery Sergeant Ernest Janson's fighting position.

A moment earlier, out of the corner of his eye, the forty-year-old Janson had caught sight of more than a dozen *Stahlhelm* helmets weaving through the underbrush in front of his foxhole. Janson leapt into the infiltrating column of Germans, who had positioned five machine guns to annihilate the 49th Company. He impaled the belly of the first soldier and twisted the bayonet's keen blade, eviscerating him. Withdrawing his bayonet, the gunny lunged again, penetrating the torso of the next field-gray-clad soldier.

Hamilton described the furious fight: "Shooting to beat the devil. Not more than twenty feet from us was a line of [about] fifteen German helmets and five light machine guns just coming into action."[19] All alone, Janson lurched at the Germans.

His war cry alerted the rest of his company who, adding their efforts to Janson's heroics and baleful bayonet, killed or scattered the column, forcing them to flee and abandon their weapons. Severely wounded, the Marine veteran, with his daring charge, saved the 49th and the hill. Had the Germans been able to set up their guns, they would have obliterated the 49th and retaken the hill.

For his bravery and disregard for his own safety, Body Bearer Gunnery Sergeant Ernest Janson would become the first recipient of the

Medal of Honor for the AEF.* But that was not his only decoration. As a result of his "conspicuous gallantry and intrepidity above and beyond the call of duty,"[20] Janson received both the Navy Medal of Honor and the Army Medal of Honor;† the Purple Heart; the Médaille pour la Bravoure Militaire from Montenegro; the Cruz de Guerra, Third Class, from the Portuguese government; the Croce di Guerra from the Italian government; and the Croix de Guerre with Palm, the French Fourragere, and the Médaille Militaire from the French government.

Throughout the rest of the day and night, the Germans relentlessly counterattacked Hamilton's tiny force of Marines holding the hill. Through a runner who had to weave his way past the Germans, Hamilton sent a desperate message to his battalion CO, Major Julius Turrill:

> Our position is not very good because of salient. We are entrenching and have four [captured German] machine guns in place. We have been counterattacked several times but so far have held the hill. Our casualties are *very* heavy. We need medical aid badly, and cannot locate any hospital apprentices and need many. We will need artillery assistance to this line tonight.

---

* Janson spent months recovering from his wounds before Pershing presented him with the decoration. His citation read, "For conspicuous gallantry and intrepidity above and beyond the call of duty in action with the enemy near Château-Thierry, France, June 6, 1918. Immediately after the company to which he belonged had reached its objective on Hill 142, several hostile counter-attacks were launched against the line before the new position had been consolidated. Sergeant Janson was attempting to organize a position on the north-slope of the hill when he saw twelve of the enemy, armed with five light machine guns, crawling toward his group. Giving the alarm, he rushed the hostile detachment, bayoneted the two leaders, and forced the others to flee, abandoning their guns. His quick action, initiative, and courage drove the enemy from a position from which they could have swept the hill with machine-gun fire and forced the withdrawal of our troops."

† Usually, Marines are eligible for only the Navy Medal of Honor. However, because the Marines worked so closely with the US Army during WWI, five Marines who served during the Great War, including Janson, received both the Army and the Navy versions of the medal for a single action. After World War I, the military discontinued the practice of awarding multiple Medals of Honor.

Ammunition of all kinds needed. . . . All my officers are gone.
9:50 a.m. George W. Hamilton[21]

The Marines held the hill. Later on the afternoon of June 6, reinforcements trickled into Hamilton's position. The first to arrive were the
missing companies earmarked for the initial assault: 1/5's 17th Company
and the 66th Company along with the 8th Machine Gun Company,
followed by a company of Army combat engineers whose spades and
pickaxes could dig deeper entrenchments into the hill.

Captured machine guns and accurate rifle fire kept the Germans
at bay. The marksmanship of Hamilton's men had a chilling effect on
the Germans. One Marine reflected, "Aimed sustained rifle-fire that
comes from nowhere in particular and picks off men—it brought the
war home to the individual and demoralized him."[22]

Nowhere was the war "brought home" more than with the
wounded. Suffering from multiple injuries, Janson struggled to stay
alive. Wounded and dying men carpeted the fields and hill. The stifling sun and lack of water drove men mad. Germans cried out: *"Ach,
Himmel, hilf, hilf! . . . Liebe Gott!"*[23] ("Oh, heaven, help, help, for the
love of God!") In the midst of the carnage, shells rained down on the
hill in a killing pattern, searching for men with their deadly shrapnel
and by concussion.

Immediate battlefield medicine was brutal and crude. Navy corpsmen assigned to the 49th and 67th worked overtime tending to the
wounded, exhausting their limited supply of bandages. At the beginning
of 1917, the US Navy Hospital Corps had just seventeen hundred men
in its ranks. A vigorous recruitment effort brought the total number of
corpsmen up to six thousand, or about 3.5 percent of the total Navy
and Marine personnel just prior to America's entry into World War I.*

---

* By the end of 1918, the Hospital Corps would have seventeen thousand men—about
ten times the number it had less than two years earlier. Hospitals across the country
set up a crash-course school to train the large numbers of new pharmacists' mates in
the basics of care.

Because the Marine Corps had no medical personnel of its own, the Marines used Navy corpsmen to tend to the wounded. Typically five to seven corpsmen accompanied each rifle company, with another five to seven assigned to the battalion aid station; in all, the 4th Marine Brigade contained 350 Navy medical personnel. Serving alongside the Marines in France was one of the most difficult assignments a corpsman could receive. Despite the prominent Red Cross armbands on their uniforms, the corpsmen were common targets for the enemy.* Hamilton required more to tend the scores of wounded Marines.

German stretcher-bearers worked in the fields, and initially, the Americans allowed them to perform their duty and collect the wounded. But the vicious German counterattacks and the dwindling numbers of Marines changed the calculus. One incident galvanized Hamilton's men. Wind lifted the blanket on one of the German stretchers. Through their field glasses, the Marines could see that, instead of a wounded soldier, the stretcher party was transporting a light machine gun—a blatant violation of laws of war. Under the terms of the Geneva Convention, the enemy medics became a legitimate military target, and accurate Marine rifle fire killed the group. News of the Boche ruse quickly spread, and the Marines didn't take chances with the lives of the few remaining members of the 49th and 67th Companies. A letter taken later from a dead *Feldwebel* (deputy platoon leader) summed up the Germans' viewpoint of the lethal new enemy they faced: "The Americans are savages. They kill everything that moves."[24] Dispatches from the German front line to headquarters also alluded to the ferocity of their Marine opponents, referring to the Leathernecks by the moniker *Teufel Hunden*† (Devil Dogs)—a title the Marines proudly use to refer to themselves to this day.

---

* Nearly half the Navy corpsmen with the 4th Marine Brigade were wounded, killed, or captured during the war. In recognition of their heroic devotion to duty, the corpsmen of World War I received two Medals of Honor, fifty-five Navy Crosses, thirty-three Distinguished Service Crosses, 237 Silver Stars, and countless Purple Hearts.

† *Teufel Hunden* is actually inaccurate German—it should be *Teufelshunde*. It is likely the term was passed orally to a Marine from a captured German, causing the word to be scrambled.

*   *   *

Buoyed by the successful attack on Hill 142, Harbord and French General Degoutte launched the second phase of the attack: an assault on the town of Bouresches and Belleau Wood itself. Inaccurate French sources deemed the woods weakly defended. The Marines gathered intelligence that contradicted the French, but they had no clear protocol for obtaining and quickly processing actionable information and moving it up the chain of command to the French.* In reality, hundreds of Germans had transformed the boulder-strewn, ravine-etched former hunting preserve into a fortress. The Allies' plan to take Bois Belleau by June 6 was a fantasy.

Ignoring intelligence that the Germans were defending the area in depth and with minimal time to prepare, Degoutte ordered an assault. Only Hamilton, Janson, and those on the ground could convey how miraculous taking and holding 142 had been. They had attacked with no preparation, minimal artillery, and erroneous intelligence that suggested the Germans did not hold the hill in force. Against all probability and through the many extraordinary actions of individual Marines, they improvised, adapted, conquered despite nearly impossible odds, and seized and held the hill. The difference between victory and defeat boiled down to the toughness and resilience of individual Marines. But instead of considering the fierce fight a harbinger or taking the advice of the 2nd Division's chief of staff, Colonel Preston Brown, who advocated stormtrooper-like infiltration tactics and saturating the German positions with artillery,[25] Degoutte seized the initiative and scheduled the 6th Marines and 3/5 to strike northeasterly from Lucy-le-Bocage and clear Belleau Wood and Bouresches. Lacking infiltration tactics, they

---

* Marine Lieutenant William A. Eddy infiltrated behind German lines "Indian style" to collect intelligence. Fearless and daring, Eddy spoke German and several other languages. After WWI, he earned a PhD and taught at Dartmouth and American University in Cairo. An expert on the Middle East, he later served as an intelligence officer in North Africa with "Wild Bill" Donovan's Office of Strategic Services and played a key role in the Allied invasion of North Africa in WWII.

would make a frontal assault, straight into machine guns, with limited artillery to maintain the element of surprise.

Bullets ripped the bark from trees and tore through the wheat in the field that lay before the Marines. Coiled in the trees facing the wheat, the 6th Marines and 3/5 prepared to cross four hundred yards of open rolling ground.

When the jump-off time arrived, the Devil Dogs to the right of Hamilton faced their own bloodbath as they fought through the open wheat fields to Bouresches. Benjamin Berry's 3/5 faced some of the hottest German fire, "a veritable hell of hissing bullets."[26] Tens of thousands of rounds per minute sailed through the wheat, "a death-dealing torrent."[27] Despite the forlorn assault, the *Teufel Hunden* marched forward in rank and file, as one participant noted, "as though facing a March gale." The Germans maintained air superiority over the area, and their sausage observation balloons wafted in the sky miles from the fields, providing accurate and deadly artillery fire on the advancing Marines.

Colonel Albertus W. Catlin, commanding officer of the 6th Marines, watched his men. "It was one of the most beautiful sights I have ever witnessed," he said. "The battalion pivoted on its right, the left sweeping across the open ground in four waves, as steadily and correctly as though on parade. . . . My hands were clutched and all my muscles taut as I watched that cool, intrepid, masterful defiance of the German spite."[28] Minutes later, a sniper's bullet would pierce his chest. He survived; however, his role in the Great War was over.

Stunned by the sight of Americans advancing in straight lines as if they were on parade, German gunners fired their Maxims on the waves of Marines stepping through the wheat.* "The Germans could not have desired better targets," a German lieutenant colonel later wrote. "Such a spectacle was entirely unfamiliar to them. German troops would have

---

* Borrowing a French tactic, the attack force anticipated that the first three waves would be annihilated, absorbing the German fire. Cold-bloodedly, they calculated that the fourth wave, charging over the bodies of their brothers, would break through and seize the objective. The hideous losses compelled the Marines never to employ the tactic again after the battle of Belleau Wood.

advanced in thin lines of skirmishers following one another in waves, or in small separate units of shock troops, moving forward in rows with their light machine guns, utilizing whatever shelter was offered by the terrain until they were in a position to open fire."[29]

Somewhere in the midst of the charge, a forty-four-year-old first sergeant saw men in his platoon from the 73rd Machine Gun Company waver.[30] The slightly built, five-feet-six Marine, "with bronzed cheeks from the wind and sun of the seven seas," raised his bayoneted Springfield over his head and yelled these immortal words:

"Come on, you sons-o'-bitches! Do you want to live forever!?"[31]

First Sergeant Dan Daly was the real deal, and when he shouted, Marines listened. Like Janson, Daly belonged to a core group of seasoned Marines who had fought in the Philippines, Santo Domingo, Peking (Beijing), and Veracruz, Mexico. Combat veterans with years of experience filled the ranks from gunny sergeants to the battalion majors. A true badass, Daly had single-handedly defended the Tartar Wall in Peking during the Boxer Rebellion in 1900. Against hundreds of armed Chinese, Daly alone guarded the wall outside the American consulate. Most likely carrying a M1895 Colt-Browning machine gun, he fought against hundreds of "Boxers," anti-foreign and anti-Christian Chinese nationalists who believed their bodies could not be harmed by bullets. They attempted to storm the building and kill everyone inside, but Daly stood in their way. Hundreds of men, armed with rifles and swords, charged the wall all night. Daly held the wall.

On another occasion, Daly, along with thirty-five other Marines, defeated approximately four hundred Caco bandits, peasant revolutionaries, and mercenaries who had infiltrated Haiti from the Dominican Republic in the fall of 1915. Backed by the German government, the Cacos were attempting to overthrow the Haitian government. President Wilson sent the Marines, including Daly, to the island nation to oppose the rebels and occupy the country. Surrounded by bandits in a walled compound and having lost his machine gun earlier in the day when crossing a river, Daly took matters into his own hands. The spry gunny escaped the siege in the middle of the night, evaded rebel patrols, found the river, dove into its muddy water, and miraculously found the missing gun. Strapping the heavy weapon on his back, Daly lugged it through the rebel lines and infiltrated back into the compound. With the recovered machine gun, the Marines under his command held off the hundreds of bandits. Daly received his second Medal of Honor for his extraordinary derring-do.

In response to his words and leadership, Daly's platoon broke through the wheat on June 6. Later, Daly single-handedly took out a machine-gun nest with his .45. A day earlier, he had rushed into a blazing ammo dump and extinguished the fire, preventing the death of scores of Marines. For those actions, his commanding officer recommended he receive his third Medal of Honor; however, it was later changed to the Navy Cross.

Charging with the Marines through the wheat was intrepid war correspondent Floyd Gibbons of the *Chicago Daily Tribune*, who recorded Daly's words. Gibbons followed 3/5's battalion commander, Major Benjamin Berry. As hundreds of deadly rounds whizzed through the field, Berry shouted, "My hand's gone." A bullet "tore through muscles and nerves in the forearm and lodged itself in the palm of his hand." As Gibbons crawled over toward the major, a bullet clipped his biceps; another the top of his left shoulder. Moving forward, he lay prone on his toes and elbows to make himself less of a target. "Then there came a crash. It sounded to me like someone had dropped a bottle into a porcelain bathtub. A barrel of whitewash tipped over, and it seemed that everything in the world turned white."[32]

At enormous cost, the Marines took the bulk of Bouresches (the Germans still held the stone train station at the edge of town) and penetrated the southern portion of Belleau Wood, losing many veterans in the process. Weeks and hundreds of lives were lost clearing the heavily defended woods and defeating numerous large German counterattacks.

Prior to marching into the wheat with the Marines, war correspondent Gibbons had crafted a sensationalized advance story and turned it over to Pershing's censors. Gibbons's story had captured the bloody events of June 6. His words (and those of others) would change the Marine Corps and the course of the war

CHAPTER 10

"THE MARINES ARE FIGHTING LIKE TROJANS"

US MARINES SMASH HUNS: CAPTURE MACHINE
GUNS, KILL BOSCHES, TAKE PRISONERS
—*Chicago Daily Tribune*

Am I dead? Gibbons asked himself. Maxim bullets had pierced his left arm and left eye, ripping part of his skull out of his head. After wiggling his fingers and left foot, he recalled, "I knew I was alive."[1] With his remaining eye, he saw Major Berry, commander of 3/5, his left arm mangled, get up and lead several Marines in destroying a machine gun. Gibbons and another reporter lay in the field until 9:00 p.m., when they crawled off and made their way to an aid station. His other press comrades thought he had died in the charge.

Gibbons's story lay in the hands of one of Pershing's censors back in Paris. The censor's job was to ensure that the press did not reveal anything of intelligence value to the Germans. To that end, the AEF enforced strict policies that forbade journalists to identify divisions or other units by number or state. They prohibited the use of the words "regiment" and "battalion," even precluding the identification of the US Army's service branches, such as artillery, infantry, and engineers. Bland and anonymous, the resulting articles failed to connect meaningfully with the readers back home.

After the Battle of Belleau Wood, rumors surfaced that Gibbons had died. The censor in Pershing's headquarters, a friend of Gibbons's, read through what he thought was the last report of a dead man, and he approved the identification of Marines in the story. "This is the last thing I can ever do for poor old Floyd,"[2] the censor murmured, and he permitted the story to go to print. The commentary overstepped the bounds of anonymity by portraying the valor and accomplishments of the Marines as a distinct unit within the AEF. That humanization touched and moved the audience in a manner previous articles had been unable to achieve. Recognizing its inherent value, the editor of the *Chicago Daily Tribune* ran Gibbons's piece on the front page. He added headlines that blew the success of the battle out of proportion. The words "US MARINES SMASH HUNS" marched in large, bold letters right beneath the masthead. Subheads added, "CAPTURE MACHINE GUNS, KILL BOSCHES, TAKE PRISONERS," and "TEUTONS SHIFT THEIR ATTACKS TO OISE."[3]

Gibbons lavished praise upon the Marines in colorful, effusive prose. "American Marines wrote another glorious page in their history Tuesday night and Wednesday, beating off two determined German attacks on the Marne battlefield," the story began. "Last night they wiped out a large enemy patrol. This morning they charged and captured enemy machine guns and this afternoon killed many of the enemy and took prisoners."[4]

The story poured on the accolades. "The Marines are fighting like Trojans and have no desire for sleep." Gibbons added, "Their French comrades say they showed the greatest skill and accuracy while under fire."[5]

Gibbons's story gave a face and a name to the men fighting in Europe. Suddenly, everyone thirsted to learn more about what "our Marines" were doing in France. The article went viral, and headlines around the world brought attention to the Corps and the battle. Gibbons bestowed everlasting glory upon the United States Marine Corps. Credited with saving Paris, the Marines became the toast of the town— even though the battle was far from over.

After the story ran, Congress approved a massive increase in the number of men in the Corps, and Marine recruitment jumped by more than 100 percent in the days following its publication. An article in *The New York Times* reported, "[A recruiter,] on duty at the Marine headquarters in East Twenty-Fourth Street, said yesterday that about 10,000 men had enlisted in various parts of the country since Congress authorized the Corps' increase from 30,000 to 75,000 men."[6]

With so much focus on the Marines, the Army was not receiving proper credit for its own heroic activities. The majority of the public believed that the entire 2nd Division was composed of Marines, when in actuality the unit consisted primarily of Army personnel. Naturally, the press reports led to bad blood between the two branches of the military; some in the Army regarded the Marines with a combination of jealousy and contempt.

Meanwhile, Belleau Wood morphed into a contest of wills among nations. Alarmed by the headlines, General Max von Boehn, commander of the 28th Division, wrote in a special order on June 8, "An American success along that front, even if only temporary, may have the most unfavorable influence of the attitude of the Entente and the duration of the war. In the coming battles, therefore, it is not a question of the possession of this or that village or woods, insignificant in itself; it is a question of whether the Anglo-American claims that the American Army is the equal or even the superior of the German Army is to be made good."[7]

The German high command moved the elite 5th Prussian Guards Division, known for its formidable battlefield prowess, into position against the Marines. The high command also shifted the 28th Division—which had been victorious at Verdun, Cambrai, and the Somme—from the Noyon-Montdidier sector, where they were facing the French, to Belleau Wood against 1/5 and Hamilton's 49th Company, which was holding Hill 142. The Germans pitted more than half a dozen other divisions and units against the Marines as well. Despite being understrength from days of fighting, these were some of the most elite German troops in the field. A military intelligence report noted, "A [28th] Division order (dated Mar. 3, 1917) found on a corpse praises the heroism of the valiant troops of the 28th Division and calls its regiments 'The conquerors of Lorette.'"[8]

The focal point of the Allied attack shifted to Belleau Wood—a natural fortress that could not be left in German hands. The thick trees of the forest provided cover for the enemy fighters and artillery. From within its shaded depths, they could sally forth and launch attacks. To ferret them out of their hiding places, the Marines planned to sweep through the woods and engage the Germans man-to-man. Tragically, this approach played into the German strategy. The Marines were about to march into a meat grinder.

Rather than attack immediately after the Marine assault on June 6, Brigadier General James Harbord first consolidated his lines and held back the Germans as they counterattacked. On June 7, replacement troops began filtering into his decimated units, which included Body Bearer Ernest Janson's 49th Company. Those infusions included Private Elton Mackin, a member of the 1st Battalion 5th Marine Regiment. Hailing from Lewiston, New York, Mackin had enlisted in 1917 at the age of nineteen, against the wishes of his family. After training at Parris Island, which he affectionately referred to as "the toughest military school under the American colors,"[9] he shipped over to France in April 1918. Mackin volunteered for one of the most perilous jobs in the 5th Regiment: runner. Because of their high mortality rate, men who served as runners were often said to be in the suicide club. The stalwart New Yorker relayed messages between units, traveling alone in hostile territory, often under shell and machine-gun fire. This job gave him a unique and expansive vantage point on the 5th Marines' and 49th Company's battlefield experiences.

Their replacements also included Lieutenant John Thomason, who would pen his own narratives of the battle. Born in 1893 and descended from several Confederate officers, Thomason was working as a cub reporter and part-time illustrator in his hometown, Huntsville, Texas, when his paper carried an advertisement seeking men to volunteer as

Marine Corps officers. In 1917, Thomason was engaged to be married. Within a year, the twenty-five-year-old found himself leading Marines in France. A gifted artist, Thomason brought a sketch pad to war and captured battle scenes in pencil and in pen and ink. His experiences would later become the grist for more than sixty short stories, magazine articles, and several books, most of which he illustrated himself.

Beginning on June 6, the Germans mercilessly counterattacked Hill 142 and shelled the 49th Company. The Americans remained on the hill for more than ten days until relieved. While Body Bearer Ernest Janson fought for his life in a field hospital near Paris, Thomason, Hamilton, and the 49th endured German shells and a silent, deadly killer: gas. As they prepared to fight, massive high-explosive shells and mustard gas drenched the 49th's shallow fighting holes. Men fought and lived in their bulky, uncomfortable masks.

Gas shells detonated with a quiet *thump* before emitting clouds of deadly fumes. Although there were also reports of the French using chemical weapons, the Germans were the first to use poison gas in World War I. A Jewish German, Fritz Haber, led the country's chemical warfare program.[10] Ironically, some of the very chemicals he developed would exterminate his fellow Jews during the Holocaust. The Germans first fired gas-filled shells at the Battle of Bolimów in January 1915, but the cold weather froze the gas, making it ineffective. They tried again at 1915's Second Battle of Ypres, and this time the consequences were deadly. On April 22, German troops opened 5,730 gas cylinders of chlorine gas by hand. The French suffered more than six thousand casualties as a result—most dead within ten minutes of exposure. However, many of the Germans who deployed the gas died, as well. Unprepared for this initial attack, Allied officers told their men to urinate on handkerchiefs and hold them over their faces to filter out the gas, but this provided little protection against the chlorine and mustard.

Known as the "king of gases," mustard gas, or sulfur mustard, is a dirty, yellowish-brown color in its weaponized form and has an unmistakable odor that many people compare to that of mustard, garlic, or horseradish. In cold temperatures, it would hover near the ground within shell holes and trenches, often lingering for days. When the weather warmed up, the mustard would rise into the air once more, injuring or killing unprepared troops.

Four hundred thousand casualties during WWI resulted from exposure to the deadly mustard. The gas—or more accurately, its oily droplets—assaulted the skin, eyes, lungs, and internal organs. The effects could appear immediately or take up to twenty-four hours to manifest. Victims first experience itchy rashes that bloom into pus-filled yellow blisters, accompanied by epiphora (watery eyes) and, in some cases, blindness. When inhaled, it ravaged a victim's lungs, leading to a painful death. And even if they appeared to recover completely, those afflicted were likely to develop cancer years or decades later.

No treatment or antidote existed. When those who had been exposed were treated in field hospitals, corpsmen and medics removed victims' uniforms and washed their skin in soap and water. They shaved off contaminated hair and rinsed the eyes in a saline solution. Recovery was invariably painful, and screams from the afflicted punctuated the atmosphere of field hospitals. Tragically, many men endured the anguish alone while lying injured on the battlefield without receiving even the meager benefits provided by the aid stations.

Unlike mustard, phosgene gas smells like fresh-cut hay or grass when released. Although colorless in its liquid form, it materialized as a green cloud on the battlefield, alerting the men to protect themselves. Often mixed with chlorine to allow for propagation across a broader distance, phosgene could kill men not wearing masks. It destroyed the lungs, causing inflammation and a buildup of fluid. Afflicted soldiers essentially drowned in their own bodily fluids, often spending their last moments gasping for air like a fish out of water. While some victims reacted to the nefarious gas immediately, the symptoms of exposure could take up to twenty-four hours to evince; troops affected by the noxious gas could put up a fight one day only to become incapacitated the following day.

To defend themselves against the chemical attacks, US Marines carried two different gas masks: either the British Small Box Respirator (SBR) or the Corrected English Model (CEM, a version of the British SBR that the Americans began producing in 1917) and the French M2. Over the course of the war, French factories churned out more than 29 million M2s. Initially, the Marines generally employed the French model as a backup. Because a single shrapnel puncture in the body of a mask could prove deadly, possession of two masks was essential.

The masks required a tight seal around the wearer's face. For Marines in the field, shaving made the difference between life and death, but conditions on the battlefield were far from ideal for maintaining proper grooming. The men had minimal food and water for drinking—let alone for shaving. And even with a close shave, the seal around the wearer's face was often not airtight. To compensate, the mask contained a painful spring-type nose clip that closed the nose and forced the wearer to breathe through his mouth. The Marines then clenched mouth guards between their teeth, and tubes jammed in their mouths connected to a hose that fed a box containing the filter. The whole experience was awkward and claustrophobic in training—made far worse by battle and bad weather. The masks limited peripheral vision, and rain exacerbated the problem, causing the masks' glass eyepieces to fog up. Marines' jaws ached from clenching down on the mouthpieces, and their noses ran. While wearing the masks, they couldn't speak. Because gas attacks could come at any time, and came frequently at night, men often slept in their masks—even though the maximum time a wearer could don the device was three hours. When they reached the limit, men often ripped the bulky contraptions off in desperation. Despite the intense discomfort of wearing a gas mask, it beat the alternative.

Hamilton, Thomason, and the 49th defended Hill 142 for days, defeating several massive German counterattacks. In mid-June, Major Turrill also dispatched a platoon from the 49th to fight in Belleau. Snipers, machine guns, and nightly raids and counterattacks added to the deadly fighting, and around Belleau Wood the battle dragged on for weeks as German artillery blasted the area. Some shells came from German heavy artillery, forming enormous craters that vaporized groups of men. Each day the odds of survival in the forest grew slimmer. One Marine recalled, "A thousand machine guns could not give one that helpless feeling brought on by the approach of the overawing, merciless shells. They would carry him instantly to oblivion by covering him in his hole or with their terrible force blow him to atoms. These monsters of powder and steel put fear in a man's soul."[11]

One survivor described the brutal subhuman conditions of fighting in Belleau Wood: "We were covered with body lice, hungry, and thirsty. We were bruised in body and soul, tired and weary, dirty and weakened by dysentery, that messy kind that requires lots of paper and sanitation, but we had none. There was human blood on our hands that had to go for many days before they could be washed."[12]

Another wrote, "It has been a living hell since I started this. We are shelled all night with shrapnel and gas shells. At times I wished that one would knock me off, but still life is very sweet at its worst."[13] The paper upon which he penned those lines was punctured multiple times by shrapnel before it reached its recipient.

The American command brought in the 7th Regiment of the 3rd Division from French reserves. The 7th's regimental commander demanded artillery support and one thousand grenades, but even with the additional munitions, he predicted the attack on the German line in the wood would fail. The Army attack went nowhere, and General Harbord turned back to his Marines. He ordered Major Maurice Shearer, the replacement for Major Berry who had lost his hand in the wheat field, to lead the 3rd Battalion, 5th Marines and clear the northern woods of Germans.

Once again, Harbord underestimated the strength of the Germans. He directed Shearer to clear the woods by employing snipers and wire to contain the enemy and reduce Marine losses. Intelligence gleaned from a captured prisoner and battlefield reconnaissance from the 5th Marine commander later revealed that the Germans still held the northern part of Belleau in strength; however, Harbord again ordered Shearer to attack, insisting upon the impracticality of withdrawal of the Marines that would enable artillery to plaster the woods. Harbord memorialized the fog of war and his lack of information about the German position, writing, "The undersigned has been misled as to the affairs in that end of the woods, either consciously or unconsciously, ever since its first occupation by the battalion under command of Lieutenant Colonel Wise and later by the battalion of the 7th Infantry."[14]

At 7:00 p.m. on June 23, Shearer and 3/5 pounced. Scores of men dropped like flies in the doomed assault on the formidable German defenses. Deadly cross fire from machine guns with interlocking positions created a kill zone. Lieutenant Laurence Stallings commanded a supporting platoon that supplied fresh bodies to the Marine line, replacing the dead or wounded.* He ordered his men to ignore the wounded, warning that the administration of first aid would delay plugging up the gaps in the Marine lines. His men crawled over the bodies, "hugging the ground, the blood on their sleeves, and hands, their faces. This last failure in Belleau Wood would be remembered by some as the worst afternoon of their lives no matter what fortune later befell them."[15]

Stopped cold by the Germans, Shearer ended the attack. He told Harbord, "The enemy seems to have unlimited alternate gun positions and many guns. Each gun position covered by others. I know of no other way of attacking these positions . . . and I am of the opinion that infantry alone cannot dislodge enemy guns."[16]

Shearer's report had an effect. Harbord met with General Omar Bundy, the 2nd Division's commanding officer, and they planned a fourteen-hour artillery bombardment, something that should have occurred weeks earlier. On June 25, following the barrage, 3/5 charged "like a bunch of wild cats springing at a band of hyenas."[17] The Marines passed the mangled corpses of the enemy. A few German survivors battled on,

---

* Stallings would later infuse his recollections of the battle into novels, films, and onstage productions. He cowrote the Broadway smash *What Price Glory?* which was later made into two films, the second directed by the esteemed John Ford.

but others surrendered. At approximately 7:00 a.m. on June 26, Shearer sent Harbord the following message: "Woods now US Marine Corps' entirely."[18]

Major Frederick Wise, summed up the battle at Belleau Wood: "The only thing that drove those Marines through those woods in the face of such resistance as they met was their individual, elemental guts, plus the hardening of the training through which they had gone."[19] With the wood in Marine hands, the 2nd Division and its Army brigade turned their attention to Vaux on the eastern flank of the battlefield.

CHAPTER 11

EDWARD YOUNGER: VAUX

On July 1, 1918, Sergeant Edward F. Younger watched as Allied artillery blasted Vaux, located to the east of the Marines. Within hours he would participate in a fight that nearly took his life. For three weeks prior, Younger, who was in Company A of the 1st Battalion 9th Regiment, had defended the right flank of the Marines in front of Vaux. The 3rd Brigade, composed entirely of Army personnel, included soldiers from the 9th and 23rd Infantry Regiments. The constant German shelling and trench raids had taken a large toll, killing more than three hundred men and wounding fourteen hundred from the 3rd Brigade during the month of June.

Younger was a quintessential doughboy who did his duty and had the wounds to prove it. Born in Chicago in 1898, he attended school only through the eighth grade.[1] Above average in height, he had a stocky build and broad shoulders. His hair was dark, and photographs from the period often depict him with a somber expression. His father died when Edward was twelve, and his mother remarried. The desire to help the Allies was strong in his family, and his brother Frank, sixteen years older, enlisted in the British Army after the Americans refused him for being too old. In February 1917, at the age of eighteen, Edward Younger joined the US Army "just out of excitement—or curiosity maybe."[2]

Critical to the defense of Paris, Vaux bisected the Paris-Metz road that led to the French capital. For the assault, the Allies had a secret weapon: a French stonemason who had worked in every house in the village provided detailed information about the location of all the buildings in the town.[3] German prisoners filled in details about enemy troop placements, giving the assault force an unusually good picture of what they were entering.

The assault commenced on the afternoon of July 1. Learning lessons from the unsupported attacks at Belleau Wood, Allied artillery plastered the defenses in Vaux and the nearby forest known as the Bois de la Roche (Wood of the Rock). Gas and high-explosive shells hammered the town, focusing on German strongpoints identified by the mason. The intensity of the shelling alerted the Germans that an assault was on its way; however, they were helpless to do anything about it. One member of the 9th remembered a close call from shrapnel that dented the top of his helmet. "We saw the systematic destruction of the part of Vaux across the creek or river that divided the American and German troops. In the first thirty minutes of the barrage every house was blown down, and by the time the troops made their attack there was no place to hide and the few Germans left in the town were in basements where they were taken prisoner or killed."[4]

At six in the evening, the 3rd Brigade, including Younger's 9th Infantry, the regimental machine-gun company, and a company from the 2nd Engineers, jumped off. They quickly overwhelmed the resistance, and by 7:00 p.m., they had taken control of Vaux. The German commanders immediately planned a counterattack and scheduled it for 2:15 a.m.[5] But as the skirmishing around the outskirts of Vaux continued, the Germans realized they had no hope of prevailing and called off their riposte.

The American artillery had disabled the German field telephone lines earlier in the day, and few German runners were able to relay messages. In the chaos, the message about the canceled German counterattack did not make its way to one of the German battalions, which advanced as originally ordered.[6] As the unit approached the railroad on the outskirts of town, the Americans sliced it to pieces.

In all, the Germans endured 250 men killed, 160 wounded, and more than 500 captured. On the American side, losses totaled 46 dead and 270 missing or wounded. The latter category included Younger, who received multiple gunshot wounds to his head, neck, and left arm but miraculously made a full recovery. It would not be the last time.

French Sixth Army Commander General Degoutte later wrote, "In view of the brilliant conduct of the 4th Brigade of the 2nd US Division, which in a spirited fight took Bouresches and the important strong point of Bois de Belleau stubbornly defended by a large enemy force, the General commanding the Sixth Army orders that henceforth, in all official papers, the Bois de Belleau shall be named 'Bois de la Brigade de Marine.'"[7]

Although Belleau Wood itself was largely tactically meaningless, what happened there was not. The 2nd Division's stand at Belleau Wood proved decisive. The Americans blunted the Germans' momentum—and the Germans never recovered it. During the second phase of the battle, the Germans moved in some of their most battle-hardened troops to deal a crushing defeat to the Americans. The German elite units had rarely been defeated while in a defensive position. The Germans wanted to show the green American troops and the world who controlled the Western Front. As a result of true grit and enormous American casualties, Belleau Wood become a turning point in the war. Now Americans had beaten some of the best German troops—and hundreds of thousands more US troops were pouring into France every month. Although some modern historians dispute it, General Robert Lee Bullard bluntly stated, "The Marines didn't 'win the war' here, but they saved the Allies from defeat. Had they arrived a few hours later, I think it would have been the beginning of the end."[8]

General Matthew Ridgway, the legendary WWII airborne commander and later General Douglas MacArthur's successor in the Korean War, thought Belleau Wood was a waste. Commenting from the perfect vision and hindsight of history, he panned the battle as a "prize example of men's lives being thrown away against objectives not worth the cost . . . and [Belleau Wood was] a monument for all time to the inflexibility of military thinking in that period."[9] Clearly, the battle taught the Marines and their Army commander horrendously deadly lessons about the need for artillery preparation, infiltration tactics, and the intelligence and planning. It was the 2nd Division's first major battle, and they were learning. Through blood and fire, the cauldron of battle forged the modern Marine Corps.

After the battle, the Germans grimly noted, "The [American Marine] personnel must be called excellent . . . a very good division, if not an assault division . . . attacks of the Marines carried out smartly and ruthlessly. The moral effect of our fire did not materially check the advance of the infantry. The nerves of Americans are still unshaken."[10]

In an attempt to turn the tide, the Germans would hit the Americans again as the Boches launched their final offensive of the war.

Armed with sharpened shovels, flamethrowers, and light machine guns, the Stosstruppen, the tip of a *feldgrau** spear thousands of troops deep, surged across the pontoon bridges that German engineers had placed across the Marne River. Once over the waterway, the steamroller crashed into G Company of the 38th Infantry Regiment of the US Army's 3rd Division. On the sticky summer evening of July 15, 1918, Quartermaster General Erich Ludendorff launched his fifth offensive, which was geared at widening the Aisne-Marne salient and seizing the vital rail hub at Reims. Logistics remained the crucial weak point of the salient. Only one rail terminal, located in Soissons, sustained the massive German thrust that earlier had supplied German armies battling at Château-Thierry and Belleau Wood. But Reims was just the first objective—the Germans still had Paris in their sights.

G Company fought hand to hand on that summer night more than twenty-five miles to the east of Belleau Wood, the forefront of an elastic defense that stretched hundreds of yards behind them into Surmelin Valley. The valley formed one of the few gaps in an east-west line of ridges, providing a crucial path to the French capital. Two German

---

* *Feldgrau* (field gray) was the traditional color of German military uniforms. The word is also used as a metaphor for the Imperial German Army.

divisions plowed through the 38th's position, wiping out nearly an entire platoon of about sixty men.

The German advance would have been even greater had it not been for a deserter who tipped off the Allies on the eve of the battle. The Americans plastered German jumping-off trenches with a massive barrage, killing or wounding hundreds of Germans before they crossed the pontoon bridges. As a result, the Germans had to replace some assault units with fresh troops.

Sustaining heavy losses, the 38th boldly counterattacked, throwing the enemy offensive off schedule. German Lieutenant Kurt Hesse, who barely survived the melee, reflected, "Never have I seen so many dead men, never such frightful battle scenes. . . . The American had nerve; we must give him credit for that; but he also displayed a savage roughness. 'The Americans kill everybody!' was the cry of terror of July 15th, which for a long time stuck in the bones of our men. . . . Of the troops led into action on July 15th, more than 60 percent were left dead or wounded, laying [sic] on the field of battle."[11]

The 3rd Division held up the German offensive, allowing Allied guns to pulverize the German units. The epic stand earned the 3rd the immortal nickname "Rock of the Marne." It also laid the groundwork for the Allies' counteroffensive, which they had been preparing around the German salient for weeks. Having learned the painful lesson from Belleau Wood, the 2nd Division, utilizing its own artillery, went after the German Achilles' heel in the Marne salient: Soissons.

IV

COUNTEROFFENSIVE
1918

CHAPTER 12

TURNING POINT: SOISSONS

Body Bearer and Color Sergeant James W. Dell rode on the back of a caisson as the team of six horses towed one of the four 75 mm guns that struggled through the chocolate-brown, soupy French mud at night in the middle of another downpour. Plutonian in its darkness, the Renz Forest was jammed with traffic, which contributed to an air of confusion. As the infantry marched through the pitch darkness, each man kept one hand on the shoulder of the man in front of him to maintain a column. Some men fell asleep marching or became lost under the dark canopy of the forest where the narrow roads took on a tunnel-like quality. Dell served in the horse-drawn Headquarters Battery of the 15th Field Artillery Regiment. His was one of three field artillery regiments for the 2nd Division, which was making its way to the jump-off area for the offensive against Soissons. One of Dell's fellow artillerists recalled the slog to the jump-off point: "[We] traveled all night and the following day without rest. Several times I fell asleep on my horse. . . . The roads were filled with trucks carrying shells for 75s and 155s. I never saw so many shells in my life. We passed a number of horses cut clean in two, and one had been blown into a tree. It was a task to get our horses past the dead bodies as they displayed great fear of the gruesome sight."[1]

Field artillery, also called light artillery, accompanies an army onto the field of battle. Unlike heavy artillery, which typically remains stationary for an extended period of time, field artillery requires flexibility to advance or retreat rapidly in direct support of the troops. During World War I, it had to be light enough for a team of horses to transport over rough terrain. As a result, the field artillery at this time primarily consisted of cannons possessing a fairly limited range of fire, with calibers between 75 mm and 84 mm.

In 1897, France created the first field gun with long-barrel recoil—a technological breakthrough that made field artillery far deadlier. A cannon barrel previously had a rigid connection to its mount; upon firing a projectile, the entire mount would roll backward, as Newton's third law of motion dictates. Before discharging their weapons again, the artillery crews would return them to their correct positions—a time-consuming task that limited the guns' rate of fire. The novel French design placed the gun barrel in a cradle that slid backward, absorbing the recoil. A braking mechanism prevented the mount from rolling backward after each shot. The gun crews could now fire rounds in rapid succession, and this required them to carry many more rounds for their weapons.

Dell's horse-drawn battery towed four of these effective French field guns—the Matériel de 75 mm Mle 1897. American manufacturers had yet to ramp up their weapons production; therefore, most US artillery units utilized foreign-made weapons. Of superior design, this model, also known as the "French 75" or "Soixante-Quinze," had become the standard field gun for Allied armies. Developed in secrecy, the 75 also leveraged earlier advancements: single-piece (fixed-cartridge) ammunition, smokeless powder, and a rotating screw breech. By the time France declared war on Germany, the French had stockpiled about six thousand of these guns, and they added eleven thousand to their arsenal before the war ended.[2]

Considered by many to be the first modern artillery piece, the 75 regularly fired fifteen rounds per minute, and an experienced crew could sometimes deliver as many as thirty shells per minute. The range of the weapons—8,500 meters, a little more than five miles—allowed Dell and his men to remain back well behind advancing lines while raining down deadly fire. They could also move several degrees laterally to provide "sweeping fire." A four-gun battery could blanket parts of the battlefield with thousands of pieces of shrapnel in minutes.

Its creators had intended the 75 to shoot time-fused shrapnel shells, ideal for taking out rows of advancing troops. These sixteen-pound shells each contained 290 tiny lead balls. When the shells exploded, these balls would radiate outward, slicing through flesh and bone. As the tactics on the battlefield shifted and trench warfare became the norm, the Allies began using the weapon to launch high-explosive shells. Insidious in their design, the high-explosive rounds would bounce off the ground and then detonate five-hundredths of a second later, precisely when they would reach the level of an average man's head. Later, the 75s also delivered poison gas shells and had an anti-aircraft variant.

Prior to the Battle of Soissons, the 75 had already proven its worth during the First Battle of the Marne in 1914 and at Verdun in 1916. At Marne, the 75s tore through advancing columns of German troops who had outrun their own heavy artillery.

The 75 weighed three thousand pounds and had a barrel nearly nine feet long. Transporting a 75 required a team of six horses, with another six to pull the caisson containing the ammunition. Six men, each with a very specific job, loaded and fired the weapon. A complete battery required more than 160 horses and 160 men, led by three officers.[*3] Renowned for his excellent character, Dell had the honor of carrying the regimental colors in official ceremonies. Standing five feet, nine and a half inches and weighing 150 pounds, Dell had blue eyes and a fair complexion. He was born September 1, 1876, in Henry County, Kentucky, a small rural county in the northern part of the state that had fewer than ten thousand residents. He attended school only through the eighth grade and first enlisted in October 1897 at the age of twenty-one. A crack shot, one of the best in the AEF, Dell won several pistol competitions. In fact, in a pistol competition after the war, he easily beat the younger man selected to represent the United States in the Olympic Games.

Before heading to the Great War, Dell had already served several deployments, including one as an artillerist in the Philippine Insurrection in 1900, and he took part in the occupation of Veracruz, Mexico, in

---

* During World War I, one field artillery commander was future president Harry S. Truman, who served in the 35th Division.

1914. President Wilson believed that the Mexicans were receiving arms shipments from the Germans, and he ordered an arms embargo, called for the overthrow of the Mexican president, and sent American troops to the port of Veracruz. Marines, sailors, and soldiers fought the local population and took control of the city.* During that time, Dell wrote a letter home that the local paper published. "The people here seem to be very well contented with us," he wrote. "In fact, some of them told me they would be sorry to see us go. But while they treat us with perfect civility, I fancy that down deep in their hearts they despise us. And why not? Did not our Navy kill 200 or more of their people in taking the city, and have we not quartered troops in their public buildings, stopped their bull-fighting, and closed their gambling joints? While our rule has been paternal and kind, it is bound to be regarded as a yoke."[4] The US troops left soon after the Mexican president stepped down, but approaching the brink of war increased the hostile feelings between the countries. It also gave the troops, including Dell, combat experience. By the time of the Battle of Soissons, he was a battle-hardened, gray-haired forty-one-year-old veteran with more than twenty years of service to his credit.

Dell's battery unlimbered their field guns behind the infantry. Germans often looked for the placement of the field artillery because it was potentially a tip-off for the beginning of a new Allied offensive. The Allies maintained strict secrecy; the French released details of the offensive to only the most senior Allied officers. The French purposely kept Dell's 15th Field Artillery back, rushing them toward the front at the last minute in the middle of the night with the rest of the 2nd Division.

Because the Retz Forest masked the Allied buildup, the Germans had no idea that long lines of French camions, often driven by Asians from France's far-flung colonies, had been quietly transporting thousands of American troops to the front lines. An official report from

---

* General "Fighting Fred" Funston oversaw the subsequent occupation and administration of the port.

the 2nd Division described the process: "Hour after hour, the column lumbered in darkness along the tree-lined National Highways of France, rolling ever northward into the unknown. . . . No lights betrayed the secret march to any hostile aviator."[5] The cloudy, rainy weather proved ideal for the surprise attack.

The onslaught marked the beginning of an offensive that the French referred to as the "Second Battle of the Marne" and the Americans named the "Battle of Soissons." Two American divisions, the 1st and the 2nd, spearheaded the main portion of the attack. Sandwiched between the Americans were the battle-hardened assault troops of the French Army: the 1st Moroccan Division, whose ranks included the French Foreign Legion, which counted a few American volunteers among its members.

The 2nd Division Marines and soldiers, including Dell, were attached to the French Tenth Army, led by General Charles Mangin, nicknamed "the Butcher" because of the number of men sent to their graves under his command. Expecting the worst under Mangin's command, leadership in the 5th Regiment ordered their officers to leave behind twenty men, who would not participate in the initial attack. When one officer complained that he did not have sufficient men, command informed him, "They will be needed as a nucleus to build new companies [to replace the dead] after the attack."[6]

The 23rd Infantry made up the 2nd Division's right flank; Dell's 15th trailed behind them with the horse-drawn 75s. The French held the 6th Marines and 6th Machine Gun Battalion in corps reserve. The 9th Infantry, including Sergeant Younger's Company A, had the center while the 5th Marines, which included Ernest Janson's 49th Company, took the left flank and liaised with the French.

For hours, the Marines of the 49th Company, still under the overall command of the indomitable Captain George Hamilton, had marched each holding one hand on the pack of the man in front of him to prevent getting lost in the darkness. A sheeting downpour and arcs of white lightning illuminated the pitch-black sky. The men had not eaten for more than a day, and they were bone-weary from the nightlong march to the jumping-off point. The 2nd Division operations report noted, "For miles it was necessary to march the troops in single file in the slippery clay ditch along the right of the road. There was very little straggling, although many of the men were on the verge of exhaustion. The darkness and the uncertain footing increased the difficulty of the march."[7]

To maintain operational secrecy, the Americans had moved into position as quickly as possible, but that left them no time to reconnoiter the ground in front of them where they would soon be fighting. Coils of barbed wire, miles of trenches, dozens of machine-gun nests, and numerous field artillery pieces lay in front of them.

Early in the morning on July 18, 1918, hundreds of guns in the French Tenth Army, including Dell's 75, opened up, catching the Germans by surprise. A member of Dell's 15th Field Artillery Regiment described how the earth shook as they fed their 75s shell after shell: "We opened fire at 4:30 in the morning. It sounded as though thousands of guns were in action at one time, all firing at top speed. The ground shook with the violence of the firing."[8]

Dell's men laid down a deadly rolling barrage, sowing a swath of destruction that advanced with the 2nd Division's frontline units, including the 49th Company. The 49th and the rest of the 5th Marines first had to push through a portion of the Retz Forest composed of dense conifers and deciduous trees. Within minutes of the commencement of the counteroffensive, the artillery uprooted the forest, cleaving many of the great trees in half.

Deadly mustard gas fired by the Germans spread and misted around the shell holes as the men worked to breach huge coils of German barbed wire.

One Marine in the thick of the fighting yelled to the long file of his charging men, with their bayonets glinting through the leaves and foliage as they lunged into a German defensive position, "By the right flank, Let's go!"[9]

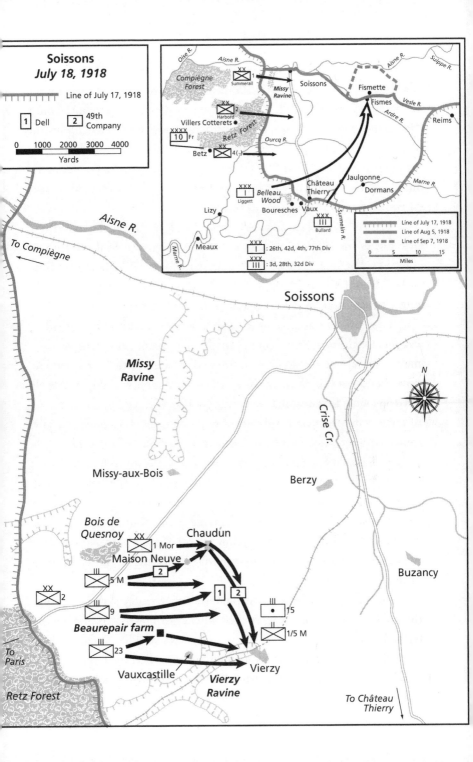

Soissons
July 18, 1918

┬┬┬┬┬┬	Line of July 17, 1918
[1] Dell	[2] 49th Company

```
0   1000  2000  3000  4000
Yards
```

Line of July 17, 1918
Line of Aug 5, 1918
Line of Sep 7, 1918

```
0        5        10        15
Miles
```

26th, 42d, 4th, 77th Div
3d, 28th, 32d Div

Oise R.
Aisne R.
Compiègne Forest
Summerall 1
Missy Ravine
Soissons
Fismette
Aisne R.
Suippe R.
Fismes
Vesle R.
Harbord 2
Villers Cotterets
Retz Forest
Ardre R.
Reims
10 Fr
Ourcq R.
Betz 4(-)
Château Thierry
Jaulgonne
Marne R.
Dormans
Liggett 1
Belleau Wood
Lizy
Bouresches
Vaux
Surmelin R.
Meaux
Marne R.
Bullard

To Compiègne
Aisne R.
Soissons

Missy Ravine

Missy-aux-Bois

Crise Cr.

Berzy

N

Bois de Quesnoy
Chaudun
1 Mor
Maison Neuve
[2]
[1] [2]
2
5 M
9
15
1/5 M
Beaurepair farm
23
Vauxcastille
Vierzy
Vierzy Ravine
Buzancy

To Paris
Retz Forest

To Château Thierry

The Marines crashed into a barrier of tree limbs and barbed wire, tearing their legs and puttees. Grenades flew. Some men sank into a concealed German trench. The Marine company commander leading the charge recalled, "I clawed out my automatic and fired twice without having much idea of what I was shooting at. A bullet clipped a brass ring from my belt and a rifle barrel thrust between my legs. I tripped, caught myself, and hurdled a line of foxholes. Our entire company surged over, smothering the Germans' position."[10]

The Allied barrage silenced a portion of the German counterbattery, giving the infantry a small measure of comfort. Still, they knew plenty of danger lay ahead. As Lieutenant General Robert Lee Bullard direly noted, "Artillery fire is not what kills men; it is the machine guns."[11] Captain John W. Thomason of the 49th Company remembered, "Machine guns raved everywhere; there was a crackling din of rifles, and the coughing roar of hand grenades. Company and platoon commanders lost control—their men were committed to the fight—and so thick was the going that anything like a formation was impossible. It was every man for himself."[12]

After fighting their way out of the forest, the 49th emerged into golden, rolling wheat fields. Allied planes thundered overhead as columns of men surged forward. Behind lumbered Color Sergeant James Dell's field artillery, and the sabers and lances of squadrons of archaic cavalry riding in the distance glistened in the sun. Here the eighteenth century met the twentieth century. French tanks snorted and rumbled into battle alongside the 2nd—a first for the men of the division, who had never before seen these modern marvels. Many of the tanks were the Renault FT, also called the FT-17. Revolutionary for its time, the design of this light tank remains influential to this day. While rotating turrets had become common in armored cars, this was the first widely produced tank to feature a fully rotating turret, and like most modern tanks, it had the crew compartment in the front and the engine in the rear. More than sixteen feet long and nearly six feet wide, the FT-17 weighed about seven tons and carried a crew of two. Quarters were extremely cramped, and the vehicles were so noisy that the commander often communicated with the driver by kicking him in the back to indicate what direction to turn in.

For armament, FT-17s had either a Puteaux SA 1918 37 mm gun or an 8 mm Hotchkiss machine gun, and the fuel tank could hold enough gas for eight hours of operation, giving it an operational range of about 34 miles at a snail-like speed of 4.3 miles per hour. Over the course of the war, the French manufactured more than three thousand FT-17s, and the Americans also licensed the design from the French (although none of the tanks the Americans produced saw service in World War I). The light tank's creators envisioned a swarm of small, agile vehicles that would be able to assault the enemy en masse. Given its fairly small size, the vehicle proved nimble enough to navigate through forests. All in all, it was considered a success, and some FT-17s remained in service even into World War II.

The armored vehicles proved to be of "great assistance" to the army. The Germans had hidden machine-gun nests in the wheat fields surrounding the woods, and the infantrymen had difficulty locating them. Heedless of the machine-gun fire bouncing off their plating, tanks flattened the fields and located many of the nests. "Whole batteries were captured, and the guns were turned on the retreating Germans," the operational report explained.[13] At the same time, the tanks became artillery magnets, and incoming German shells demolished many, along with the troops that accompanied them.

The Americans made swift progress in the opening hours of the offensive, but the terrain slowed them down. Several miles behind the German front lines lay the incredibly steep, canyonlike Vierzy Ravine. "This ravine had been, for some hours on the 18th of July, an interesting place. There were Boche support troops in it, and broken units from the woods had reformed there and fought. It angled from the wheat in front of the woods across to the right, toward the town. The dead were very thick as you approached it; they lay together in German feldgrau, and American khaki," Thomason reflected.[14] Taking full advantage of the ground, the Germans had positioned their guns deep within the ravine, where Allied artillery could not reach them. To eliminate the stronghold, American infantrymen descended into the ravine, battling through German strongpoints one at a time, hacking away at the enemy's defenses until they had eliminated the threat.

As the counteroffensive unfolded, different units were crossing over into one another's lines of control. The 49th fought on the left flank, acting as a liaison with French units in that sector. Thomason recalled, "The attack waves got off on time; they advanced and continued to advance. They lost formation but retained so much individual energy that the German formations on their front were destroyed or rendered incapable."[15] On the plateau near the ravine, Marines became intermixed with a detachment of Senegalese. The Germans were terrified of being captured by the Moroccans and Africans. "These wild black Moham-medans from West Africa were enjoying themselves," one Marine noted. "Killing, which is at best an acquired taste with the civilized races, was only too palatably their mission in life. Their eyes rolled, and their splendid white teeth flashed in their heads. . . . They were deadly. Each platoon swept its front like a hunting pack, moving swiftly and surely together."[16]

Later in the day, the Marines captured several German prisoners, and walking-wounded Marines took on the task of taking the prisoners to the rear area. Along the way, a group of Senegalese troops threatened to take the prisoners. An odd phenomenon occurred, with the captives briefly becoming the allies of their captors. "When the Marines prepared to resist this attempt to rob them of their prisoners, the Germans looked around for their weapons and lined up with the Americans against the Muslim Colonials," Thomason recalled.[17]

In another incident, one German fought to the death to avoid being taken prisoner. One of James Dell's men supporting the infantry with the field guns related, "I came across a most interesting sight this afternoon. There laid a German, a man I should judge about thirty years old; he looked about six feet tall, lying on his stomach, his head towards our lines. Facing him in practically the same position was a little Moroccan about five feet three inches tall. Both were dead; both were cut something terrible; both had their trench knives in their hands. It must have been a terrible struggle, a fight to the death. Both paid the penalty. They had made the supreme sacrifice. They surely were enemies when they met."[18]

As the 49th fought through the ravine toward the town of Vierzy, they encountered a German aid station under a cliff. The 9th Infantry had seized the station along with a full complement of German doctors, whom the Americans pressed into service to tend to the wounded and dying. A redheaded surgeon from the 9th had the impossible task of caring for "acres of casualties."[19] In the midst of the carnage, he tugged on a burlap bag clutched in the viselike grip of a wounded Moroccan. The surgeon could not break the wounded man's grasp until "the soldier swooned into unconsciousness and released his hold on the burlap bag. The captain picked up the bag and looked in and found a German soldier's head that had apparently been severed with a knife (apparently a bolo which most of those troops carried)," recalled one member of Younger's unit.[20]

James Dell and the 15th advanced behind the infantry to provide close support "firing day and night until the 20th."[21] The regiment captured numerous 77 mm and 105 mm German artillery pieces and turned the guns against the Germans. Here, near Vierzy, Dell distinguished himself and was cited for gallantry in the general orders. The men fired yellow-cross gas shells and German high-explosive rounds at the enemy.

After fighting through the ravine, the Marines and soldiers of the 2nd Division tried to capture the heavily defended town of Vierzy from the northern side, but the Germans drove them back with gas and machine guns on July 18. The town lay near the boundary between the Army's 3rd Brigade and the Marines' 4th Brigade, and the two units crossed over each other's lines of control. The 49th Company remained in the thick of the fighting with 1st Battalion 5th Marines under the temporary command of the 2nd Division's 3rd Brigade, led by the indomitable Colonel Hanson Ely, soon to be promoted to brigadier general. Hailing from Iowa, and a former professor of military science with a long list of combat assignments, Ely was a hard-core, professional officer known for his courage and hands-on approach. A broad-shouldered "giant," with a reputation as a brawler in his youth, Ely was a man of action. He personally organized and led the attack on Vierzy. Nicknamed "Steamroller"[22] by his men, he angrily confronted the commander of the 1st Battalion, 5th Marines, Major Julius Turrill, demanding to know why Turrill had not taken the town.[23]

One of the participants later recalled that when Turrill said that they were held up, Ely, who spoke in a gruff manner with clenched teeth and rarely smiled, responded, "Held up, hell, you were supposed to take that town by four o'clock, and here it is six thirty and the sun is going down! Go get that—"

"But sir, I've sent for help from the two companies. I've got to have some men."

"Men? Men? Jesus! You want men? What's the matter with all these men around you in the ditches here—are they Boy Scouts?" Ely acidly retorted.

"But [General], these are runners, clerks, and orderlies and such as that. They're only armed with pistols and I've only forty, more or less. They can't—"

The participants recalled that Ely lowered the boom on Turrill: "At that point the colonel made a silken purr, loud enough for all to hear, you could feel his satisfaction. One could easily picture someplace where gyrenes [slang for Marines] had stolen glory and a fair share of the news from this old soldier's own good army outfit." Ely then asked, "They are Marines, aren't they, major?"[24]

With that backhanded compliment, Turrill retreated with an "Aye, aye, sir." A platoon of the 49th and elements of Turill's battalion secured most of Vierzy, with Ely's 23rd Infantry Regiment clearing the remainder of the town.[25]

* * *

Eventually, the Commanding General of the 2nd Division, James Harbord, committed his reserve, the 6th Marines. The 5th and 9th pursued an enemy retreating to the northeast; now the Germans had consolidated behind their defenses. "The advance to the front lines was a severe test of the morale and discipline of the 6th Marines," said an after-action report. "This attack caused about 40% losses."[26]

In addition to the threat on the ground, the Germans were able to bring their airpower to bear. The Red Baron's Flying Circus, now led by Hermann Göring after the Red Baron was shot down, conducted bombing and strafing runs, killing scores of men. One Marine refused to take the onslaught. An officer wrote in his diary, "A Marine in a trench by himself had fallen heir to a German machine gun with apparently [an] unlimited supply of ammunition. He amused himself all afternoon shooting at [German] planes."[27]

The diary also recorded other details of the assault:

At 8:35 A.M. we jumped off. . . . Wallace, hit in the leg, went down in the short wheat. . . . Overton was hit by a big piece of shell. . . . His heart was torn out. . . . A man near me was cut in two; others when hit would stand, it seemed an hour, then fall in a heap. . . . Captain Woodruff . . . . his hand all tied up, coat torn in rags, left arm helpless, thigh cut up and in general a mass of blood, but his eyes sparkling.

At 10:30 we dug in; the attack just died out. Watched some men near the beet field dig in. You don't know how fast it can be done till you have to. Cates [Clifton Cates, future commandant of the USMC] had his trousers blown off and was slightly wounded. . . .

In a shallow trench . . . I found three men blown to bits, another lost his legs, a fifth his head. At one end of the trench sat a crazy man who . . . with a shrill laugh, pointed and said over and over again, "Dead men, dead men." The man who had lost his eyes wanted me to hold his hand. Another with his back ripped open wanted his head patted.[28]

Despite the rough tactical start at Soissons, the Allies pushed the Germans out of the Marne salient, across several crucial rivers, and back toward their prepared defenses on the Hindenburg Line. The 2nd Division lost many men in the counteroffensive: 3,788 men killed, wounded, gassed, and missing. Artillery vaporized and shredded men on the battlefield, reducing many of their bodies to mere remains—"unknown soldiers." Included in the "butcher's bill" were 187 men from Dell's 2nd Field Artillery Brigade.[29] The 2nd Division captured 66 German officers, 2,899 enlisted men, 9 pieces of heavy artillery, 66 light artillery guns, 2 trench mortars, and more than 200 machine guns.[30]

Soissons marked a turning point on the Western Front, rocking the Germans on their heels and putting them on the defensive. George Marshall, a key planner of operations on Pershing's staff, summed up the impact of Soissons: "The entire aspect of the war had changed. The great counteroffensive on July 18 at Soissons had swung the tide in favor of the Allies, and the profound depression which had been accumulating since March 21st was in a day dissipated and replaced by a wild enthusiasm throughout France and especially directed toward the American troops who had so unexpectedly assumed the leading role in the Marne operation."[31] Marshall, who had witnessed the ebb and flow of the war and shock of the German spring offensives, further reflected, "Only one who has witnessed the despair and experienced the desperate resolution when defeat is anticipated can fully realize the reversal of feeling flowing from the sudden vision of a not-too-distant victory."[32]

In the British sector, several weeks later, the Allies followed up Soissons with a massive tank assault at Amiens, smashing the German salient created by Operation Michael. The British Fourth Army achieved a near breakthrough, advancing twelve miles. German discipline cracked, and units fled on August 8, 1918, which Ludendorff later dubbed the "black day" of the German Army.

Although the Americans had halted the German drive on Paris, the Europeans still had been dubious about the capabilities of their US allies and constantly sought to use the Americans as replacements and cannon fodder within their own depleted armies. "The European looked upon the American as a soldier of doubtful value," said the 2nd Division Report of Operations. "Europe knew the strength of the American dollar, but the merit of the American soldier yet had to be demonstrated."[33] Tens of thousands of Americans, such as Body Bearer James W. Dell, would prove the point with their individual and collective actions.

Pershing was closer to achieving his goal of gaining recognition as a separate, independent American army. Several American divisions spearheaded a major French offensive, and two Army corps—General Hunter Liggett's I Corps and Lieutenant General Robert Lee Bullard's III—participated in the offensive. The AEF, the only force growing in number among its exhausted Allied counterparts, now numbered more than 1.2 million, with 200,000 more pouring into France every month.[34]

Thousands of those new American arrivals, including water tender Charles Leo O'Connor, traveled on the USS *Mount Vernon*, which would become a target for a stealthy German U-boat.

V

BY SEA
1918

CHAPTER 13

CHARLES LEO O'CONNOR:
USS *MOUNT VERNON*

Water tender and Body Bearer Charles Leo O'Connor toiled in hell. Intense heat bathed the Boston native and his fellow bluejackets as they worked in the cavernous steel bowels of the USS *Mount Vernon*. Sweat poured down their filthy bodies as the men shoveled brimstone— black, dirty nuggets of coal—into the blast furnace–like engines of the troopship. With the rank of petty officer, the brown-haired, hazel-eyed O'Connor had one of the dirtiest jobs in the Navy: tending the fires and boilers in the mighty ship's engine room. Hailing from Cambridge, Massachusetts, the thirty-one-year-old O'Connor stood five feet nine and weighed a beefy 212 pounds; much of that bulk was muscle resulting from five years spent shoveling coal for the US Navy.

Mount Vernon, the third ship so named by the US Navy, was originally the German ocean liner SS *Kronprinzessin Cecilie*. In the summer of 1914, it was carrying 1,216 passengers and a whopping $10,679,000 in gold and $3,000,000 in silver in its cargo holds when the war broke out. The liner sought refuge in the then-neutral United States to avoid capture by the French Navy or Royal Navy. The four-funnel, three-masted steamer was nearly the size of *Titanic*. Interned in Bar Harbor, Maine, the vessel languished until 1917, when the United States Shipping Board seized the ship and the gold.

In the years leading up to the Great War, the number of US ships had shrunk to lower than Civil War levels. This forced the United States to take drastic measures, and it confiscated hundreds of ships.

The board turned the SS *Kronprinzessin Cecilie* over to the US Navy, which converted the liner into a troop transport, stripping the great ship of its finery and outfitting the vessel with thousands of bunks. The Navy later painted the ship gray, black, blue, and white in a wild, bold dazzle-camouflage pattern. It commissioned the USS *Mount Vernon* on July 28, 1917, and assigned her a crew, including O'Connor.

Since her commissioning, *Mount Vernon* had completed several transatlantic voyages transporting thousands of American troops to France. Following the nation's entry into the Great War, the US Navy's primary mission, along with working with her allies, was to transport the nation's soldiers to Europe. At the insistence of the British, in May 1917 the Allies implemented a convoy system to transport America's troops to France. Gone were the days of gun crews like Body Bearer James Delaney's protecting lone ships from prowling U-boats on the high seas. Instead, massive convoys of Allied warships and merchant ships slowly crept across the Atlantic. Armed with anti-submarine countermeasures, such as depth charges and additional deck guns, the warships served as a powerful deterrent against submarine attacks, and U-boat losses soared. While the large convoys of ships were only as fast as the slowest, they nevertheless greatly reduced the Allies' shipping losses. Hundreds of thousands of Americans were arriving in France every month.

A rainbow, a sailor's warning for veteran mariners, arced across the dawn sky on the clear morning of September 5, 1918. Most of the passengers on board *Mount Vernon* had been seriously wounded in combat or had contracted influenza. They were focused on the voyage back to the United States and the opportunity to see their families and sweethearts, ignoring the foreboding sign. Having finished her seventh voyage transporting troops across the Atlantic, the ship was headed home. Belowdecks, it seemed like any other morning for O'Connor. He had just relieved his counterpart, who had been on watch from 4:00 a.m. to 8:00 a.m. in the No. 8 fire room—another routine day.

Everything changed when a massive explosion suddenly rocked the ship.

O'Connor fell to the deck, "instantly enveloped and almost fatally burned in the flame of gases driven from the furnaces."[1] The high pressure of the boiler room forced a sheet of fire into the compartment. As the power cut out, the overhead lights went dark. A shower of scalding coal dust and debris rained down on his head, scorching his body as the searing heat burned his throat and lungs. Before he could catch his breath, a torrent of seawater rushed into the compartment.

A torpedo had struck *Mount Vernon* amidships, not far from O'Connor's position. Thirty thousand tons of metal were lifted, twisted, cracked, and bent from the explosion. Tons of water rushed into the ship. Within minutes, *Mount Vernon*, sinking fast, dangerously rode ten feet below her normal waterline. Fatefully, the explosive had struck some of the fire rooms and boilers, where the stores of coal compounded the force of the blast.

The captain of *Mount Vernon*, Douglas E. Dismukes, a veteran mariner with ramrod-straight posture and a commanding presence, ran a tight ship and had taken precautions against a torpedo attack—to no avail. He later recalled, "The whole side of the fire room, including the outer and inner skin and the bulkheads of the intervening bunkers, were torn away, plates being crumpled up like so much paper crushed in one's hand."[2]

O'Connor knew that his chances of further survival were slim. Far below the waterline, the fire room was a death trap. At any second, the remaining intact boilers on *Mount Vernon* could explode. With the sea flooding in and the ship riding perceptibly lower, the water tender had limited time to make his way to safety. Tongues of flame still flickered in parts of the room. But rather than escape, he immediately set about doing whatever he could to save the ship. Staggering in the swirling water, he struggled to his feet and turned to close a watertight door leading to a large coal bunker behind him.

Four men currently occupied the bunker, their lives in peril. The compartment extended the entire width of the ship. When completely filled, this compartment alone could hold about twelve hundred tons of water—enough to pose a substantial threat to the vessel. Still reeling from the blast, O'Connor pulled on the hydraulic lever to close the watertight door.

The water tender's valiant efforts later awed Dismukes. "The fact that O'Connor, though profoundly stunned by the shock and almost fatally burned by the furnace gases, should have had presence of mind and courage to endeavor to shut this door is as great an example of heroic devotion to duty as it is possible for one to imagine."[3] Another officer wrote in the ship's official report, "It is probable that [O'Connor] might have escaped from this fire room with less burns, had he immediately taken to the ladder, which was quite near the point where he stood."[4] Taking the time to close the door resulted in painful injuries and scars, which O'Connor would bear for the rest of his life. However, his self-sacrifice very likely saved the ship and the lives of his fellow crew members.

Two days earlier—Tuesday, September 3—*Mount Vernon* had arrived at its destination in Brest, France. With the harbor full of transports unloading thousands of Americans, *Mount Vernon* had to wait her turn. Not until the next morning were the troops off-loaded, a seven-hour operation. Wasting no time, the crew quickly loaded three hundred tons of coal and set sail for New York at 5:20 in the evening on Wednesday, accompanied by the USS *Agamemnon*, *Connor*, *McDougal*, *Nicholson*, *Wainwright*, *Wilkes*, and *Winslow*.

To avoid U-boats, the convoy pursued a zigzagging course with the vessels maintaining a strict formation. On the morning of September 5, 1918, they were approximately 250 miles from the coast of France, heading west at 18 knots. Just a few minutes before 8:00 a.m. on Thursday, a member of the 7.5-inch gun crew on board *Mount Vernon* sighted something ominous: a German periscope.

Since June 5, 1918, Kapitänleutnant Heinrich Middendorff had commanded *U-82*, the vessel whose periscope poked above the water.

In just four months, he had sunk five ships.[5] Having torpedoed the SS *Dora* and sent it to the bottom of the Atlantic a day earlier, his crew were flush with success and feeling confident in their abilities. For the past hour they had been pursuing *Mount Vernon* like a cat stalking its prey.

At first, *Mount Vernon's* gunnery officer believed that the report of the enemy vessel was likely a false alarm. But seconds later, the officer of the deck's order, "Man gun 1, train 45°," had him hurrying to the lookout position.[6] The gun crew fired a shot at the periscope, which immediately ducked back under the water. The bluejacket watched from the starboard side to see where the shot landed. "The splash was easily picked up immediately and was about 5,000 yards from the ship, two points forward of beam," he recalled.[7]

Then the U-boat attacked.

"There she is. She has just fired a torpedo. I can see her wake," the chief quartermaster, who was manning the bridge, called out.[8] The executive officer rushed to the starboard side; from there he could see the unmistakable and horrifying sight of a torpedo closing in on *Mount Vernon*.

"Bearing 45 degrees, distance 500 yards," he said.[9]

The officers and crew watched helplessly as *U-82's* torpedo sliced through the water, heading directly toward *Mount Vernon*. "Right full rudder!" commanded the officer of the deck. "Emergency speed ahead."[10] The piercing sound of the ship's whistle filled the air as the officer sounded the alarm to warn the men that a collision was imminent.

With a concussive blast, the torpedo exploded on impact, striking nearly amidships, near the bulkhead separating the No. 3 and No. 4 boiler rooms, killing around three dozen men and nearly ending O'Connor's life.

When he heard that the crew had sighted a periscope, Captain Dismukes rushed from his cabin to the bridge. He had made it as far as a ladder when the explosion hit. The blast was "terrific," Dismukes recalled. "For an instant it seemed that the ship was lifted clear out of the water and was smashed to pieces." All over *Mount Vernon*, men fell to the deck, some of them temporarily losing consciousness. The force even knocked one of the 7.5-inch guns out of its mounting position. Almost immediately, the starboard side of the ship dropped, listing a few degrees.

Within "two or three seconds after the explosion," the captain made it to the bridge and took charge.[11] "Sound collision quarters," he ordered.

Dismukes knew that no large Allied ship had ever survived two direct torpedo hits from a German U-boat. Every split second counted. The situation was dire, and he had to maneuver his vessel out of harm's way. Placing distance between the ship and the submarine was crucial. If *U-82* fired another torpedo and hit the crippled ship, *Mount Vernon* was doomed. Dismukes immediately ordered fire control to drop a pattern of five depth charges about six seconds apart. Simultaneously, he fired six shots from the aft guns, hoping to take out the German U-boat that had attacked his ship.

U-82 never returned to the surface. Dismukes was uncertain whether they had repelled the U-boat or if it was merely biding its time to attempt another attack in the dark of night.

After the torpedoing, *Mount Vernon* rode about ten feet lower in the water than usual, but it did not seem to be sinking any deeper. If the ship sank just two and a half feet more, it would lose the ability to float. Stopping the flow of water into the vessel became paramount.

Mount Vernon's executive officer sprang into action and began inspecting it to make sure that watertight doors were sealed. Alarmed, he espied water pouring into several areas, most notably the flooded No. 3 and 4 boiler rooms, near where O'Connor was fighting for his life. Would the vessel's compartments hold? The ship had reached a critical phase.

Reports trickled in. Although two of the boiler rooms had sustained damage and four fire rooms had flooded, the forward boilers remained fully functional. The engines, having avoided a direct hit, could limp along, propelling the ship without the two demolished boilers.

At the time of the attack, most of the off-duty men were in the mess hall for breakfast. The force of the blast tossed them—and their half-eaten food—around the compartment. While most of them were still dazedly making their way back to their feet, one man jumped up and addressed the crowd: "Remember, boys, we are all Americans, and it's only one hit."[12] Believing that their ship could not possibly be sunk by just one torpedo, the men calmly proceeded to their collision stations to begin repairs.

Putting distance between *U-82* and *Mount Vernon*, Dismukes ordered the crew to turn the ship back toward Brest and to begin repairs as soon as possible. Fully aware that the lives of all those on board depended upon how swiftly they could repair the damage and pump out the water the ship had taken on, *Mount Vernon*'s carpenter detail and crew mobilized. As thousands of gallons of frothy ocean water poured in, they shored up the bulkheads with massive wooden timbers while the men feverishly manned the pumps. For the officers and crew, "there was no sign of confusion and no thought of abandoning the ship; in fact, the call was not even sounded."[13] Navy doctrine holds that any ship, no matter how disabled, can be saved with enough hard work. Believing this maxim to be truth, "officers and men worked untiringly on pumps, handy-billies [a portable pump], and buckets, putting additional shores on bulkheads and reinforcing hatches and doors until arrival of the ship in port."[14]

Several officers heaped praise on the crew for their behavior during the encounter. "It was what had been done by the officers before the torpedo struck, what the men did afterwards that saved the ship," one recalled. "Very few orders were necessary."[15]

Despite their efforts, seawater continued to make its way into *Mount Vernon*. Two feet of water covered the deck in the mess room and galleys, and although the vessel at first seemed stable, it began slowly but inexorably to list more and more to port. At first, the list was only three degrees, but as the wind picked up and more water filled the holds, the angle became more alarming. By midnight, it had rolled to ten degrees. *Mount Vernon* was in danger of capsizing.

The human carnage caused by the torpedo was unmistakable. The wounded, such as O'Connor, suffered horrendous burns, and several sailors lost limbs. Scores of lifeless bodies remained entombed in the watertight compartments filled with seawater. At the instant the torpedo struck, a new group of O'Connor's fellow crewmen had just arrived on watch; therefore, twice as many men as usual were in the boiler rooms. The explosion killed thirty-five men immediately and injured thirteen, two of whom later died of their injuries. In every case, the cause of death was the same: flames shooting out from the boilers had seared their bodies, resulting in brief but agonizing pain before claiming their lives.

The torpedo attack and its aftermath were not the only dangers affecting the ship. *Mount Vernon* was a plague ship; influenza threatened the lives of those on board, including the Navy officers and crew. In addition, more than a hundred Army personnel had contracted influenza during the voyage to Europe and remained behind in the ship's hospitals on the return. Also on the vessel were several VIPs—Senator J. Hamilton "Ham" Lewis of Illinois, Congressman Thomas David Schall of Minnesota, and Schall's wife, Margaret.

At the time of the attack, the senior medical officer on *Mount Vernon*, was caring for a sick Army officer. He rushed to the ship's hospital to find the rest of the medical staff "very active without displaying the least evidence of confusion."[16] He noted that "in less than three minutes time, fifty-eight patients, most of whom were absolutely helpless and the remaining few requiring individual attention and assistance, were in life boats and bedding had been provided for their comfort and protection."[17] As those injured in the attack arrived, the staff dressed their wounds, provided them with food—and, in keeping with standard procedure for the time, cigarettes—and cared for their needs as well. Those unable to walk remained in the lifeboats until dark, and "the wants and needs of these unfortunates were so thoroughly provided for, that most of them preferred remaining in the boat overnight, where they slept undisturbed until morning," recalled the medical officer. "A case of pneumonia not only enjoyed sleeping in the boat but showed evidence of improvement in his condition after eighteen hours of it."[18]

* * *

Throughout the war, only seven hundred of the more than one hundred thousand Americans who died perished as a result of enemy attacks at sea, but thousands died of influenza and pneumonia they contracted during the voyage across the Atlantic.[19] More deadly than German bullets, the savage pandemic, later known as "Spanish influenza," took the lives of more American soldiers and sailors than the number who died in battle.[20] Worldwide, half a billion people contracted the illness, and approximately fifty million perished as a result.[21] It was the worst plague to afflict the human population since the Black Death of the Middle Ages.

Although experts disagree about the worldwide source of the virus, some trace its origins to Haskell County, Kansas. There, some of the first to contract the disease resided and trained at Camp Funston, the second-largest training camp in the United States, which was named after Wilson's original choice to lead the AEF.

However, no one disputes the ease and celerity with which the virus spread. When patients first contracted the disease, they would experience the typical coughing, sneezing, aches, and fever that are normally associated with the flu. With every cough or sneeze, they would disseminate millions of droplets of contagion. As the disease progressed, the passage virus morphed and became lethal. Many patients developed severe pneumonia, which often caused their cheeks to turn blue as they struggled to breathe. Many of those who died "drowned" slowly in their own phlegm as the virus ravaged their lungs.

Most strains of the flu are more dangerous to infants and the elderly, but the 1918 epidemic was hardest on young men and women in the prime of their lives—exactly the age group that nations were sending to the front lines of the war. The close confines of barracks and transport ships proved to be the perfect breeding grounds for the devastating disease, presenting President Wilson with a thorny decision. General Pershing was begging for troops to replace the 150,000 American soldiers in Europe who had come down with the illness, but crowding men onto ships would certainly sentence thousands of them to death as well. On the other hand, halting the flow of American troops might provide the Germans the advantage required to win the war.

Army Chief of Staff Peyton March assisted the president in making his decision. "Every such soldier who has died [from influenza] has just as surely played his part as his comrade who has died in France," he said. "The shipment of troops should not be stopped for any cause."[22] When March warned him of the threat posed by the plague, Wilson stared out the window and bizarrely recited a children's song: "I had a little bird, its name was Enza. I opened the window, and in flew Enza."[23] The president agreed to continue sending the ships even though he knew he was condemning many of the men on board to death. The transport ships maintained their relentless crawl across the Atlantic, and thousands of young doughboys met their fate before ever seeing the shores of Europe.

After *Mount Vernon* arrived in port and unloaded the wounded, including Body Bearer Charles Leo O'Connor, members of its medical staff had the grisly task of locating and removing the bodies of those killed in the explosion. "These men went into any and all compartments where any one or a combination of the following existed: heat, water, wet coal dust, danger of being hurt or burned, and intensely hard work," the medical officer recalled. "Not one displayed evidence of a lack of interest and continued to assist in preparation of the bodies recovered, for transportation to the United States after nearly twelve hours of hard gruesome work where these men had met their death and continued to work until two o'clock in the morning, this following the two days and sleep-disturbed nights of anxiety and trying ordeal."[24]

Severely burned and near death, O'Connor lay in sick bay. Undoubtedly, he recounted his life. He had enlisted on March 10, 1913, at the age of twenty-six, and served for four years. Now his life hung by a thread. Defying all the odds, he survived.

Safely making it back to the French port also presented the captain with an opportunity to express his thanks to the crew. He called out O'Connor's group specifically, noting, "The entire crew has acted manfully, as Americans are expected to act in the time of danger, but the Captain desires especially to express his admiration for the brave men of the Engineers' Force who unhesitatingly, and to a man, stuck to their posts of duty, facing the possibility and even the probability of death at any moment during the critical time immediately following the attack. This devotion to duty unquestionably saved the ship from a second and perhaps fatal attack."[25]

Writing about O'Connor and another of the heroes aboard the *Mount Vernon*, Captain Dismukes later noted, "With a brave and disciplined body of men, however strong may be their momentary impulses for self-preservation, their secondary and controlling impulses are to stand by their stations and do their duty. I can conceive of no more trying ordeal of one's courage than that was presented to the men in the fire rooms of groups 1 and 2. The profound shock of the explosion, followed by instant darkness and falling soot and particles, the certain knowledge that they were far below the water level, enclosed practically in a trap, with the imminent danger of the ship sinking, and the added threat of the exploding boilers. All these dangers, and more, must have been apparent to every man below, and yet not one man wavered in standing by his post. In at least two instances men who were actually in the face of death and badly wounded did actually forget, or at least held in abeyance, their instincts for self-preservation and endeavored to do what appeared to them to be their duty."[26] For his "voluntary heroic conduct in battle Charles L. O'Connor, Chief Water Tender, US Navy, is recommended for the Medal of Honor."*[27]

The lives of Charles Leo O'Connor and his fellow crewman were intertwined with the trial of fire and combat on September 5, 1918. Upon the ship's return to the United States, Secretary of the Navy Josephus Daniels addressed O'Connor and the crew: "There are expressions that come out of this war that will live. I hear one of the boys who

---

* Although recommended for the Medal of Honor, O'Connor actually received the Distinguished Service Medal.

was at Chateau Thierry, Argonne, and other battles calling his comrade, 'Buddie'; saying Buddie did this or Buddie did that. . . [It] meant they were kin, nearer than blood kin; kin in mutual service, mutual sacrifice, mutual brotherhood of the brave."[28]

That naval brotherhood contributed to Body Bearer James Delaney's survival in an ongoing, already yearlong captivity in the harsh and desperate conditions of deprivation and starvation in a German prisoner of war camp.

CHAPTER 14

JAMES DELANEY: BRANDENBURG

After Delaney and his crew's capture by *U-61* in June 1917, the men spent the next year in hell in a German prisoner of war camp.

Weeks after capture and shortly after the prisoners left the destroyer where they faced interrogation, the guards ordered Delaney and the others from *Campana* into a shower at Brandenburg prisoner of war camp. In a scene that eerily foreshadowed the descriptions of concentration camps from World War II, the Germans forced the prisoners to scrub themselves down with some sort of limelike powder. "After this we were put under a shower, and all the hair left our bodies."[1]

For his POW uniform, each man received only a small coat and a pair of wooden shoes. Next came the bedding: "two blankets made from paper, and a mattress, which consisted of straw and shavings."

After searching the prisoners from *Campana*, the guards moved them into a spartan barracks. "All of our clothing was gone through and our money was taken from us, and we were given German money in exchange," Delaney explained. "No jewelry was taken from us."

Delaney and the others shared a room with three Russians. Two guards stood watch—one on the inside and one on the outside of the cell. Intimidatingly, both were armed with bayonets that looked like saws. In fact, they were the same sawback bayonets that the soldiers in the trenches used for cutting barbed wire and causing brutal injuries to their enemies.

The food in the barracks wasn't much better than it had been on the submarine. In the evening, the men received some salt and two pieces of bread and were told to "make salt sandwiches." The morning coffee was made from burnt acorns. "This coffee, we afterward found out was very hard on the system, causing kidney trouble, etc." At noon, they received a hot meal, usually vegetable stew.

After several days in the barracks, they were awakened at four in the morning, given their usual salt sandwiches for breakfast, and loaded onto a train. They spent a day and a half on the train with no food and only a little water to drink before arriving at the prisoner of war camp at Brandenburg, home to more than ten thousand captive prisoners of war, many of them Allied sailors. By now, to the great relief of the Americans' families, the Germans informed the US government that Delaney, his gunners, and Captain Oliver were prisoners of war.

Brandenburg belonged to a category of camp that Germany called *Mannschaftslager*. These basic camps housed men in wooden shacks. Around 250 men were assigned to each 30-by-150-foot barracks and given straw or sawdust beds to sleep on. A 9-foot barbed wire fence surrounded the camp to contain the prisoners. Hunger was a constant companion. Their daily ration consisted of a little bread, "one small bowl of coffee, made from acorns, etc., and a bowl of soup at noon, and coffee at night." Hundreds of prisoners, primarily Russians, died of starvation. Delaney said that he and his fellow Americans would almost certainly have shared that fate except that the American Red Cross issued them relief parcels of food. Still, the parcels rarely arrived unspoiled as the Germans regularly searched them before delivering them to the prisoners. "If it appeared that Germany was winning, all our cigarettes were broken in two," Delaney said. "Syrup, coffee, tea, and all articles would be opened and poured into one basin, and mixed together."

Complaints about these abuses fell on deaf ears, and more often than not, resulted in punishments for those who dared to speak up. Often, they were put in "strafe," or confinement, or the parcels were put in strafe and not given out for weeks at a time. One of the officials told Delaney, "[He] was going to run his sword through me because I made complaints about parcels being robbed."

The Germans begrudgingly doled out meager supplies of wood that the prisoners could burn for warmth and cooking. "The fuel issued to us in the wintertime was one big root of a tree every other day," Delaney recalled. "This would last about twenty minutes in the barracks stove." To keep warm, the Americans often traded food for wood with the Russians who worked outside the camp and "had the opportunity of stealing." To heat their meals, the Americans cooked in buckets on the sand of the camp "beach," which was really the banks of a sewage dump. Angry guards would sometimes put out the fires and kick the polluted sand into the food, spoiling it.

The housing at the camp wasn't any better than the food. The shacks were made from boards covered in tar paper, and a single light-bulb was available for a very large room. The toilets were nothing more than "open sheds with boards placed lengthwise." Delaney described the sleeping area as "filthy." He said the bunks "were literally covered with bed bugs, fleas, and lice." The prisoners were allowed to bathe only once every two weeks, and this contributed to the stench and disgusting conditions. Any men who wanted to clean the barracks had to purchase brooms themselves, and after thirteen hours a day of hard labor, they had little time or energy for housekeeping.

The only medical treatment in the camp came by way of the British Red Cross. "If a man was sick and saw the German doctor, he was just looked at and told he was well and sent to work again." Allied doctors in the camp arranged for men who were ill to be housed in a shed used as a hospital, but with no medicine, there was little anyone could do for the sick. Many died. In the close quarters, viruses spread like wildfire, and during one three-month span, nearly all the Americans, including Delaney, caught influenza. The Red Cross gave them a supply of quinine for treatment, but the German guards failed to distribute it to the men.

When the Spanish ambassador visited the POW camp, Delaney lodged a complaint about the conditions, the handling of the Red Cross packages, and the manner in which two of his petty officers had been forced to work. Delaney had been elected president of the Brandenburg American Red Cross Camp Committee, and he took his responsibility to look after the other Americans seriously. His complaints earned him a visit to the camp commandant, who asked why Delaney had been trying to contact the ambassador. "I told him that our shipments of parcels from Berne were being lost and pilfered, anywhere from seven to eleven packages being lost out of each shipment," Delaney remembered, "and that two American merchant officers were given three days confinement for refusing to pull a wagon, like a horse, after parcels." Although his complaints afforded no improvements, Delaney said that "great praise should be given the Spanish Ambassador for the interest shown by him in behalf of the Americans."

The guards in the camp didn't have much better food than the prisoners, and they were eager to buy or trade anything the prisoners had to offer. "Most of the prisoners received pay amounting to from thirty to fifty *Pfennigs* [a German coin roughly equivalent to a penny] per day," and they often used this money to buy things to trade. According to Delaney, "The German soldiers tried to buy tea and coffee or anything with grease in it, offering the greatest of prices. Same with cigarettes and tobacco." The Russian prisoners often benefitted the most from the deals and "made thousands of Marks through this trading."

Their deprivation also made the guards susceptible to bribery. Delaney noted that they would look the other way during an escape attempt in exchange for nothing more than "a few biscuits and a piece of corned beef." Taking advantage of the situation, the American attempted to escape four times, but each time, the Germans caught Delaney and brought him back. The penalty was severe: ten to fourteen days of bread-and-water rations after each unsuccessful attempt.

In the coming months, the commandant again called Delaney in for questioning, along with the others from *Campana*. The authorities in Berlin had launched an investigation into the battle and seemed convinced that *Campana* must have been a Q ship. "We would not give them any information as to what they asked us," Delaney recalled.

Despite their willingness to trade, the guards were otherwise harsh in their treatment of the prisoners. "If you failed to work fast enough you ran chances of being shot or bayoneted, as this occurred to French, Russians, and a few British," Delaney recalled. "One American civilian was beat senseless by a soldier." Delaney and his men feared for their lives.

Allied offensives on the Western Front would change their fate.

VI

OFFENSIVE
1918

CHAPTER 15

ST. MIHIEL

August 30, 1918,
General Pershing's Headquarters in France

From each side of a table, two of the great personalities of WWI faced off. On one side was Marshal Ferdinand Jean Marie Foch, serving as Supreme Allied Commander. On the other, was John J. Pershing, commander of the American Expeditionary Forces.

Tension arced through the air as Foch made his demand. The Frenchman insisted that Pershing scale back his intended attack on a bulge in the Allied lines known as the St. Mihiel salient and instead break off a portion of the American army to fight in the Argonne.

For Pershing, this idea was completely unacceptable. President Wilson had given his general an order: the American troops must fight as a single unified American army and must not be broken up. In addition, Pershing had been preparing the St. Mihiel initiative since his arrival in Europe. Asking him to give up the attack seemed like one more example of European disdain for US military capabilities. From a practical sense, the salient threatened the right flank of Foch's offensive in the Meuse-Argonne—it had to be reduced.

Pershing acidly retorted, "Marshal Foch, here on the very day that you turn over a sector to the American army, and almost on the eve of an offensive, you ask me to reduce the operation so that you can take away several of my divisions. . . . This virtually destroys the American army that we have been trying so long to form."[1]

The argument soon became more heated. Eventually, Foch asked Pershing a pointed question, "Do you wish to take part in the battle [in the Argonne]?"

"Most assuredly," Pershing firmly answered, "but as an American army and in no other way." He continued, "Marshal Foch, you have no authority as Allied commander in chief to call upon me to yield up my command of the American army and have it scattered among the Allied forces where it will not be an American army at all."

Bristling with anger, Foch snapped, "I must insist upon the arrangement."

But Pershing was not willing to give in. "Marshal Foch, you may insist all you please, but I decline absolutely to agree to your plan. While our army will fight wherever you may decide, it will not fight except as an independent American army."

With that exchange, both men rose from the table, their argument far from over.

The great counteroffensive at Soissons had shifted the momentum of the war in favor of the Allies. The generals knew that now was the time to capitalize on the turning tide of the war, but they disagreed—often vehemently—about how to do that. To Pershing, the St. Mihiel salient seemed an obvious target for the newly formed American army. Enough American divisions had finally arrived to form several corps, known as the First United States Army. Now Pershing held two roles: commander of the American Expeditionary Forces and commanding general of the First United States Army.

During the First Battle of the Marne in 1914, the German Army had pressed forward around the town of St. Mihiel, about twenty-five miles southeast of Verdun, creating a bulge in the lines shaped roughly like an arrowhead. The Germans later used the area as a staging ground to launch the attack against Verdun in 1916. For the past several years, the French repeatedly tried to destroy the German bulge, only to be repulsed with massive losses. Since his arrival in France, Pershing believed First Army ideally suited to eliminate the St. Mihiel salient.

Foch disagreed. He did not consider the attack at St. Mihiel vital to Allied efforts; he preferred that the Americans, instead, begin the long journey northwest to attack German lines between the Meuse River and the Argonne Forest. To accomplish his plan, the supreme commander proposed segmenting the newly formed independent First Army that Pershing had spent more than a year forming. For several days following their contentious meeting, Foch and Pershing continued their verbal sparring.

On September 2, they reached a compromise: the two met again, this time effecting a covenant that would grant each man the essentials he desired. Pershing would maintain an intact American First Army and employ it to attack St. Mihiel on September 12; however, his men would have little time for the operation. He promised Foch that the American army would be in position less than two weeks later for the offensive in the Meuse-Argonne that would begin September 26.

Pershing achieved most of what he wanted, but at a terrible price. His staff hurtled into overdrive to redraw battle plans for the offensive at St. Mihiel, now just ten days away. If the First Army flattened St. Mihiel, they would have no rest before moving more than five hundred thousand men, all their equipment, and over two thousand artillery pieces sixty miles to fight in the Meuse-Argonne. Each giant American division required scores of trains and/or hundreds of trucks, forming a cavalcade that stretched miles. To keep the second offensive a secret, hundreds of thousands of men (including several of the Body Bearers), horses, and trucks would have to move at breakneck speed under the cover of darkness. In addition, Pershing had to take into consideration the capabilities and morale of his men. Some of America's greenest units, with virtually no fighting experience, would be pitted against the veteran, resilient, and highly flexible German Army that in a crisis could move tens of thousands of reinforcements to hot spots, furiously counterattack, and prevent breakthroughs in their lines. Pershing dared to attempt the seemingly impossible: committing his inexperienced army, which had never fought as a unit, to fight in two back-to-back complex operations.

Pershing and his staff had mere days to plan the twin offensives—a logistical nightmare. Major George Catlett Marshall, future five-star general and secretary of state, was the mainspring behind planning St. Mihiel and, later, the Meuse-Argonne Offensive for the Americans. First Army's combat debut required a massive combined arms operation involving tanks, planes, artillery, and infantry—all of it synchronized as a cohesive unit, a nearly insurmountable goal in such a short period of time.

The loose lips of Pershing's soldiers as they visited the brothels and restaurants of Paris had made the St. Mihiel initiative practically an open secret to the Germans. To keep the enemy guessing on the timing of the operation and possibly convince them that an offensive would occur in another region of France, Pershing ordered a sub-rosa deception plan. The initial part of the operation involved sending General Omar Bundy's VI Corps south to the town of Belfort. The Belfort Gap and the strategic city of Mulhouse could be a likely avenue of an Allied offensive. Pershing instructed Bundy that his corps would lead a major offensive and that St. Mihiel was a feint. (He would not be informed of the actual truth until after the battle commenced.) Accompanying Bundy to make the magic of the deception happen was Colonel Arthur Conger, a young intelligence officer and Harvard graduate. After moving his corps south, Bundy set up his headquarters in a posh hotel in Belfort. Conger sent out probes, raided German lines, and spread rumors. Tanks rolled around day and night to give the appearance of preparation for a major attack. Next, Conger typed in triplicate a faux situational report on the proposed attack. Suspecting that German intelligence had been casing the hotel, he balled up the carbon copy, threw it into the trash, and left the room. Within hours, the carbon copy went missing; it was likely that housekeeping was on the German intelligence services payroll.

However, the ruse had minimal impact, and the Germans shifted few reserve units toward the phantom attack at Belfort.

Around the bulge in the Allied lines, Pershing arrayed three corps on the south side of the salient with a few other American divisions held in reserve. The 26th and a corps of the French Army advanced on the western side of the salient. Pershing held four of his untested American units in reserve in the event the operation began to fail. The 2nd Division would attack toward the French town of Thiaucourt, roughly near the top eastern corner of the arrowhead.

Mountains of barbed wire entanglements encased the German defenses. Initially, the Allies planned for British heavy tanks to spearhead the attack and clear paths through the wire, which could otherwise gore a man. But the Allies diverted the rhomboid-shaped tanks to another operation. Artillery could pulverize the wire with a day of bombardment, but that would eliminate the element of surprise. Instead small groups of engineers, armed with wire cutters, would lead what the soldiers of the American Revolution would have called a "forlorn hope" because the likelihood of survival was so low. One of the men on that mission was Body Bearer Corporal Thomas D. Saunders of the 2nd Engineer Regiment.

CHAPTER 16

THOMAS DANIEL SAUNDERS: BREACHING THE WIRE

On September 12, under the cover of early-morning darkness and with rain pelting his face, Saunders crept forward through the mud-caked, pitted ground of no-man's-land. A brilliant star shell illuminated the inky darkness as tracer rounds from a Maxim whizzed by their position. An American Indian of the Cheyenne tribe, Saunders, at the vanguard of the advancing American army, had volunteered for a suicide mission. By his side, he had only one companion: Private Alfred Wilkerson from Youngstown, Ohio, another volunteer from the 2nd Engineers.

In front of them lay forests of tangled, rusty barbed wire. And somewhere beyond the wire, the German Army was melting away toward strong defenses at the base of the salient—part of a planned retreat, dubbed "Plan Loki," that began a day earlier. They carefully withdrew, holding key strongpoints just long enough that the bulk of their men and guns could withdraw. To cover their retreat and slow the Allied advance, the Germans left behind machine-gun nests and carpeted the battlefield with artillery fire. The Germans had not completed their withdrawal on September 12; the swiftness and timing of the American offensive caught them by surprise. Order disintegrated and confusion reigned in some German units that had been hit from multiple flanks. Behind Saunders and Wilkerson, the 9th Infantry and the rest of the 3rd Brigade of the 2nd Division were poised and ready to thunder through no-man's-land, but not before these two men and scores of their counterparts could breach the wire.

Armed with heavy two-handed wire cutters, Saunders and Wilkerson expeditiously cut through loop after loop of corroded wire, advancing at a steady pace. At several other points along the line, other squads of wire cutters tackled the same task.

German machine gunners opened up, targeting the shadowy figures of the two men, dimly visible in the morning light. Although they took cover, the Americans did not stop their steady snipping at the wire. By 5:00 a.m., the roar and flash of hundreds of Allied guns, including Body Bearer James Dell's 75s, opened up on the Germans, taking some of the pressure off the wire cutters. The 15th's guns provided a rolling barrage that lifted their range as Saunders and the infantry of the 3rd Brigade advanced.

Behind Saunders and Wilkerson, other engineers chopped through wooden posts and moved the tangles of wire to the side; slowly but surely, the 2nd Division drew ever closer to the German lines.

Prior to the battle, the men had received special training for the wire cutting. A typical squad included four men: two in front to cut the wire, a third carrying an axe to break down the wooden fence posts, and the final man tasked with clearing aside a wider path. According to the official history of the 2nd Regiment of Engineers, "After three days' practice, these wire-cutting squads became very efficient, and in a test against time, they cut a path through a 60-yard belt of ordinary smooth wire in about two minutes, that is, they cut about one-fourth as fast as the marching rate."[1]

Saunders was a member of Company A of the 2nd Engineer Regiment, known as "combat engineers," or in other armies as "sappers" or "pioneers."[2] Combat engineers have three main tasks: building, repairing, or blowing up infrastructure. They construct bridges, roads, and fieldworks; operate captured trains; and breach trenches and other fortifications. Combat engineers also facilitate movement across a battlefield for an advancing army by filling in tank traps and building or repairing bridges crossing waterways, or laying a path of destruction to impede an adversary from catching an army in retreat. In addition, the 2nd

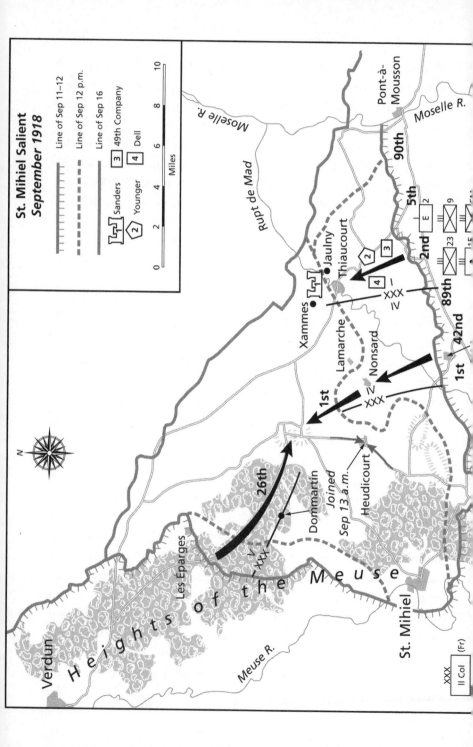

St. Mihiel Salient
September 1918

Line of Sep 11–12
Line of Sep 12 p.m.
Line of Sep 16

⌐T¬ Sanders   3 49th Company
② Younger   4 Dell

Miles
0   2   4   6   8   10

Moselle R.

Rupt de Mad

Pont-à-Mousson

Moselle R.

90th

5th

E 2   9

2nd

23   15

89th

3

② ④ I

XXX

IV

42nd

Jaulny
Thiaucourt

⌐T¬
Xammes

Lamarche

Nonsard

1st

IV

XXX

1st

26th

V

XXX

Dommartin

Joined
Sep 13 a.m.

Heudicourt

Les Eparges

H e i g h t s   o f   t h e   M e u s e

Verdun

Meuse R.

St. Mihiel

XXX
II Col (Fr)

Regiment also fought as infantry at many of the inflection points in battles where the 2nd Division was engaged.

As Saunders and Wilkerson became more visible after dawn, German snipers found them through their sights and squeezed off numerous rounds. Making what use they could of the limited cover, the pair somehow evaded both the machine-gun bullets and the rifle rounds. Intrepidly, they made it through yards of wire and became some of the first men to cross into German lines, a feat they would repeat as the operation to reduce the St. Mihiel salient unfolded.

Corporal Saunders was born in Medicine Bow, Wyoming, a tiny town over one hundred miles northwest of Cheyenne. Today it is practically a ghost town with barely 250 residents, but at the turn of the twentieth century, this popular waypoint on the railroad was home to the finest hotel in the state. Its main street full of saloons and stockyards, Medicine Bow fit the stereotypical image of a western town, and both Indian attacks and train robberies were common. Saunders later moved to Cheyenne, and at the age of twenty-five, he enlisted at Fort Logan, Colorado, on May 12, 1917. Only a decade earlier, the US government had been pitted in a savage war against Saunders's Native American father and grandfather.

Unwittingly, Saunders would eventually be an integral element of the commencement of a healing between Native Americans and the United States. Saunders was one of approximately ten thousand American Indians who served in the US forces in World War I.[3] Native Americans had played a role in every major conflict involving the United States and, before that, the thirteen colonies. As far back as the American Revolution, members of the Stockbridge, Passamaquoddy, St. John's, and Penobscot tribes chose to fight alongside the colonists and, with their blood and sacrifice, helped forge the United States; others remained neutral or chose to fight alongside the British. Throughout the nineteenth century, the American Indians and the US government openly engaged in numerous small wars and battles.

During WWI, the Onondaga and Oneida were the first tribes to declare war on Germany. In 1914, a circus promoter hired sixteen Onondaga to perform Wild West shows in Europe. When conflict broke out, German mobs attacked the Native Americans, arresting some and charging them as spies. In protest, the tribes declared war.

At the time, nearly a third of American Indians were not officially US citizens and thus were exempt from the draft.* Not until 1924 did the Indian Citizenship Act or Snyder Act grant citizenship to all tribe members. However, a large number chose to sign up for military service for their own personal reasons. Economic forces were a powerful motivator for some—most Indians lived in squalor. In 1916, the average Native American earned a paltry $91.66 per year, while the average enlisted man earned $528.[4] Others considered the war an opportunity to travel, and some were attracted to the thrill of combat. Many viewed joining the military as a continuation of their tradition as warriors—an opportunity to earn honor for themselves and their tribes. Numerous Native Americans volunteered, believing in their patriotic duty to fight.

Some tribes were more eager than others to join the American military. By several estimates, 40 percent of eligible men from Oklahoma's Osage and Quapaw tribes enlisted. Conversely, the percentage of Navajo signing up was very low. Their fellow soldiers generally revered the American Indians who joined the US forces. Stereotypes held that Indians had mythic abilities to move silently through the forest, find their way in the dark, travel long distances with limited rest and food, and defeat any enemy in hand-to-hand combat. As a result, officers frequently assigned Native Americans to some of the most dangerous jobs, such as serving as scouts, messengers, and snipers. While it's tempting to dismiss these ideas about Indian warriors as mere legend, many of them did distinguish themselves in battle. Throughout the course of World War I, ten American Indians (including Saunders) were awarded

---

* The US Constitution originally stated that Indians were not taxed, and before the twentieth century, the courts held that this meant they were also not citizens by birth. However, many chose to become naturalized citizens or obtained citizenship by marrying whites, serving in the military, or paying taxes.

the French Croix de Guerre, and more than 150 received other medals such as the Distinguished Service Cross, an award second in precedence to the Medal of Honor. Saunders was one of a few who received both—ultimately becoming one of America's most decorated Native Americans in the AEF. One US officer observed, "When an Indian went down, another Indian stepped immediately to the front. . . . They were always at the front; if a battle was on, and you wanted to find the Indians, you would always find them at the front."[5] Having battled against tribes in his early career as a cavalryman, Pershing also respected the Indians' abilities.

In addition to serving bravely in battle, the American Indians also performed one other vital service for the Allies. Because many Germans spoke English, transmitting radio messages or telephone calls in English could potentially reveal Allied plans to the enemy. While the US government officially discouraged Indians from speaking their native tongues, many remained fluent in their tribal languages. Several commanders asked the Native officers to transmit vital secret information in Choctaw or other Native American languages. Because these languages were completely unknown to the Europeans, it provided airtight secrecy.

For their part, the Germans were fascinated by American Indians. In fact, they became so obsessed with their romantic view of American Indians that one researcher coined a word for the phenomenon: "Indianthusiasm." Before the outbreak of war, Germans flocked to Wild West shows and devoured media reports on the topic. A couple of decades later, Adolf Hitler would exploit this fascination with Indians, likening himself and the Germans to legendary Native warriors. And the swastika that Hitler would adopt as his symbol was common in some tribal art as well as in several other cultures.

This phenomenon also had an impact on the battlefield. The Germans were terrified of the Native Americans, believing them to be practically invincible. German media even tried to suppress stories of Indians' involvement in battles so as not to upset morale. As the St. Mihiel offensive unfolded, Saunders headed into a hornet's nest: the commanding officer of the German 97th Landwehr ordered snipers to pick off Indians when they were recognized.

Yards behind Saunders, Sergeant Edward Younger of Company A, 9th Infantry—the man who would later select the remains of the Unknown Soldier—pushed forward in the mist and rain. Machine-gun bullets whizzed through the blackness as the rest of the 9th went over the top. Donning masks to protect themselves from gas, Younger's platoon, struggling to see through fogged-up eyepieces while the nosepieces incited mucus to stream down their faces, moved out ahead. The Chicago native, still recuperating from the wounds he received on July 2, led his sixty-plus-man platoon into no-man's-land.

Within hours, he was part of the force that captured the 9th's primary objective: the French town of Thiaucourt, which served as a German headquarters, and where nearly six months earlier, the Germans had taken American prisoners of war from the Seicheprey Raid.

The Marines of the 49th Company and the 5th Regiment, not yet recovered from the devastating losses they sustained at Soissons, followed behind Younger and the 9th Infantry. One "Fighting Fifth" Marine recounted trundling forward: "We followed them [9th and 23rd Regiments] at a walking pace, enjoying the show. . . . Older fellows scoffed at replacements because they walked in awe and half fear.

"Hell, man, ya shoulda been in Soissons."

"The old Boche fought us there."

"Why, kid, this ain't no battle, just a walk-away for troops like us."[6]

Shells fell; machine guns roared. However, a lull in combat proved nearly as dangerous. "That evening a fellow in the company pulled a fork out of his pocket. One of the prongs caught in the pin of a hand grenade in the same pocket, setting off the detonator. After pulling the pin you have five or six seconds to throw it before the explosion, just as a firecracker being lit. He was trying to get the grenade out of his pocket when the explosion occurred, killing him."[7]

*   *   *

The attack at St. Mihiel would rely heavily on the 2nd Engineers. For nearly four years, the Germans had held the well-fortified position. The 2nd Division, to root them out, would drive north and cross the river at Thiaucourt. As the official history noted, "It was evident that the Engineers must make preparation to cross the river at Thiaucourt, and must assist every one in getting over 'No Man's Land'; the Artillery needed help; the tanks needed help; and we had plenty of work of our own to prepare the bridge for crossing."[8]

To achieve the 2nd Engineers' objectives, the officers subdivided the regiment into several different groups. Serving as wire cutters, Corporal Saunders and the bulk of two companies risked their lives, clearing the way for the rest of the troops who would follow. Nine squads accompanied the small tanks, and six joined the artillery. Two other platoons scoured for tank traps that could potentially retard the advancing army. Four platoons remained in reserve as a quick reaction force in case of emergency. Saunders and his brothers were fighting engineers, used frequently to plug the holes in the line caused by German counterattacks or to hold a position, a role they would repeat throughout the war. The map section and the rest of the engineers would follow, reporting on the terrain and repairing the roads.

By noon on September 12, the 2nd Division's 9th Infantry Regiment, including Sergeant Younger's Company A, had reached Thiaucourt. Small patrols pushed farther north and northeast to the villages of Xammes and Jaulny, with the engineers in the vanguard.

Corporal Saunders led one small group into Jaulny, a tiny township about two and a half miles northeast of Thiaucourt. Resting on the east bank of the Rupt de Mad, and constructed on rocky high ground in the second century, the Château de Jaulny was, by far, the largest building in the hamlet; the stone castle controlled one of the few river crossings in the area during the Middle Ages. Within the château's thick stone walls lay a labyrinth of four levels of cellars, originally designed to provide protection to the village's residents during a time of attack. Recognizing the safety the château could afford, the Germans had seized the structure, employing it as a barracks and hospital.

Braving artillery and sniper fire, Saunders and Wilkerson rushed toward the château. Before they reached the castle, they had to traverse an area pockmarked with trenches, foxholes, and machine-gun nests. As machine-gun and sniper fire whizzed nearby, they first encountered eight Germans in a dugout and subsequently took them all prisoner. Not yet satisfied, Saunders and Wilkerson pressed on. Although the Germans were in retreat, they had left behind a rear-guard detachment to facilitate the withdrawal. Heedless of their own survival, the two Americans cautiously entered Château de Jaulny, its medieval interior a maze of twisting hallways and passages that could easily hide an enemy soldier around every corner. Room by room, they cleared the structure, taking prisoner those who surrendered. Slowly, they descended into the lower-level dungeons (called *caves* in French), where they found dozens of the enemy. Remarkably, the two men took fifty-five more prisoners, bringing the total haul to a mind-boggling sixty-three, an astounding achievement for which Saunders eventually received the Distinguished Service Cross. Along with the prisoners, Saunders and Wilkerson also captured the key German strongpoint in Jaulny.[9]

Engineers played a role in the combat debut of an American legend: Lieutenant Colonel George S. Patton. Born into a military family, Patton attended Virginia Military Institute and West Point but was only an average student. An accomplished fencer, he competed in the 1912 Olympics and designed a saber. Patton believed strongly in destiny. "A man must know his destiny," he said. "If he does not recognize it, then he is lost. By this I mean, once, twice, or at the very most three times, fate will reach out and tap a man on the shoulder. If he has the imagination, he will turn around and fate will point out to him what fork in the road he should take, if he has the guts, he will take it."[10] Throughout his military career, Patton saw his fate and seized it.

Patton ostensibly commanded the nascent American tank corps at St. Mihiel, leading two battalions with a total of 144 FT-17 tanks, driving into the heart of the German defense a couple of miles to the west of the 2nd Division.* The thirty-two-year-old veteran had already gained fame as a cavalry officer when he pursued Pancho Villa into Mexico. When he saw the situation in Europe, he understood that technology was making horses obsolete as weapons of war and that the cavalry of the future would be mounted on tanks. "Tanks are [a] new and special weapon—newer than, as special, and certainly as valuable as the airplane," he opined.[11]

In 1917, Patton, then a captain, set up the first light tank school in Bourg, France. The United States had grand plans for thousands of tanks, but American industry could not ramp up production fast enough, delivering a measly ten tanks to France at end of the war. Instead, America depended entirely on French and British production. Patton organized several light battalions built around the French FT-17. The Americans also stood up heavy battalions around the British rhomboid-shaped Mark V or Mark V Star tanks, which raced across the battlefield at a whopping five miles an hour. A crew of eight manned the tank's 57 mm main gun and four Hotchkiss machine guns.

Patton's view of tanks differed from that of most army officers. They tended to use the armored vehicles as mobile pillboxes acting in support of infantry. But Patton believed that tanks could be very effective in independent actions, much like the horse cavalry that had been a major part of his career.

While Saunders's team breached the wire, combat engineers from another unit escorting Patton's FT-17s would prove particularly critical, scouting for large holes that could impede the unwieldy vehicles' advance. The sticky mud of the French countryside also hindered the tanks; the engineers frequently had to extricate them from the morass. Patton wrote that he saw the technological marvels "getting stuck in the trenches . . . it was a most irritating sight."[12] Notorious for his irascible temper and colorful language, Patton, upon discovering an opportunity to express some of his frustration with the tanks' slow progress, was quick to pounce. "I

---

* Brigadier General Samuel D. Rockenbach actually commanded the American tank corps, but Patton led it in the field.

saw one fellow in a shell hole holding his rifle sitting down," he wrote. "I thought he was hiding and went to cuss him out." But the dressing-down was not to be, as Patton ascertained "he had a bullet over his right eye and was dead."[13] Patton intensely led by example and here, literally, by one of his axioms: "A good plan, violently executed now, is better than a perfect plan next week."[14]

CHAPTER 17

THE SKIES ABOVE AND VICTORY

Undoubtedly, as Saunders, Younger, Color Sergeant James Dell, and Ernest Janson's Marines of the 49th Company peered into the morning sky over St. Mihiel on September 12, they felt dismayed by the lack of American planes. The same misty weather instilling misery in the ground troops was also preventing the aircraft from taking off; the American planes did not get into the air until the afternoon.

Although airplanes could provide invaluable intelligence and provide cover for the men on the ground, flying during World War I was perilous. The Americans flew De Havilland DH-4s, often called "flying coffins" given the frequency with which the fuel tanks caught fire. The canvas-covered aircraft, sometimes with wooden frames, burned quickly, and many pilots met a fiery end. Open cockpits exposed the pilots to small arms and artillery fire from the ground. And frequently, the pilots flew without parachutes; therefore, if the plane were to ignite, it became a death trap. The DH-4s were also uncomfortable. Their Liberty engines were lubricated with castor oil, which often leaked onto the pilots, who sometimes managed to ingest the oil; this resulted in searing abdominal pain. American aviators jumped at the opportunity to fly French aircraft like the SPAD S.XII, armed with a massive (for biplanes) 37 mm semiautomatic cannon that ran through the center of the engine and fired through the nose of the plane, and a synchronized 7.7 mm machine gun mounted on the starboard side of the nose. The SPAD 12s being in short supply, the French typically passed on, in the form of a hand-me-down, the Nieuport 28, sporting a 160-horsepower engine and a pair of fixed forward-firing Vickers machine guns. Despite its near obsolescence, many of America's aces piloted the Nieuport.

Following the weather delay, the dogfights over the St. Mihiel salient were epic, emerging as one of the great air battles of World War I. More than five hundred German planes took to the skies, opposed by a combined force of nearly fifteen hundred American, French, Italian, British, and Portuguese aircraft—until that time, the largest concentration of military aircraft the world had ever seen. American Colonel William "Billy" Mitchell commanded the Allied aerial operations. Although later called "the father of the US Air Force," at the time, Mitchell had only limited combat experience after serving as a private in the Spanish-American War. However, as the son of a wealthy senator from Wisconsin, Mitchell had plenty of connections and quickly rose through the ranks. In 1912, when he was thirty-two, Mitchell became one of the youngest officers then serving on the general staff. Ironically, when he became temporary head of the Aviation Section in 1916, he was too old to qualify for military aviation training. Mitchell paid for flying lessons out of his own pocket at a cost of $1,470, about $33,000 in today's money.[1] A man who began his flying career as a lowly junior officer and paid for his own flying lessons ultimately would have a profound impact on the evolution of aviation warfare. Mitchell pioneered strategic bombing and devised airborne concepts, proposing to outfit the 1st Division with parachutes and drop them behind German lines. After the war, he proved that airplanes could sink battleships, changing the course of naval and aviation history.

Mitchell laid out several objectives for the air campaign at St. Mihiel, including destroying enemy planes, obtaining intelligence of German positions in order to direct artillery fire, and taking out ground targets, specifically rail lines and artillery.

As the battle began, Mitchell had his planes "put into a central mass and hurled at the enemy's aviation, no matter where he might be found, until complete ascendancy had been obtained over him in the air."[2] He attacked German aircraft "both night and day, so as to force [the enemy] either to arise and accept combat, or to lose his airplanes in the hangars themselves on his own fields."[3] Although their pilots and crews were inexperienced, the Allies did have two factors working in their favor: a three-to-one numerical advantage and the element of surprise. They would put both to good use.

America's greatest WWI ace, Captain and Squadron Commander Eddie Rickenbacker, took part in the battle. Because he was a former race car driver, the Army had first assigned Rickenbacker the task of driving General Pershing's car. But the boring job of chauffeur held little attraction for the adrenaline junkie, who soon sought and received a transfer to the 94th Aero Squadron, nicknamed the "Hat in the Ring." The 94th initially consisted largely of Ivy League graduates, who considered Rickenbacker a country bumpkin. One Yale alumnus sneered, "[Rickenbacker] was a lemon on an orange tree."[4] Rickenbacker described receiving his orders to attack as "an exciting moment in my life." He recalled, "At 60 feet above ground [flying] straight east to St. Mihiel, we crossed the Meuse River and turned down its valley towards Verdun. Many fires were burning under us as we flew, most of them well on the German side of the river. Villages, haystacks, ammunition dumps, and supplies were being set ablaze by the retreating Huns."[5] Despite being grounded throughout the morning by the bad weather, Rickenbacker remarkably managed to shoot down four German planes.

The Germans initially mounted a stiff resistance to the American-led air campaign at St. Mihiel, downing nearly as many Allied planes as they lost themselves. However, the Americans had a greater number of aircraft and pilots at their disposal, which ultimately allowed them to gain the upper hand.

In the middle of the St. Mihiel salient, the 1st Division (the "Big Red One"), fighting on the same side of the bulge as the 2nd Division, met and linked up with the 26th Division, which initially jumped off on the opposite side. The salient was bisected and collapsing, cutting off many Germans in the process. On the evening of September 13, the Marines of the 4th Brigade began to relieve Sergeant Younger's 9th Infantry

Regiment and Dell's 15th Field Artillery. One 5th Regiment Marine recalled approaching Jaulny, which lay only a few hundred yards away:

> It was shelled by the Germans quite regularly, but their main object seemed to be the small bridge across a stream at the edge of the town. Large shells fell at intervals just below us a short distance. We could hear the shells coming, and when they hit, the old earth fairly shook and trembled.
>
> An old Frenchman, leaving the town, while the leaving was good, stopped to talk to three other fellows and me. He had all his possessions in a bundle on his back. He was so glad that the town had been retaken, as he and all others in the town had been under German rule for nearly four years. Knowing that the old fellow was without money, we all gave him five francs apiece. He was so overjoyed that he kissed us every one on the cheek.[6]

The Marines moved into Jaulny and took over the château that Body Bearer Saunders had liberated. The danger was not over. Shells continued to rain down on the town, taking their toll. A massive shell from a German heavy gun struck one corner of the castle, pulverizing two Marines. Earlier they had buried bodies of German soldiers killed around the property and put a suffering horse wounded by artillery out of its misery with a .45. Numbly, the burial party went back to work. The sergeant in command bellowed, "Hell, fellows, more work! We may as well bury them now; then we can go get a drink of water."[7] The men lifted the bodies of their comrades into the shell hole.

Eventually, the US Army, with the Marines and other Allied units, pursued the Germans to the base of the salient where they strongly dug in along the Hindenburg Line and successfully repelled several American thrusts.

It was an overwhelming victory for First Army. Over the course of four days, the Americans captured fifteen thousand German prisoners, along with hundreds of artillery pieces and machine guns, all while losing fewer than nine thousand of their own men. Publicly, Pershing expressed

Body Bearers for the Unknown Soldier from left to right. Front Row: Color Sergeant James W. Dell, USA; Sergeant Samuel Woodfill, USA; Gunnery Sergeant Ernest A. Janson, USMC; Chief Water Tender Charles Leo O'Connor, USN. Second Row: Sergeant Thomas D. Saunders, USA; First Sergeant Louis Razga, USA; First Sergeant Harry Taylor, USA; Chief Torpedoman James Delaney, USN. This august group included two Medal of Honor recipients and several men who received the Distinguished Service Cross, the Navy Cross, and other decorations of valor.
Source: United States Marine Corps (USMC)

John J. Pershing, commander of the American Expeditionary Forces in World War I, reviewing the elite 2nd Division (Regular). Commander Pershing had the final say in the selection of the Body Bearers for the Unknown Soldier.
Source: USMC

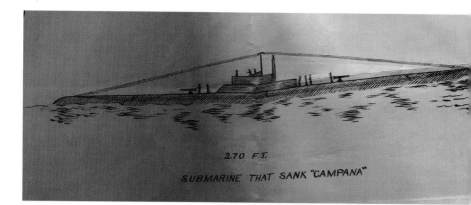

270 FT.

SUBMARINE THAT SANK "CAMPANA"

U-Boat 61, most likely drawn by Body Bearer James Delaney. Delaney, chief gunner's mate on the SS *Campana*, and his deck crew were involved in a four-hour running gun battle with the sub, each side firing more than one hundred rounds. During the battle, the U-boat struck several vital areas in the American ship and *Campana* surrendered. Delaney and several of his men became some of the first US prisoners of war captured by Germany, and they witnessed war under the sea as *U-61* sank additional ships and was itself depth-charged. *Source: National Archives and Records Administration (NARA)*

German U-boat sinking a merchant ship in the Atlantic. *Source: Wikipedia*

Body Bearer Ernest A. Janson received the Medal of Honor for his bayonet charge into several German machine guns. His actions saved the crucial Hill 142 near Belleau Wood. *Source: USMC*

Major George Hamilton, the commanding officer of Janson's 49th Company, is considered one of the great Marine officers of WWI. The book chronicles the 49th Company's experiences of trench warfare around Verdun to the deadly and tragic night crossing of the Meuse River on the final night and day of the conflict. *Source: NARA*

German *Stosstruppen*, or stormtroopers, pioneered modern assault tactics. Squads of men took advantage of whatever cover they could find and then laid down suppressing fire to force their opponents' heads down and hamper them from returning fire. Meanwhile, other groups of troopers charged forward, flanking the enemy, and if possible, annihilated their foes. *Source: Wikimedia*

Captain John Thomason, executive officer of the 49th Company. Thomason carried a sketch pad throughout the war, capturing battle scenes in pencil and in pen and ink. His experiences later became the grist for more than sixty short stories, magazine articles, and several books, most of which he illustrated himself.
Source: USMC

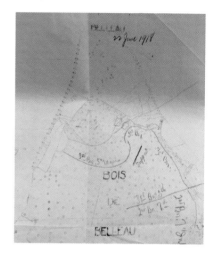

Field overlay map of Belleau Wood, the battle that forged the modern Marine Corps and thwarted a German drive on Paris in June 1918.
Source: NARA

Marine officers, survivors of Belleau Wood. *Source: USMC*

An M1917 trench knife named "Hun killer" by the Marine who used it. A WWI Brodie helmet affixed with an Eagle, Globe, and Anchor with the hand-painted Indian Head insignia from the 1st Battalion, 5th Marines. A gas mask. A Chauchat ammunition bag inscribed with the battles in which the Marine participated. *Author photo*

The brutal hand-to-hand combat of Belleau Wood, where men fought to the death with knives, clubs, pistols, and bayonets.
Source: USMC

Author (on left) and two members of the USMC Wounded Warrior Regiment at Belleau Wood. The author served as a volunteer guide for the 5th Marines and Wounded Warrior Regiment and earlier was an embedded combat historian with several men in the Battle of Fallujah, as recounted in *We Were One*. The idea for *The Unknowns* came from these trips. *Author photo*

Field artillery crew forced to don their protective masks to prevent the deadly effects of poison gas. In the background is one of the famous French 75 mm field guns. Body Bearer Color Sergeant James W. Dell was a member of the field artillery that manned the 75s.
Source: USMC

Sergeant Edward Younger, a doughboy with the 2nd Division's 9th Infantry Regiment, who went over the top in many battles and later selected America's Unknown Soldier.
Source: gallica.bnf.fr

The USS *Mount Vernon* five minutes after a German torpedo hit the ship. The captain of the vessel nominated Body Bearer Chief Water Tender Charles Leo O'Connor for the Medal of Honor and considered his efforts vital in saving the ship. *Source: NARA*

Torpedo hole in the USS *Mount Vernon. Source: NARA*

Members of the 91st Wild West Division. Farmers, loggers, ranchers, cowboys, and others who prided themselves on self-reliance and rugged individualism, hailing from the nine western states and the territory of Alaska, formed the backbone of the division. Blending among the rough-hewn men of the Wild West were filmmakers from the nascent industry in Hollywood. Body Bearer Harry Taylor and his regiment in the 91st made what amounted to a "Charge of the Light Brigade" at Gesnes in the Argonne. The unit took the town after suffering catastrophic casualties but was ordered to withdraw after units on its flanks crumbled under withering German counterattacks. *Source: Military History Institute (MHI)*

Wire cutters typical of those used by Body Bearer Sergeant Thomas Saunders, an American Indian who participated in "forlorn hope" suicide missions to sever German wire and breach defenses in no-man's-land. *Source: Scott Kraska*

Sergeant Stubby, the 102nd's Regiment's brindle-patterned bull terrier mascot, fought ferociously despite being wounded in the foreleg by a German grenade. The courageous canine endured through gas attacks and major battles to survive the war and later become the mascot of Georgetown University following World War I. *Source: Wikimedia*

The Great War saw the advent of the tank on the battlefield. Pictured are FT-17 tanks with American troops in the field. *Source: NARA*

The battlefield at Gesnes, where the Wild Westerners attacked and sustained bloody losses. *Source: MHI*

Body Bearer Sergeant Samuel Woodfill, Medal of Honor recipient, whose actions destroyed several German machine-gun nests in the Meuse-Argonne Offensive. Woodfill dispatched one German gunner in hand-to-hand combat with a pickaxe. Pershing considered him one of the greatest American soldiers of World War I. *Source: NARA*

An eight-inch howitzer of the type used by Body Bearer Louis Razga's gun crew. *Source: Library of Congress*

On the final, bloody night of the war, Thomas Saunders's 2nd Combat Engineers built a flimsy floating footbridge that spanned the Meuse River. Under heavy fire, Marines crossed the bridge, and many tragically lost their lives in vain on an operation that had no military or strategic significance. *Source: NARA*

Camouflaged German pillboxes on Blanc Mont. *Source: NARA*

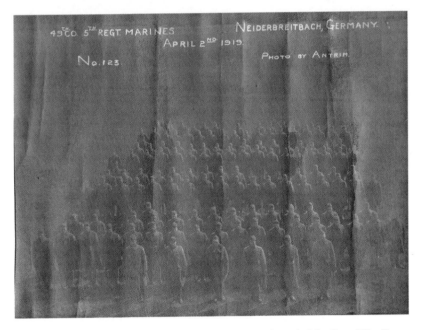

49TH CO. 5TH REGT. MARINES NEIDERBREITBACH, GERMANY.
APRIL 2ND 1919.
No. 123.   PHOTO BY ANTRIM.

Haunting photo of the members of the 49th Company at the end of the Great War. Few of its original men from the inception of the war were still alive or not wounded in the spring of 1919 when this picture was taken. The 49th Company of the 1st Battalion, 5th Marines engaged in some of the toughest fighting at Belleau Wood (taking and holding the crucial Hill 142), Soissons, Blanc Mont, and the Meuse-Argonne. They crossed the Meuse River under a hail of machine-gun and artillery fire on footbridges constructed by Body Bearer Sergeant Thomas Saunders. *Source: Scott Kraska*

Procession of the Unknown Soldier moving from Châlons, France, where Sergeant Edward Younger selected the Unknown from four flag-draped caskets. Younger prayed silently while he paced by the remains. As if summoned by some invisible force, he homed in on one of the flag-swathed caskets. "I know this man," he thought. His arms seemed to move of their own accord, placing the roses he held atop the coffin. *Source: gallica.bnf.fr*

At a ceremony in Le Havre, André Maginot awarded the Grand Cross of the Legion of Honour, France's highest military decoration, to the American Unknown Soldier. *Source: USMC*

Marines and sailors secured the coffin bearing the Unknown Soldier in the bow of *Olympia*, where it remained throughout its transatlantic voyage. *Source: USMC*

In gray, drizzly weather, the Body Bearers carried the Unknown Soldier from *Olympia* to the awaiting horse-drawn caisson that transported the body to the US Capitol. Various military officers, including General Pershing, saluted as the casket passed by. *Source: USMC*

Thousands of Americans lined the path to Arlington National Cemetery, many of them holding up small American flags in somber tribute as the funeral procession passed. *Source: USMC*

The Quantico Marine Corps Band played solemn hymns as marches to accompany the Unknown Soldier on his journey to the cemetery. *Source: USMC*

The Body Bearers carried the body down the steps of the Memorial Amphitheater in Arlington National Cemetery. *Source: USMC*

The Body Bearers carried the casket to the prepared burial site in Arlington National Cemetery. Visible in the front, from left to right, are Corporal Thomas D. Saunders, Chief Torpedoman James Delaney, and Sergeant Samuel Woodfill. *Source: USMC*

Thousands of mourners gathered for the graveside service to honor the Unknown Soldier. Electric amplifiers, high-tech equipment for the time, broadcast the speeches and music of the ceremony to those at the cemetery and across the country to specially designated listening places in several cities. *Source: USMC*

One final American stepped forward to honor the Unknown on behalf of his people. Chief Plenty Coups, present throughout the ceremony, removed the feathered war bonnet from his head and placed it on the sarcophagus alongside his coup stick. The symbols were meant to honor the sacrifices of the many American Indians who, like Body Bearer Corporal Thomas D. Saunders, had served their country heroically. The Unknown Soldier was then slowly lowered into his final resting place. *Source: Library of Congress*

America's most sacred monument is guarded twenty-four hours a day, every day of the year, regardless of weather conditions, by Tomb Guard sentinels, all volunteers from the US 3rd Infantry Regiment (The Old Guard). *Author photo*

The Tomb of the Unknown Soldier. Every year on Veterans Day and Memorial Day, US presidents lay a wreath at the Tomb in remembrance of all unidentified Americans who died in battle. *Author photo*

pleasure with the American army's performance in its first battle fighting as a cohesive unit. "We gave 'em a damn good licking, didn't we?" he bragged.[8] An independent American army was born, and would fight as such. Talk of breaking up the First Army and filtering American battalions into the French and British Armies finally died down.

Critically, the offensive sent the Germans into a state of disorder and confusion about where the American hammer wielded by First Army would fall next. Foch wanted to stay on the offensive to keep the Germans off balance and prevent them from recovering.

Saint Mihiel also brought to light many problems in how the AEF fought, particularly regarding coordination and logistics. (An American division was more than twice the size of the average French or German division, which at times could make them unwieldy.) Getting supplies and replacement troops to the front where they were needed had remained a nightmare during the offensive. Men on the front lines went without food and water while supply trucks sat stuck in traffic jams. Poor communication had resulted in units' becoming lost and a lack of coordination between the artillery and the infantry. To solve the logistics problem that emanated from the French ports and the unloading of troops, munitions, and supplies, Pershing dispatched his favorite general, James Harbord. Command of the 2nd Division had also passed to Marine Major General John Archer Lejeune.

With no time to bask in the victory, the First Army, many of the Body Bearers, and Sergeant Younger now faced another enormous challenge. As a result of his deal with Foch, Pershing had committed to launching another major offensive. He had only two weeks to conduct the Herculean task of moving his army and artillery more than fifty miles north to the Meuse-Argonne.

CHAPTER 18

"A NATURAL FORTRESS ... BESIDE WHICH THE WILDERNESS IN WHICH GRANT FOUGHT LEE WAS A PARK": THE MEUSE-ARGONNE

Brilliant hues of red and gold sunlight bathed the rolling hills of France; blue skies and white clouds marked a beautiful start to autumn. The success of St. Mihiel confused the Germans about where the AEF would attack next. For appearances' sake, a few convoys roved along the rolling French roads during the day to mislead German reconnaissance into thinking the front remained static.

But by night, hundreds of thousands of men in Pershing's army clogged the roads, a juggernaut that rumbled northeast toward the Meuse-Argonne. "Prowling skulking, preparing, stalking, half a million armed human beings accompanied by acres of guns—paraphernalia covering the earth—a blanket of destruction ten miles deep, thirty miles long, gliding by inches," remembered the future founder of the Cleveland Clinic, George Crile, then one of the soldiers in the dense column.[1]

In a miracle of logistics, the American army moved five hundred thousand men, two thousand guns, and nine hundred thousand tons of ammunition from areas around St. Mihiel more than fifty miles to staging areas near the Argonne. Each division occupied twenty miles of road space and would first have to march or ride twenty-five miles southwest from St. Mihiel to Bar-le-Duc, and then turn north toward staging areas outside the Argonne. As an added challenge, the AEF accomplished the movement behind French troops also traversing the roads. Most challenging, the entire operation required completion under the cover of darkness over the course of many nights in an attempt to maintain secrecy.

A forgotten hero of the Great War unsnarled the massive potential logjam. For years the French had been moving large numbers of troops to the front, and the agency in charge of the road movement of troops was the Service Automobile des Armées. The chairborne command with supreme power to move mountains and men fell on the shoulders of a lowly major, Joseph Édouard Aimé Doumenc.[2] What Doumenc lacked in rank he made up in skill and experience, and with his American counterparts, he performed wizardry in logistics and transported Pershing's men to the Argonne on time.

Fresh off their success in the St. Mihiel operation, Pershing and his principal planner, Major George Marshall, quickly turned their attention to the Meuse-Argonne. A series of fortifications that stretched from Arras to Laffaux, it was some of the most heavily defended real estate on the Western Front and the site of the American contribution to the Allies' grand offensive along the Hindenburg Line.

The Germans had converted the Argonne into a fortress. A strip of rocky, mountainous woods about six miles long, the forest provided defensive cover and murderous, natural kill zones through which an attacking army would have to battle. American officers compared the terrain to that of the Battle of the Wilderness in the Civil War, notable for its heavy underbrush and equally heavy casualties. One described the Argonne as a "natural fortress . . . beside which the Wilderness in which Grant fought Lee was a park."[3]

The Germans had spent the better part of three years constructing and gradually improving the defenses until they were seemingly impregnable. They had created a series of three and, in some areas, four lines of defense, with names from Richard Wagner's *Ring* cycle of operas. The first, the Etzel-Giselher Stellung, lay three miles behind the main line and contained mountains of barbed wire, a maze of interlocking trenches, and concrete pillboxes designed to lure incoming attackers into dead ends where German heavy artillery and field guns were poised to rain down showers of death. Machine guns, manned by expert gunners, were set in concrete bunkers and redoubts and had interlocking fields of fire aimed at goring attackers with enfilading (flanking) fire. Montfaucon (Mount of the Falcon), a strongpoint on a 1,122-foot-high butte, dominated the center of the Etzel-Giselher Stellung. Its height afforded the Germans an excellent view of the battlefield and the ability to direct their artillery fire.

If they survived and fought through that deadly defensive line, an opposing army would next encounter the Kriemhilde Stellung, part of the vaunted Hindenburg Line. Taking maximum advantage of the natural topography, the Germans used various high points to create funnels to trap and kill opposing troops. About the Kriemhilde, one American general said, "This was the most ideal defensive position I have ever seen or read about. Nature had provided for flank and crossfire to the utmost in addition to concealment."[4]

Several miles behind the Kriemhilde lay the less formidable final line of fortifications before the Meuse, Barricourt Ridge and a partially completed position known as the Freya Stellung. One American general described the Meuse-Argonne as "the most comprehensive system of leisurely prepared field defense known to history."[5] The American infantry and the Body Bearers entering the forest were largely equipped with light weapons, rifles, grenades, and light machine guns but would have to fight through a factory of death.

Rather than assault the Argonne directly, the Americans would attack the forest from the southeast while the French approached from the southwest. If the offensive succeeded, the Allies would link up behind the German defenses. Facing encirclement, the Germans would be forced to retreat from the Argonne. The British around Cambrai would keep up the pressure and also attack east. The Meuse-Argonne

Offensive was part of what has been dubbed "the Grand Offensive" with all the Allies moving on several axes of attack to advance the front toward Germany. The ultimate objective of the Meuse-Argonne Offensive would be the city of Sedan, an important railroad hub about fifty-two miles north of Verdun. The city sat just across the border. The Germans had seized it early in the war and, since then, had been using it to transport supplies to their troops. If the American army could cut the rail lines at Sedan, they would deprive the enemy of a critical link in its supply chain, effectively pulling the kaiser's troops out of their fortifications in the forest.

For what would prove to be the largest battle in American history, Pershing planned to attack initially with 225,000 men, divided into three corps with three divisions each. After St. Mihiel, which utilized veteran divisions, such as the 1st and 2nd, Pershing would be forced to employ largely inexperienced men in the first wave. This would prove to be a flaw in the planning, which later bogged down the offensive.

As they did at St. Mihiel, the First Army would once again face off against a portion of the Heeresgruppe Gallwitz, about five divisions in an army commanded by General Max Karl von Gallwitz.[6] Decorated, efficient, and competent, Gallwitz began his service in the 1870 Franco-Prussian War. By the start of WWI, he commanded a German Army on the Eastern Front and received Germany's highest decoration, the Pour le Mérite. At the close of 1915, he transferred to the west and commanded an army at Verdun and the Somme.

The prodigious resilience and flexibility the Germans displayed in four years of warfare on the Western Front remained of grave concern to Pershing. Within twenty-four hours, von Gallwitz could reinforce his front with four new German divisions. In twenty-four more hours, an additional two would arrive, and by seventy-two hours, nine more could pour into the German fortress. Time was of the essence: if Pershing did not move swiftly, he faced a force with the potential to mushroom into a formidable twenty-five divisions, possibly allowing the Germans to hold the area for months.[7]

* * *

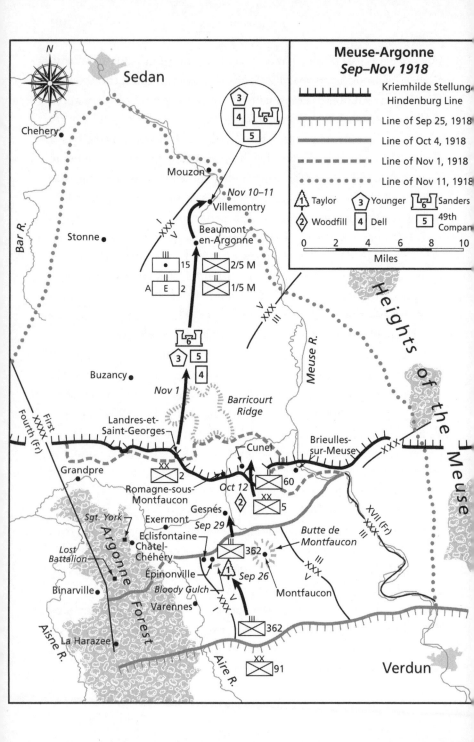

Meuse-Argonne
Sep–Nov 1918

⊥⊥⊥⊥⊥⊥⊥	Kriemhilde Stellung Hindenburg Line
⊤⊤⊤⊤⊤⊤⊤	Line of Sep 25, 1918
━━━━━━	Line of Oct 4, 1918
━ ━ ━ ━	Line of Nov 1, 1918
• • • • •	Line of Nov 11, 1918

Taylor ① ③ Younger ⌐6⌐ Sanders
Woodfill ② ④ Dell ⑤ 49th Company

0   2   4   6   8   10
Miles

Sedan

Chehery

Mouzon

Nov 10–11
Villemontry

Beaumont-en-Argonne

Stonne

Bar R.

XX
V   15

A E 2

2/5 M
1/5 M

XXX
III V

Meuse R.

Heights of the Meuse

⌐6⌐
③ ⑤
④

Nov 1

Buzancy

Barricourt
Ridge

Landres-et-
Saint-Georges

Brieulles-
sur-Meuse

Fourth XXXX First

Grandpre

XX
2

Romagne-sous-
Montfaucon

Cunel

Oct 12

XX   60
XX   5

Sgt. York

Exermont

Gesnés

Sep 29

Butte de
Montfaucon

XVII (Fr)
III XXX

Eclisfontaine
Châtel-
Chéhéry

III 362

Lost
Battalion

Argonne Forest

Épinonville

Sep 26

Montfaucon

XXX
III V

Binarville

Bloody Gulch

Varennes

①

XXX
V   I

La Harazee

Aisne R.

Aire R.

III 362

XX   91

Verdun

Just before midnight on September 26, 1918, the windows shook in General von Gallwitz's headquarters deep behind the German front lines. More than twenty-four hundred guns of a variety of calibers started a rolling barrage.

Ludendorff and Gallwitz had known the French would attack the Champagne region of France and expected a smaller attack in the Argonne. But the Germans were caught by surprise at the staggering size and scale of the offensive on the Argonne. As the deafening onslaught continued throughout the early morning hours, the three American corps got what sleep they could before starting their assault at 5:30 a.m.

Chapter 19

Harry Taylor and the Wild West Division

When Body Bearer First Sergeant Harry Taylor's watch clicked over to 5:30 a.m., a sudden roar of artillery shook the ground like an earthquake. One participant in the battle described the massive deluge of flying steel and high explosives: "The whole sky flickered from horizon to horizon as if in the flares from hundreds of blast furnaces. And over our heads, now with quick, pert, almost frivolous whistles; now with long-drawn, lazy moans; and now with a rushing sound of a departing express train, the shells began racing over into the enemy's lines."[1]

As shells streaked across the sky, the order went out: "Fix bayonets!" Armed with 220 rounds of 30-06 rifle ammunition, grenades, and a light load of reserve rations that would have to last for more than three days, Taylor and his fellow doughboys hurtled out of their jumping-off trench.

Sergeant Harry Taylor looked every inch a cowboy. Ruddy, brown-eyed, muscular, and standing five feet ten and a half inches tall, the rugged horse-soldier had spent his entire career in the saddle. After enlisting in 1901 as a young man at Fort Yellowstone, Wyoming, Taylor rode with the legendary 1st Cavalry, which had fought in every major American conflict since the Mexican War. A model soldier, Taylor earned a reputation as a crack shot with a pistol and an expert with the saber. His skills were anachronistic in the age of the machine gun and heavy artillery, but his leadership abilities were still highly valuable. His superiors rated Taylor's character as "excellent" on his progress reports.[2] The start of the Great War coincided with Taylor's fifth three-year enlistment with the US Army. Throughout his career, each of his assignments had been the same—cavalry and "H," or headquarters, troop.

Fittingly, when the United States entered World War I, the Army assigned Taylor to the 91st, known as the "Wild West Division." Farmers, loggers, ranchers, cowboys, and others who prided themselves on self-reliance and rugged individualism hailed from the nine western states and the territory of Alaska to form the backbone of the division. Among the rough-hewn men of the Wild West were filmmakers from the nascent industry in Hollywood. As the 91st Division trained and built up for Europe, the Army, as usual, assigned Taylor to headquarters troop. Frequently mounted, this group often performed recon and could rapidly move among the various units within the division. Taylor and his brothers were formidable fighters, but with the advent of modern weapons and technology, the cavalry's days were numbered.

After forming in San Francisco, the Wild West Division traveled by train to the East Coast. The journey had a galvanizing effect on Taylor and the men who traveled with him. Along the way, they encountered scenes such as the "motherly gray-haired old woman standing in front of her little cottage on the broad prairie of Montana, alternately waving a flag and brushing away tears she could not restrain." At the same time, "the journey gave many citizens, especially in the East, a better conception of the high quality of manhood the West was contributing to the United States Army."[3]

Arriving in Europe in July 1918, the 91st served as Corps Reserve during the St. Mihiel Offensive but did not see any action. Then in the early hours of September 26, 1918, the 91st entered the fray in the Meuse-Argonne. Taylor and his brothers-in-arms prepared to go over the top at dawn. The division's four regiments—the 361st, 362nd, 363rd, and 364th (in reserve)—formed the left flank of the Fifth Corps. As in much of the AEF, untested recruits and draftees filled the ranks of the division. Leadership from experienced NCOs like Taylor would hold the conscripts together later that day as they assaulted formidable defensive positions manned by the toughest army in the world at the time.

Fortunately, the Allied shells had pummeled the ground in front of the men, transforming the terrain into a moonscape as the artillery collapsed bunkers and flattened the German wire. Taylor and his Wild Westerners met no enemy fighters the first two miles into the German defenses. The troops appeared to have left quickly before the attack began. One participant recalled that the only living creature he encountered in his sector was a fox terrier "that gave a glad welcome"[4] to one of the first sergeants. Meeting no resistance, the Wild West men began to crack jokes and wave at each other as they marched.

With headquarters troop, Taylor moved among the various regiments, but he spent the bulk of his time with the 362nd Infantry.

After marching through the woods for more than an hour, Taylor and the others finally got their first real taste of battle. With a sudden, terrifying roar, German machine guns opened up on the doughboys. To eliminate the nests, the commander of the 362nd organized "gangs" of thirteen to seventeen men. Each had two scouts, five automatic riflemen, two rifle grenadiers, two hand-bombers, and two to six riflemen. Ranging ahead about one hundred to five hundred yards, the scouts ferreted out the nest locations by drawing enemy fire. Improvising upon Pershing's concepts of "open warfare," the Wild Westerners and other Americans innovated and developed their own tactics for overcoming the enemy defenses. Maintaining plenty of space between them, soldiers then moved into position to flank the machine guns while the heavier weapons remained in the back to bombard the nests. The tactic worked well, and the 91st slowly cleared out the Germans.

However, snipers and artillery took a heavy toll on the 91st. As Taylor emerged from the woods, German artillery began bursting with increased frequency and deadly accuracy. "One minute there were maybe two or three specimens of perfect manhood, the next minute nothing but raw carcasses or groaning wounded with stumps for arms or legs."[5] It is possible that Taylor may have entered the battle mounted, in which case he would have been a larger target. The shells did not discriminate between beast and man, and they blew one of the 91st's horses fifteen feet into a tree where the carcass dangled, suspended from the branches like a gory piñata.

Pressing forward relentlessly, Taylor and the 362nd passed through an orchard and a muddy creek that snaked through a deep valley. The men later dubbed the place "Death Valley" or "Bloody Gulch" for the carnage that would unfold there in the coming days.

On the 362nd's flanks, the 91st's other regiments encountered stronger German defenses that prevented them from keeping up, leaving the regiment's flanks exposed as it approached the tiny hamlet of Épinonville, which now consisted of little more than the shells of several bombed-out houses and other buildings.

As Taylor and the other Wild Westerners entered Épinonville, they discovered signs of a hasty departure: half-filled beer glasses, valuable field glasses, and an expensive fur coat all left behind.[6] The Germans had exited in a hurry—and they would return just as quickly. That night, while the 362nd occupied the town, the Germans infiltrated back into Épinonville in strength, forcing portions of the regiment to retreat. Working through the night, the Germans quickly refortified the area, manning machine-gun nests and bunkers, transforming the hamlet into a fortress and kill zone. They intended to hold the town as long as possible and bleed the Americans.

When morning arrived on September 27, the 362nd set out to retake the village. They lit up Épinonville with one-pounders, a 37 mm light gun handled by a crew of several men, and machine guns. Hotly contesting the American advance, German snipers, Maxim gunners, and artillerists trained their fire on the men, making them pay for every step.

Wild Westerners died in droves. "For the first and only time doubt and indecision displayed themselves,"[7] and the 362nd staggered back as the ferocious onslaught decimated its ranks. The assault on Épinonville faltered until someone made the call to "raise the artillery."[8] Within minutes, US shells plastered the hamlet. Tragically, the rounds fell short, slaughtering many of the Americans. The green troops showed signs of panic as they made frantic calls to halt the fratricide.

In the midst of the chaos, the towering figure of Colonel John "Gatling Gun" Parker, the regimental commanding officer who loomed at least six feet, three inches tall, burst onto the scene, "brandishing a cane like a young sapling, and swearing like a trooper."[9] With a massive smoking pipe dangling from his mouth, he waved the regiment forward. His bellowing voice echoing across the field, he urged the men to find their courage and advance. Parker, a hero of San Juan Hill who would earn four Distinguished Service Crosses for his valor in battle, had recently taken command of the 362nd after proudly commanding the 102nd Regiment whose two companies survived the raid on Seicheprey. Stubby, the fearless 102nd Regimental mascot, didn't join Parker but stayed with the 102nd.

German machine guns and snipers mowed the Americans down as the 362nd inched up the side of the hill. The enemy defenses checked their advance, and Parker ordered his men to dig in. Enemy artillery raked the slope. Because the 37th Division had failed to keep pace with the 362nd, the Germans could freely hit the Westerners from the right side, and aircraft strafed the regiment.

Lieutenant Farley Granger, who after the war would own an auto dealership in Alvarado, California, and subsequently manage his movie actor son with the identical name, was a platoon leader and later a captain in an infantry company in the 362nd. Granger commanded "tough men from Utah, Wyoming, Idaho, and Montana."[10] He recalled one of their trials under fire: "Eventually the Huns' planes began to take their toll. A shell struck so close to our 'foxhole,' we were covered with mud at first and mistook it for mustard gas because of its cold damp feeling down our necks and up our sleeves. All night long terrible shelling continued. Gas masks were worn continuously and the frequent cries of 'medic on the right' and 'medic on the left' pierced the night and justified the name the men gave the mount, 'Hell's Hill.'"[11] Eventually, the furious counterattack forced Taylor and his fellow soldiers to retreat, leaving scores of dead Americans behind.

To the west, the 91st's 363rd and 364th Regiments advanced to the town of Éclisfontaine. The result was the same as at Épinonville:

the Westerners took the town but could not hold on to it when the Germans counterattacked. As the battle dragged on, food and water shortages became acute. Because of bottlenecks in the American rear, fresh supplies could not reach the front lines. For three days the men lived on the meager rations they had brought with them into battle or what they captured. Most men were forced to drink primarily from the dirty creek at the bottom of Death Valley, which was polluted with chemical weapons and other runoff from the battle.

In the aftermath of the bloodbath at Épinonville and Éclisfontaine, stretcher-bearers took the wounded men with lost limbs, fractured faces, and shattered bodies to the aid station. Those who were not carried limped or crawled to makeshift field hospitals and dressing stations in Death Valley. German artillery and gas rained down upon the area, turning the entire scene into a hellish nightmare. Eventually, on September 28, the division seized Épinonville and Éclisfontaine after withstanding several furious German counterattacks.

Several miles to the right of the 91st, the Germans maintained the crucial strongpoint of Montfaucon. The fortified butte provided a commanding view of the area and served as a key node in the Kriemhilde Stellung. The American plan called for taking Montfaucon on the first day. However, the Germans were determined to maintain possession of it, repelling several American assaults. Two days later, it fell. That delay, combined with furious German counterattacks, had thrown the entire Meuse-Argonne Offensive off its tight schedule.

Part of a defense-in-depth strategy, Épinonville and Éclisfontaine lay in front of the Kriemhilde Stellung. To the north of both hamlets, in front of the Wild West Division, lay open ground that stretched to the town of Gesnes, a strongpoint just outside the Kriemhilde Stellung that the Germans planned to hold at all costs.

CHAPTER 20

THE CHARGE OF
THE LIGHT BRIGADE AT GESNES

First Sergeant Harry Taylor and the rest of the 91st faced a suicide mission: Gesnes.

The Germans had turned Gesnes into a fortress, and a subterranean network of tunnels bored under the town connected bunkers and strongpoints. To reach the tiny French hamlet, the Americans would have to cross a full mile of open ground with no cover. And the land was "double enfiladed by machine guns and subject to the highest concentration of [German] artillery fire I have ever seen," recalled "Gatling Gun" Parker, who would lead the assault on the town.[1]

Despite the tremendous risk, V Corps headquarters had ordered Major General William Johnson, the division commander of the 91st, to attack Gesnes "with utmost vigor and regardless of cost."[2] To carry out the order, Johnson turned to Parker. Surveying the ground, Parker saw at once that this was a forlorn hope; he attempted to explain to Johnson the bloodbath that would ensue. "The position can be taken," he argued, "but only if it is desired to pay the price, which will be very severe losses."[3]

Unswayed by Parker's argument, Johnson resolutely shot back, "The whole army is being held up because this brigade has not taken all the objectives assigned to it."[4] Taylor, Parker, and the rest of the regiment would charge Gesnes.

Nearly a mile from the town, in the jump-off position, Lieutenant Farley Granger surveyed the battlefield through his binoculars.

"Every square yard was visible from the higher hills beyond, occupied by the enemy, and the concrete-box on Hill 255, and every foot swept by machine-gun and artillery fire. Protection, there was none—not even concealment for one man. The gullies between the hills were swept by enfilading fire from wooded hills above Gesnes, and the hillsides were commanded by nests hidden in flanks."[5]

To make matters worse, the 91st faced some of the Germans' most battle-hardened elite troops: the Prussian Guards and elements of several other regiments.[6] With plenty of time to dig in, these experienced veterans of the Western Front had all the advantages of bunkers, command of the high ground, and control of the flanks—the 91st's assault at Gesnes faced German attacks on three sides.

Taylor, at thirty-eight an old man in the troop, understood that the attack meant near-certain death. In Granger's opinion, "an umpire of field maneuvers would call the task impossible and rule the regiment out."[7] He recalled that in a meeting with officers of the 362nd, very likely including Taylor, one officer murmured that taking Gesnes would be "impossible, that our losses would be terrible."

Granger's commanding officer laid down the law. "The hell with the losses—read the order!"[8]

Gesnes would be taken, regardless of cost.[9]

Heading into the battle, the 91st had brought limited food and water—many were starving. German shells and constant gas alarms had kept the men awake for thirty-six hours straight. Heedless of their exhaustion, the undaunted Wild Westerners prepared to assault, moving into position about a mile outside the town.

Sunlight filtered through the slate-gray clouds and the husks of nearby trees as the members of the 91st gripped their rifles and other weapons, primed to charge into open ground. An enemy sniper picked off men from the rear as a deadly shower of German shells landed only twenty feet in front of the jumping-off position. Frequent screams of "Gas!" cut through the din of battle. At 3:40 p.m. the officers blew their whistles, and NCOs, such as Harry Taylor, on foot with the infantry, surged ahead. Many of the 362nd yelled their Western battle motto, anachronistic in the modern killing fields of the Meuse-Argonne: "Powder River! Let 'er buck!"

Unbeknownst to the mass of soldiers charging forward, according to Lieutenant William Hutchinson, a bald-headed officer in the 362nd, "the order had been countermanded, but too late—the countermand coming just after we started." He lamented, "The colonel could not be found. I do not know that he could have prevented it entirely, but it surely could have been called off before we had all the losses at Gesnes."[10]

In a charge reminiscent of scenes twenty years earlier at the Battle of San Juan Hill, Parker led from the front, in the center of the first screaming wave of men. Farley Granger's commanding officer was not as dramatic. Accepting his fate, he turned to Granger and said, "Well, Farley, let's go."[11] Taylor, Farley, and the men of the 362nd left their forward fighting positions and the last vestige of cover, leaping into a hail of German lead and steel.

Granger later described the "glorious" forlorn hope: "Perhaps the charge of the Light Brigade was more spectacular, more melodramatic and picturesque, but not more gallant. It is one thing to ride knee to knee in wild delirium of a cavalry charge under the eyes of armies; it is something else to plod doggedly on, so widely scattered as to seem alone over a barren hillside against an unseen enemy's invisible death singing its weird croon as it lurked in the air and stinging swiftly on every side. Man after man fell, but the others continued on through a 'hell' of shrapnel and machine-gun fire as would be impossible to exceed."[12]

Columns of olive drab—ranchers, cowboys, and loggers—charged, only to morph into blobs of flesh and crimson rags. Heavy shells vaporized others in a spray of blood and gore. The fields outside Gesnes harvested their share of unknown soldiers; bodies of unrecognizable men carpeted the rolling plain.

A Renault FT-17, taken in an earlier battle by the Germans, obstructed the path of the advancing tide of Westerners until Granger and a company of men led by Lieutenant William Hutchinson took care of it. Charging forward, with no body armor save steel helmets, the men swarmed the tank and shot the crew as those inside attempted to flee the vehicle. Climbing into the blood-drenched FT, they turned the steel monster on Gesnes, and the tank's machine gun tore into Boche nests.

Finally, irregular groups of Westerners topped the last crest into the town. Once inside Gesnes, Taylor, Granger, and Hutchinson had their work cut out for them. "The satisfaction of some bayonet work was given to us," recalled Granger. Small groups of men from the 362nd advanced into Gesnes, and "promptly cleared it." However, Granger cautioned, "One must not think of this as happening in an instant—over an hour of this bloody plodding along under a tornado of missiles passed before the worst was over."[13]

Several men from the 91st earned the Medal of Honor that day. As would be the case at Iwo Jima during the next world war, "uncommon valor was a common virtue." Parker said that he saw so many examples of gallantry that it was difficult to single out the men who were worthy of medals. In the 91st's general orders, the division recognized Taylor for the valor he displayed that day—he received a Citation Star, an honor later known as the Silver Star.*

Parker did not witness the capture of Gesnes. Wounded multiple times, he lay near death in a shell hole five hundred yards in front of the town for two hours. Upon learning of the capture of the town and the hill beyond, he issued an order: "Dig in, hold on, and get food for your men." In a precarious position and fearing a German counterattack, Parker "caused some wounded men near me to make a bonfire of all maps, orders, and papers in my possession, destroying everything that might possibly give any information to the enemy."[14]

A fate similar to Parker's also took out Granger: a machine-gun bullet hit him in the ankle. Granger made his way off the field with four bullet holes in the flaps of his trench coat and another drilled into his canteen.

---

* Congress established the Citation Star on July 9, 1918, and in July 1932 the secretary of war converted the Citation Star to the Silver Star. Congress formally authorized the Silver Star in 1942. The US Army and Air Force refer to the honor as the "Silver Star," while the US Navy, Marine Corps, and Coast Guard call it the "Silver Star Medal."

After taking Gesnes, the 362nd advanced, cutting down Germans with bullet, grenade, and bayonet. About two hundred reinforcements streamed in, swelling the American ranks. Some of the soldiers, led by Hutchinson and a few other officers and noncoms, seized a portion of the wood and the southern slope of Hill 255, north of the town. The doughboys took prisoners and captured several field artillery pieces. Hutchinson also discovered a nearby cabbage patch. After starving for three days, the ravenous men cut the cabbages in half and gorged themselves on the green leafy plants, "in the same variety of enjoyment that we would have had, if it been Crab Louie. We ate in the dark, eating cabbages, dirt, and worms, but how good it tasted."[15]

Scores of wounded men lay near the town, and Hutchinson attempted to find them shelter in a nearby shed. "The weather turned cold and many men suffered from loss of blood and were already shaking."[16]

After tending to the wounded, Hutchinson climbed back into a foxhole on the hill. Despite the German artillery fire raining down around him, Hutchinson, exhausted and suffering from exposure to gas, fell asleep next to the bodies of dead men.

Late that night, an officer espied the bald head of Hutchinson, who had lost his helmet earlier that afternoon, "in the scrape" next to the row of corpses, dead bodies of his friends, and shook him awake. "We are withdrawing" the officer told Hutchinson.[17]

General Johnson himself had given the order because the division was in grave danger. During the American operation to seize Gesnes, the Germans launched a massive counterattack, nearly destroying the American 35th Division on the 91st's left flank. The enemy drove the 35th back almost two miles and fell upon the 91st. Fortunately, the 2nd Battalion of the 363rd Infantry, a machine-gun company, and other units held the line—had they failed, the Germans might have enveloped the 91st.

Acting according to their orders, divisions in V Corps had attacked independently of each other, charging forward, ignoring their flanks, and as a result meeting disaster. The 37th Division on the right flank, about two and a half miles behind, also did not keep up with the rest of the force. This strategy left individual units widely isolated and vulnerable to counterattack. Disaster loomed.

As darkness fell, the retreat from Gesnes became horrific. The memory of the withdrawal was seared into the minds of Westerners. "Everyone in our sad little procession was carrying or helping carry a wounded man. It was quite cold with a strong wind blowing rain in our faces," recalled Hutchinson. "We stumbled along, floundering through shell holes and every now and then picking up wounded men who had not been brought off the field. We picked up a 2nd lieutenant who had been wounded early in the afternoon. Many times the stretchers gave way and the stretcher-bearers stumbled and fell. The wounded would groan and curse, and the column would halt until they were ready to move forward again. Our morale was all gone—we simply continued to stumble ahead."[18] The dead, far too numerous, many of them unknown soldiers, were left behind.

And then the stone-cold realization set in: the attack had been for naught. "The withdrawal finally began. We were all so tired that we did not have much feeling one way or the other at that time, but later the full truth dawned on us. We were withdrawing to the point from which we started that attack. The whole terrible afternoon and hideous night were all for nothing."[19] Taylor and the Wild Westerners had advanced more than five miles into German lines since September 26 but had outpaced the units on their flanks. Had they remained where they were, they would have been cut off, encircled, and annihilated.

What was left of the 362nd retreated from Gesnes carrying the wounded.

Granger noted, "Never have men displayed a greater devotion to duty. That is why a regiment without complete equipment or training could defeat such troops as the elite Prussian Guards, overcame positions of noted strength and still advanced, often without officers, after losing in a few minutes over 50 percent in casualties; the offensive spirit, the will to win, the fitness to win, in a word, the morale was such, the personnel was such, that victory was possible despite the greatest handicap."[20]

According to the regiment's history, the morning after the attack, Taylor and the survivors, slipped into a "loggish stupor. The men lay, their minds heavy with the horror of the last day, their bodies bruised and exhausted, with no more spirit than the mud under their feet."[21] Only handfuls of men filled out companies, which at the start of the attack had numbered two hundred men—the remainder were dead or wounded. "Captains commanded battalions, lieutenants companies, and sergeants platoons, so great had been the slaughter. One company had eighteen men left of its 179. Few companies ran as high as seventy-five [men]."[22] Back at a field hospital, Granger met the severely wounded Gatling Gun Parker. Despite his injuries, Parker boasted to the young officer, "I didn't see in the whole regiment a single case of cold feet—not a single yellow streak."[23]

While cases of desertion were minimal in the 362nd, desertion and stragglers were a sizable problem in the AEF. Estimates vary, but as many as one hundred thousand soldiers left their units in the first month of the AEF's fighting in the Meuse-Argonne Offensive—as much as 10 percent of the total American force quit fighting and meandered to rear areas.[24] In the 37th Division, which the 91st flanked, an inspector reported that 20 percent of the men in the unit may have been in the rear with the gear.[25]

Part of the difficulty in calculating the volume of stragglers is that many of the men accused of avoiding duty were actually suffering from undiagnosed injuries. The doughboys' steel helmets had no real padding, and many men experienced concussions and traumatic brain injury, also unknown at the time, after shells exploded nearby. In addition, post-traumatic stress disorder, then called "shell shock," was common. Many of the men wandering away from the front lines were not displaying cowardice but instead were dazed or impaired as a result of these medical conditions.

Some of the stragglers had just gotten off the boat, and these raw draftees had not received adequate training. (This was generally not the case with the Marines or soldiers in the elite 2nd Division.) Some could not properly fire a rifle or throw a grenade. The inspector general in the AEF dismally reported that these "men who did not know the rudiments of soldiering soon became 'cannon fodder' or skulkers."[26]

Officers toiled to combat straggling. In First Army V Corps, they formed a 4,500-man Hobo Barrage to "systematically mop up and purge all dugouts, houses, hospitals, rail heads, YMCAs, etc."[27] Some wanted to shoot stragglers, but President Wilson refused to allow the practice. Instead, officers usually arrested those found lingering at kitchens, first-aid stations, and YMCA huts. Repeat offenders faced court-martial, imprisonment, disagreeable work assignments, or in some cases, public shaming. A few officers outfitted those repeatedly found dawdling behind their comrades with large signs on their backs that read, "STRAGGLER FROM THE FRONT LINES." Not surprisingly, this strategy proved to be quite effective at encouraging the men to perform their duties. Even more effective was the technique used by one brigadier general; after his soldiers received orders to advance, he had his military police (MPs) throw grenades into dugouts behind the lines. With the rear sealed off, stragglers had no place to hide.

Desertion was not a problem in the 91st—the problem was the "butcher's bill" from the fighting. The Wild Westerners suffered about 25 percent casualties—yet they fought on in the Meuse-Argonne Offensive until the second week of October, when the First Army transferred Taylor, Granger, and Hutchinson to Belgium. There the 91st fought side by side with the British Army, distinguishing themselves during the final days of the war.

Despite the loss of many of his close friends, a part of Granger's youth remained in France—undoubtedly this feeling has haunted many soldiers since the beginning of warfare. "I want to live those days again; to see the bursting shells and hear them whistling for their victims; hear the frantic cries of 'gas!' 'cover!' 'medic!' 'Raise the artillery!' I want to go back to France once more—not to seek new joys or thrills, but to revive the dreams of old that are fading with the years," Granger recalled decades later.[28]

By September 29, 1918, Pershing's offensive largely stalled after three days of fighting. The fact that Pershing held the AEF's most battle-hardened and experienced divisions—the 1st, 26th, and 42nd, which had been delayed after spearheading the St. Mihiel Offensive—in reserve contributed to the lack of progress. The mighty 2nd Division also did not participate in the first phases of the American offensive.

But in October 1918, there was no time to reflect wistfully on the carnage. Most of the Body Bearers, including Color Sergeant James W. Dell, Corporal Thomas Saunders, and the Marines of Gunny Ernest A. Janson's 49th Company headed northwest for the Champagne, where they were assigned to the French Army and would mount a forlorn attack on another seemingly impregnable German fortress: Blanc Mont.

CHAPTER 21

MISSION IMPOSSIBLE: BLANC MONT RIDGE

September 27, 1918,
Fourth French Army Headquarters

Major General John A. Lejeune stared at the large relief map sprawled out in front of him. His eyes focused on the ridgeline where the Germans had constructed an ostensibly impregnable fortress. Hundreds of machine-gun nests, an intricate maze of trenches, concrete blockhouses, artillery pieces, and tangled masses of barbed wire awaited any force foolish enough to attack. For more than a month, Lejeune had held a divisional Army command—the first and only Marine officer ever to do so in combat. The tough commander, "a Marine's Marine" later hailed as "one of the greatest of all leathernecks," led the Army's 2nd Division, including the Marine Brigade. It was one of the finest divisions in the Allied armies. Marshal Foch, noting the 2nd's élan and battlefield prowess at Belleau Wood and Soissons, had requested the division be placed under the temporary command of the Fourth French Army, which was led by the grizzled, one-armed General Henri Gouraud.

Gouraud explained to Lejeune that the French Army had stalled in front of the high ground and his men were exhausted. He had earmarked the 2nd for the formidable task of breaking through the powerful German defenses. Gouraud's piercing eyes and bushy handlebar mustache seemed almost to pop off his face as he emotionally placed his only hand on the German fortress on Blanc Mont Ridge on the map. "General," he declared, "this position is the key of all the German defenses of this sector, including the whole Rheims Massif. If this ridge can be taken, the Germans will be obliged to retreat along the whole front thirty kilometers to the river Aisne. Do you think your division could effect its capture?"[1]

For years, the French Army had launched one forlorn attack after another on the fortress. The result: a bloodbath, thousands of men killed—gored on the seemingly impenetrable defenses of Blanc Mont.

Without hesitation, Lejeune informed Gouraud that the 2nd could seize the stronghold. Whereupon the French general ordered him to draw up an assault plan and prepare his men to attack Blanc Mont.

Sergeant Edward Younger of the 2nd Division's 9th Infantry Regiment sat in the back of the camion as it snorted down the dusty French road approaching the staging area near Blanc Mont. After dismounting from the French truck, Younger undoubtedly looked up at the bald ridge where protruding white limestone jutted out, giving the landmark its name, "White Mountain." Row upon row of machine-gun emplacements, pillboxes, barbed wire, and husks of trees dotted the lunar-like landscape, which was scarred from years of shelling.

Younger and his men maneuvered toward the French, believing they occupied trenches about a mile away from the fortress. They espied the wreckage of four years of war: bleached bones, broken equipment, and scores of lonely helmets with bullet holes drilled through their rusted metal skins. The dead lay where they fell.

Machine-gun fire and grenades erupted as Younger and his platoon from Company A approached the French trench line where they would jump off. The French had retreated early, and the Germans had retaken a portion of the entrenchment. Younger and the 9th spent several hours clearing German soldiers out of the jumping-off point.

In a few hours, the 3rd Brigade (9th and 23rd Regiments) and 4th Brigade (5th and 6th Marines) would advance across a mile or so of open ground at an oblique angle to the German defenses, which consisted of three parallel belts. Beyond lay the mighty concrete machine-gun emplacements and bunkers on Blanc Mont. The redoubts allowed the Germans to triangulate their fire. As the Allies had experienced, enfilading fire from a handful of machine guns could annihilate an assaulting force. A system of honeycombed trenches and tunnels connected the strongpoints, enabling the Germans to reinforce them or recapture overrun positions. Scores of concrete pillboxes dotted the area; their deadly fire supported the main redoubts. Each of the 2nd's brigades occupied a mile of French real estate, not contiguously linked together but separated by the Bois des Vipères (Viper Woods).

The 2nd Division was about to enter one of the most perilous kill zones on the Western Front. If they survived, the men would link up on the crest.

John Thomason from Body Bearer Ernest Janson's 49th Company described the moment when wave after wave of Marines and soldiers from the two brigades went over the top at 5:50 a.m. on October 3, charging into the teeth of German defenses: "For a moment, the sun shone through the murk, near the horizon—a smoldering red sun, banded like Saturn, and all the bayonets gleamed like blood. Then the cloud closed again." In front of them lay the result of the previous doomed French attack on the German trenches: scores of dead soldiers formed "a wedge, thinning toward the point as they had been decimated, and at that point was a great bearded Frenchman, his body all a mass of bloody rags, who lay with his eyes fiercely open to the enemy and his outthrust bayonet almost in the emplacement."[2]

Once again, the heavy guns and field artillery from Body Bearer Color Sergeant James W. Dell's 15th Regiment opened fire. The whine became a rumble as the shells arced across the sky. The French and American guns "opened with one world-shaking crash."[3] Crimson and green flames pelted the German lines; the powerful rolling barrage rained down on their defenses. The shells dropped in advance of the infantry at a fixed rate, creeping ahead while the assault pushed forward

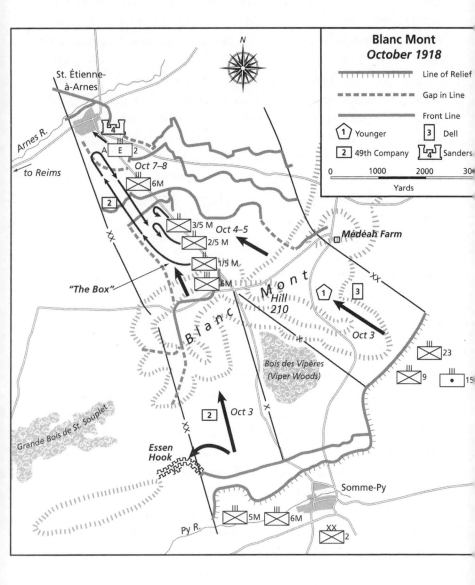

Blanc Mont
October 1918

St. Étienne-à-Arnes

Arnes R.

to Reims

Oct 7–8

6M

Oct 4–5

3/5 M

2/5 M

1/5 M

6M

"The Box"

Blanc Mont

Hill 210

Oct 3

Médéah Farm

Bois des Vipères
(Viper Woods)

23

9

15

Grande Bois de St. Souplet

2 Oct 3

Essen Hook

Somme-Py

5M 6M

2

Py R.

Line of Relief

Gap in Line

Front Line

1 Younger

2 49th Company

3 Dell

4 Sanders

0   1000   2000   300

Yards

with the hope of destroying enemy emplacements. Some shells fell short. The artillery did not range properly, and incidents of friendly fire were high. But the shelling proved deadly effective as a battlefield tactic and kept many Germans in their bunkers while the infantry charged their position.[4]

Enemy guns responded to the bombardment and hit Dell's men hard. One member of the 15th recalled, "The German artillery was raising the devil with us; one shell killed eighteen horses that were being fed in a ravine about a hundred yards back of us. Our position was continually under fire—it was a case of moving front or back. We moved ahead to within three hundred yards of our infantry. Quite a few prisoners were coming in, also several hundred wounded. The Germans were making us pay dearly for every inch we gained. They wouldn't give in. Our barrage raised havoc with the Germans. They must have tried to get away with their artillery, but the God of War must have said 'No!'—some of their horses were cut in two."[5]

Younger and his men went over the top and charged across the pock-marked no-man's-land. The 9th's 1st Battalion, including Younger's Company A, led the onslaught toward the crest of Blanc Mont. German artillery pelted down on Company A, slaughtering several soldiers within minutes. Machine-gun nests checked the battalion's advance until one of the company runners grabbed a Chauchat machine gun. Although renowned for its unreliability and tendency to jam in combat, the weapon did not fail New York Private Frank J. Bart, whose one-man charge in front of the 9th's skirmish line wiped out one nest. More machine guns held up the battalion's advance. Undaunted, Bart charged and destroyed a second machine-gun emplacement. These valiant actions later earned the private a Medal of Honor.

Behind Bart, Company A and Younger's men worked their way up Blanc Mont. On the far right of the ridge, the 9th took Médéah Farm, which the Germans had adapted into a strongpoint, and the Blanc Mont Road that ran near the ridge and northwest into the crucial town of

Saint-Étienne. To the west, the 9th stormed a German emplacement on a knoll labeled Hill 210. Then the army linked up with the 6th Marines, who led the attack up the left side of the ridge in heavy fire. Company A sustained many killed and wounded, some blown to bits by the German guns, their remains unaccounted for. To this day, many share the fate of the masses of the war's unknown fallen. Company A's casualties included Sergeant Younger; a Maxim machine-gun bullet penetrated his thigh. The wound landed the Chicago native in a field hospital for weeks, but he would make a full recovery.

Dell's 15th Field Artillery moved their guns with the advancing infantry. "Our infantry got possession of the hill and kept it," recalled a member of the 15th. "While moving out of our position, we came directly under fire of a German gun. We could hear its report, and immediately a shell would land among us. We realized we were in for a hot time. We finally made it to the field and were fortunate as only five men were wounded in getting through. We stayed on the road about thirty minutes. Our captain sent a runner ahead to notify the infantry, and in about five minutes the gun was silent. The Germans had hidden the gun in the woods, and our infantry had passed through and missed it. As soon as the infantry passed they must have pulled the gun out and commenced firing. As we moved forward, we saw the gun and gunners, all dead around the gun."[6]

By the evening of October 4, the 2nd's Marines and soldiers linked up on the crest of Blanc Mont and continued to hack, blast, and shoot the Germans fiercely fighting in concrete bunkers and trenches on the ridge.

But French ineptitude overshadowed the day's glory. The French failed to keep up with the 2nd, exposing its flanks. The Germans launched powerful counterattacks and fired upon the 2nd from the front, the sides, and even the rear. Reinforcements poured in as they steeled for an all-out attempt to crush the 2nd.

With disaster looming, Lejeune cabled Pershing and furiously informed him he would resign his commission rather than fight under French command if the Allies did not fight through toward their objectives.

Far from headquarters, the men fighting atop Blanc Mont had now gone twenty-four hours without food or water. In desperation, the men scavenged the dead for their canteens while the Germans mercilessly counterattacked, shelled, and gassed them. Against all odds, the men of the 2nd pushed forward and positioned themselves in a salient—their flanks and rear now on the opposite side of Blanc Mont. The teeth of the German defenses at Saint-Étienne lay in front of them, over a mile of open ground in the distance.

Digging in on the northern side of Blanc Mont, the 5th Marines and the 49th Company girded for their coming attack at dawn.

"Orders are to attack, and by God, we'll attack," declared Major George Hamilton. Ernest Janson's former company commander, Hamilton had heroically led the attack on Hill 142 in Belleau Wood and now commanded the 1st Battalion, 5th Marines. A yawn spoiled the dramatic nature of his pronouncement. "And now I'm going to get some sleep. Coxy, wake me at 5:30."[7]

At dawn, the 5th Marines surged forward toward Saint-Étienne. A sea of doughboys clad in overcoats and army tunics with their gas-mask bags slung around their necks advanced in columns of battalions. In the open ground, machine-gun bullets, artillery, and gas tore into the Marine phalanx. Crumpled brown figures lay in the wake of the charging battalion. "The raw smell of blood was in the men's nostrils," the 49th's Lieutenant Thomason remembered.[8] "All hell broke loose" on the 49th Company's rear from Germans dug in on the reverse slope of Blanc Mont. German shrapnel rained down. "Singing balls and jagged bits of steel spattered on the hard ground like sheets of hail; the line writhed and staggered, steadied and went on, closing toward the center as the shells bit into it . . . red flashes, full of howling death."[9] The casualties included "a girlish, pink-cheeked lieutenant" who was gleefully swinging a brand-new pair of field glasses as he accompanied several machine gunners. A shell "flattened them into a mess of bloody rags, from which a bloody arm thrust upward, dangling the new field glasses."[10]

German gas shells pummeled the advancing Marines. "[One Leath-erneck] inhaled some poison gas and left for the rear with mucus run-ning out of his eyes and nose. What a sight,"[11] recalled one member of the 5th Marines. Enfilading fire from the left flank pelted Hamilton and the others, and the Germans tried to surround the Marines. After taking enormous losses, the 2nd and 3rd Battalions of the 5th Marines began to withdraw.

"Am being shelled heavily and machine-gun fire from 270 degree of compass. I cannot hold front longer, 1st or 2nd [Battalion] must come up and take over." Major Henry Larson, the commanding officer of the 3rd Battalion, 5th Marines sent this desperate message to the 5th Regi-ment's commander, Colonel Logan Feland.[12] A Kentuckian with a BA in architecture from MIT, Feland initially served in the Army before joining the Marines after the Spanish-American War. Machine guns filled the woods on the Marines' flanks, and the Germans counterat-tacked en masse, forcing the depleted battalion—some companies with fewer than thirty men—to withdraw. Several Marines broke and ran toward the rear. Major Hamilton reported that he and another officer drew their pistols on their fellow Marines to stop the rout. One of the officers Hamilton halted included the 2nd's commander, Major Robert Messersmith, who sustained German bullet holes in the cuffs of his blouse and field glass case.*

According to the official report, "The situation became so critical that it demanded immediate and bold action. It was at this point that Major Hamilton, USMC, who commanded the 1st Battalion at the time, came to the front and showed his wonderful initiative and power of quick decision." Recognizing the danger the German machine guns posed to his left flank, Hamilton ordered his men to form up and push west, directly into the teeth of the oncoming assault. "The moment the battalion started forward, the machine guns opened up, and from then on

---

* Ultimately, an inquiry into Major Messersmith's command determined that "he displayed no lack of courage" but "displayed a lack of leadership." He was reassigned to 5th headquarters as a liaison officer to the 4th Brigade headquarters.

their fire was incessant."[13] Despite the bullets whizzing past their faces and limbs, the Leathernecks surged forward. They broke through the German counterattack and headed for the ridge outside Saint-Étienne that was their objective.

But unbeknownst to the Marines, the enemy soldiers had circled around and were now infiltrating from behind. "The fire from the ridge itself was so intense," recalled the report. "Here we were practically surrounded and receiving a galling fire from three directions. There was nothing to do but advance on up the hill."[14] Out of options, Hamilton gave the signal to move forward. In response, the Marines began their slow, inexorable climb up the ridge, even as their closest friends were falling around them. It was a day none of them would ever forget—and a day they could never fully describe to anyone who hadn't been there.

As their numbers dwindled by the second, the Marines reached the German lines. Hand-to-hand fighting took the place of machine-gun and rifle fire, and bayonets clashed as the men killed each other in the most personal of ways. Thomason wrote that one "big *Feldwebel* sprang against one of [the Marine] sergeants with the long Prussian lunge that throws the bayonet like a spear to the full reach of the arm. It is a spectacular thrust, and will spit like a rabbit what stands in its way. But the sergeant, Bob Slover, a little fiery man with a penchant for killing Germans, ran under it and thrust from the ground for the Boche's throat. And as his point touched, he pulled the trigger. The *Feldwebel*'s helmet flew straight into the air, and the top of his head went with it."[15]

Casualties continued to mount, but still the Marines pressed forward. They took the crest of the ridge by storm, rounding up nearly a hundred German prisoners and capturing the machine guns that had taken so many American lives. Still their ordeal was not over. From a second, slightly higher ridge and from the town of Saint-Étienne, machine-gun nests and artillery continued to rain death on Hamilton and the Marines. "This fire was so intense and casualties were occurring at such a rate that it meant annihilation to continue the advance with no support and no liaison on either flank. We were absolutely alone, and at this point receiving fire from all four sides," the report said.[16]

Unable to continue the advance, the Marines followed their maxim of never leaving a man behind. They collected their wounded and sought cover within the woods on top of the ridge. From there they fought their way eastward until they met up with the other two Marine battalions.

The Germans rushed reinforcements into the area. Elements from multiple German divisions counterattacked the 49th Company and the 5th and 6th Marine Regiments with the hope of plugging the breach. The loss of Blanc Mont tore into the Hindenburg Line, and the Germans were intent on destroying the Marines who were fighting for their lives in a salient dubbed "the Box." Pockets of Germans still holding on the back and top of the ridge fired upon the Allies.

After receiving orders from Colonel Feland, who was bunkered miles behind American lines in a command post, to hold and be prepared to advance, Hamilton replied, "Our forces are so much diminished that we do not extend over to the original left of the sector. . . . This battalion will go, or attempt to go where you order it. You should understand, though, that your regiment is now much depleted, very disorganized, and not in condition to advance as a front line regiment. . . . It is hard to say 'can't,' but the Division Commander should thoroughly understand the situation and realize that this regiment can't advance as an attacking force. Such an advance would sacrifice the regiment."[17]

As night fell on October 4, the 49th Company and 1st Battalion dug in despite being nearly surrounded by Germans. Artillery pounded them ceaselessly as the Marines repelled another counterattack on the left flank.

The 5th held, but the slaughter continued. High-explosive shells and shrapnel shrieked through the air, followed by the staccato rat-a-tat of the Maxims. One 5th Marine recalled the terror of the incessant shelling:

> Away out of the air we could hear the hissing of a shelling headed our way like a red-hot iron dipped in water. As it drew nearer, the hissing grew louder, and when it hit the ground with a crash, everything around us shook. I lay and trembled, as did the others

in my foxhole, so much that I could see it when we heard a shell coming we stopped trembling, stopped breathing, closed our eyes, pulled our muscles taut enough to burst, and waited; it seemed a long time, but it was possibly only ten seconds. When the shell burst and we found we still had a connection with a thread of life, we started to breathe again, opened our eyes; perfectly normal for a few seconds, then began to tremble again. As the afternoon wore away, the only activity was the First Aid men [corpsmen] running after each direct hit. . . . The idea came into my mind that this was my last day on earth. I could feel it in my bones. . . . Everything was so still. . . . I wasn't afraid because I knew there was no way out. A calm came over me. I stopped trembling."[18]

Hamilton's 1/5 was now down to around 150 Marines from an original strength of about 1,000. The American dead and wounded shared the same ground as the piles of German bodies. Forty-three Marines in the Fighting 5th alone received the Distinguished Service Cross.[19] The regimental history emphatically proclaimed, "October 4 was the bitterest single day of fighting the 5th Regiment experienced during the whole war."[20] So intense was German shelling that many men would later suffer shell shock. One victim was Major George Hamilton's runner, recently promoted Corporal Elton Mackin, who was convinced he would die from nonstop German shells pelting his position.*

The 3rd and 4th Brigades lay in shell holes within a mile of Saint-Étienne. Exhausted, the 6th Marines steeled themselves to assail a wooded hill adjacent to the town. Earlier, the 23rd had attempted to enter the village, but the Germans had repulsed them with heavy casualties. After the attack, Lieutenant Clifton Cates, a future commandant of the Marine Corps, led the remnants of two companies from the ill-fated attack. Cates later laconically reflected, "We ran into one of

---

* After years of negotiation with the VA, Mackin eventually received disability payments for his PTSD.

the largest machine-gun nests that I have ever seen, and naturally we were held up."[21]

On the evening of October 7–8, the 6th and 23rd Infantry Regiments, now preceded by a platoon of the 2nd Engineers that included Native American Body Bearer Corporal Thomas Saunders, went over the top at 6:30 a.m. once again to hit Saint-Étienne, the final line of German defenses at Blanc Mont. Braving fire, Saunders and his men employed wire cutters to clear a path through the thick web of German barbed wire. Saunders then made a night patrol to conduct reconnaissance before leading his men to attack. Saunders's sergeant major later wrote, "Such heroism is understood by a man's comrades more than can be explained in writing, as during time of stress, the one who does what Saunders did, does it with no thought of self, but only of carrying out to the best of his ability what he believes his duty to be. In my close contacts, during and since the World War with Saunders, I can state that everything he does is a bit better and with more energy than other men of equal physique would do the same thing."[22] The fighting was fierce, and the cemetery at Saint-Étienne changed hands several times. The attack, another bloodletting, cost the assault force 30 percent of its men; however, they reached their objective—a trench east of Saint-Étienne. The Germans, also weakened, barely held on to the village and cemetery. For his service in the combat patrol, Saunders later received the Croix de Guerre. This accolade, combined with the Distinguished Service Cross and other honors, made him one of the most decorated American Indians of WWI.

Several days of hard fighting remained for some of the Marine battalions. To assist, Lejeune called up his reserve troops: the green Texans and Oklahomans of the 36th Division. As usual, the Germans counterattacked, capturing scores of 36th Division men in Saint-Étienne. The 2nd Engineers remained engaged in the battle, and by October 10, the village was in American hands.

French Field Marshal Pétain later extolled the achievements of the 2nd Division, saying, "The taking of Blanc Mont is the single greatest achievement of the 1918 campaign."[23] The 49th Company's John

Thomason, who was at the sharp end of combat, took a bitterly different view: "We were shot to pieces in the Champagne—I never enjoyed the war afterward."[24]

The 2nd Division suffered 4,832 casualties; Body Bearer Ernest Janson's 1/5 had one of the highest rates of missing, wounded, and killed, including many unknown dead. "The battalion came back from Blanc-Mont Ridge. No, the battalion was still up there. But anyway, oh hell, let me get this straight. A hundred and thirty-four of us come back from Blanc-Mont ridge. We had gone up a full-strength battalion, a thousand strong," recalled Elton Mackin.[25]

"Dead" would be a word that the decimated Marines in George Hamilton's 5th Battalion became hauntingly familiar with for the first time during mail call. A Marine sergeant called the names of the dead and living alike to distribute mail from home. "When a battalion has gone through four hard fights, there are men remembered, and remembered too, that all had not gone out as soldiers do." The next name called by the mail sergeant included one such man, as Corporal Mackin recalled:

"Gil Badrow. A hard voice said flatly, 'dead.' A new word, that, from these hard men. 'Dead' He had been caught rifling the pockets of the dead of his battalion. He was dead too, [fratricide] as a man or two could tell. There are some laws that must not be transgressed."[26]

CHAPTER 22

WOODFILL OF
THE REGULARS

The first few days of the Meuse-Argonne Offensive in early October were some of the darkest in US Army history. Although the Americans experienced some initial success, stiff resistance slowly ground their forward progress to a halt. The Allies failed to capture the key German stronghold at Montfaucon on schedule, giving the enemy time to recover from the initial surprise of the attack and move additional troops into place. The men on the American front lines began to run out of food and ammunition, and the Germans not only held their lines but also pushed the Americans back in some areas.

General Max Karl von Gallwitz, sanguine that his men could hold, wrote, "On the 27th and 28th, we had no more worries."[1] Several days into the offensive, the initial plan to encircle the German forces had devolved into a near-total failure. The American attack ominously began to resemble the failed Allied campaigns of 1916 and 1917, as the Germans poured troops into the area, inflicting heavy casualties. Already forty-five thousand Americans had been wounded or killed.[2] Gallwitz masterfully reinforced the area with more than forty divisions; the prospects of an American breakthrough dimmed. The Germans stripped units from other areas of the front to hold the Meuse-Argonne, allowing the Allies to gain ground in other sectors. Nevertheless, the war appeared as if it would inevitably grind on into 1919.

General Pershing suspended offensive operations for several days while veteran divisions were rushed to the front line. The halt enraged the British and French. Georges Clemenceau, the prime minister of France, attempted to have Pershing sacked. First Army fought for their lives as their leader ruminated. In his report, Pershing wrote, "We were no longer engaged in a maneuver for the pinching out of a salient, but were necessarily committed, generally speaking, to a direct frontal attack against strong, hostile positions fully manned by a determined enemy."[3]

To break the stalemate, Pershing decided to reorganize his forces and integrate new divisions that arrived in France along with some of his veteran units. As a by-product of his reorganization, the general also created the US Second Army. Two massive field armies, the First and Second, now composed the AEF with Pershing assuming the overarching title of Army group commander. Within the sprawling American armies, commanders were fired or reshuffled into new positions. One head to roll was that of Major General John E. McMahon, the current commander of the 5th Division, who was replaced by the tough-as-nails, hard-charging Major General Hanson E. Ely. A lifelong officer, McMahon was more comfortable maneuvering the internal politics of the military than actually leading men into battle. According to accounts, he once spent forty-five seconds signing his name and slept through the St. Mihiel Offensive. His replacement, Ely, was McMahon's opposite in nearly every way. Built like a tank and possessing piercing blue eyes, Ely was known for getting things done.

Ely's 5th Division included the 60th Infantry Regiment and First Lieutenant Samuel Woodfill, who would become one of the AEF's most decorated soldiers. A veteran of the Philippine-American War, thirty-five-year-old Woodfill hailed from Bryantsburg, Indiana. His father had served in the Civil War and the Mexican-American War, and he taught Samuel to hunt and shoot at a very early age. Following in his father's footsteps, Woodfill enlisted in 1901, as soon as he turned eighteen. A career military man, he received a temporary commission when officers were needed for World War I. A few months before shipping out for Europe, he married Lorena Wiltshire, a direct descendent of Daniel Boone, and the two bought a home in Fort Thomas, Kentucky, just south of Cincinnati.

Five-foot-ten and a lean 170 pounds, with light brown hair and blue eyes, Woodfill was a lifelong hunter from rural Indiana. His first taste of combat came in the Philippine-American War, after which he spent nearly three years in the islands. Next, he quietly passed eight years stationed in Alaska before serving on the border during the Mexican Border Expedition. When the United States entered World War I in April 1917, thirty-four-year-old Woodfill was a combat veteran with more than sixteen years of experience. In July of that year, the Army awarded him his first commission as a lieutenant, and less than a year later, he set sail for France. After arriving in France, Woodfill and his men had initially spent time in the trenches in a quiet sector where they participated in a couple of raids on German positions.

Nearly two weeks into the Meuse-Argonne Offensive, Ely ordered Woodfill and Company M of the 60th Infantry Regiment to relieve the 319th Infantry, which had been holding a line south of Cunel. Artillery fire in the area had been devastating. "The woods was simply covered with rotting horses, dead men, human hands and feet, shoes half filled with flesh and bones, blood, mud, filth, and stench," Woodfill remembered.[4]

The horrors weren't limited to men and horses. Two young women from the Salvation Army had set up a kitchen in the shell of a building that had been nearly destroyed by the battle. Despite multiple warnings that they should leave the area, the women continued serving coffee and doughnuts to the men on the front lines. As men lined up for the food and drink, they drew the eyes of artillery spotters, and soon a German shell came flying into the building. "The doughnut kitchen was blown to smithereens, and both girls were killed," explained a member of the 319th. "They just buried 'em over in that field this morning. Gave 'em full military honors, too."[5]

Upon arriving in the area, Woodfill and several other officers headed for a dugout where the 319th had set up its headquarters. Near their destination, machine-gun and rifle fire crackled in a virtually non-stop cacophony as the 319th skirmished with the Germans. To get close to the building, Woodfill and his comrades would have to pass through a moonscape clearing pockmarked by shell holes and half-dug trenches. Bits of corrugated metal stood on end here and there where they had fallen after being blasted into the sky by artillery fire. Hoping that the enemy soldiers were too busy with the 319th to notice them, Woodfill and the others made a mad dash across the field.

A German machine gunner soon caught sight of the new arrivals and trained a stream of death in their direction. Immediately, the men dove for whatever cover they could find. The lucky ones found deep holes that could provide shelter, but Woodfill landed in a trench just over a foot deep. Lying as flat as possible, he got his entire body below the lip of the depression, but his backpack was clearly visible. Sensing an easy target, the German gunner turned his weapon in Woodfill's direction. "Plunk! A bullet sunk into my pack," Woodfill recalled. "Then two more ripped through it. Than a hail of them sprayed the ground hardly two feet from my head, kicking dirt all over me."[6]

More machine gunners joined the first, sweeping a torrent of fire across the field. Bullets struck the pieces of metal, clattering like hail on a rooftop and boring so many holes through the pieces of iron that they began to look like sieves.

To Woodfill's dismay, a louse began slowly crawling down his back. The vermin provided a constant irritant on the front lines, where the men went weeks without bathing or changing clothes. Woodfill didn't dare reach up a hand to scratch at the insect, because he would certainly have caught a bullet. Space was so tight in the shallow trench that he couldn't even maneuver his rifle into position to take a shot. With no way to defend himself, Woodfill figured it was just a matter of time before the enemy took him out. This thought seemed confirmed when one of the German 77 mm artillery pieces began targeting the field. One of the first shells landed just feet from Woodfill's position, sending a fresh shower of dirt over his body.

Mebbe the next one will have my name on it, he thought to himself.[7]

With little hope for survival, Woodfill chanced a bit of movement. He pulled out the picture of his wife that he always carried in his shirt pocket. With a small piece of pencil, he wrote her address on the back and began what he thought would be his final message to her. In a cramped scrawl, he wrote:

> In case of accident or death it is my last and fondest desire that the finder of my remains shall please do me a last, and ever so lasting favor to please forward this picture to my Darling Wife. And tell her that I have fallen on the field of Soissons, and departed to a better land which knows no sorrow and feels no pain. I will prepare a place and be waiting at the Golden Gate of Heaven for the arrival of my Darling Blossom.[8]

But in his despair, Woodfill had forgotten about the 319th. Eventually, they took out the German machine gunners, bringing the flood of bullets to an end. Shortly thereafter, the whine of the artillery shells also ceased. The Germans retreated, chased by the Americans.

As the noise of battle quieted, Woodfill's comrades slowly began poking their heads up above the trenches and shell holes where they had been taking cover. Somehow, miraculously, all of the dozen survived. Still loath to stand and present a target to any enemy fighters who might still be in the area, they began crawling as a group toward the farm where they had been headed. But before they had gotten very far, they heard someone calling from nearby. Moving aside a clump of weeds, they came upon "a German officer with his legs half blown off."[9]

"*Wasser, Wasser,*" the man pleaded.[10]

One of the other officers gave the man a drink from his canteen. Most of the group stayed near him while two went up ahead to check in at the 319th headquarters. When those two returned, they loaded the German onto a litter and carried him to a first aid station. That act of kindness paid off because they were able to get some important information from him.

Just as Woodfill and the other men of the 60th were assuming the positions vacated by the 319th, the Germans began another artillery barrage. With no time to dig new trenches, they took shelter in the shell holes that dotted the landscape—no more than two men to a hole in order to minimize casualties. The holes were uncomfortable, not only because they provided less cover than a well-dug trench, but also because many of them had a foot or more of water in the bottom. A torrential downpour had begun, and in no time, all the new arrivals were coated in a thick layer of slime.

Woodfill received orders to lead a patrol of eight men through the woods off to the right of the battlefield to look for any Germans. They found only mud and trees, but on their way back they ran into a booby trap. The Germans had wired a small wooden bridge. "The minute we set foot on it—whang! Bang! The shells started poppin' all around us," he recalled. "About a dozen of them came over, but luckily every one was an overshot."[11] The men dropped to all fours and crawled the rest of the way back to their shell holes, covering themselves in even more gelatinous ooze.

Later that night, Woodfill found himself crossing that bridge for a second time while directing an American machine-gun crew to the woods he had just patrolled. Once again, the Germans blasted the men as they crossed. On his way back to his shell hole, Woodfill had to cross a third time. In the darkness, he stepped on the first board of the bridge without realizing where he was. He jumped back, but not fast enough. "There was a clap of thunder right in the tree over my head," he remembered. "Then I passed out. The next thing I knew was the rain beatin' in my face. I lay there sort of fumblin' around in my mind wonderin' who I was and where and why."[12] Checking himself over for wounds, he found nothing except a bloody nose. With his ears ringing, he hauled himself to his feet and headed toward his shell hole once more. Disoriented by the blast, he stumbled into the wrong hole. The man inside lifted his bayonet.

"Hey, you! It's me!" Woodfill called out.

"Gosh, Lieutenant, you nearly got it through the gizzard that time."[13]

The man directed him to the correct hole, and Woodfill crawled in and caught some sleep.

* * *

Tanks were part of the changing nature of modern warfare, and the Meuse-Argonne Offensive provided a test for the nascent American Tank Corps.[14] Just as important, it was a test for the 304th Tank Brigade commander, Lieutenant Colonel George Patton.

The charismatic leader had at his disposal nearly 150 light Renault FT-17 tanks. He planned to deploy them in a concentrated force, sweeping in and annihilating the enemy. As the battle unfolded, however, Patton observed that some of his tanks weren't moving up from the rear as ordered. A man of action, he set out on foot to determine the source of the problem. He soon discovered that one of the heavy tanks had been unable to cross a ditch and was blocking the way, preventing the rest of the tanks from moving forward. With artillery zeroed in on their location, the men had taken shelter in the ditch or their tanks.

Putting himself in the line of fire, Patton personally roused a crew and set them to work getting the tank across the obstacle. Some of the men initially balked at leaving the safety of their shelters, and in one case, Patton maniacally hit a man on the head with a shovel to get him to obey orders. He later said that "he might have killed him. He never knew."[15] Despite their fear, the men somehow managed to dislodge the tank and get the line moving again. Patton, unharmed in spite of exposing himself to constant machine-gun fire, followed on foot. "To hell with them," he said aloud. "They can't hit me."[16]

As the tanks rumbled forward, the machine-gun fire intensified, and Patton dropped to the ground. He later explained that he "felt a great desire to run." But while he was "trembling with fear," he remembered his ancestors who had given their lives for their country. He "seemed to see them in a cloud above the German lines looking at me." The vision calmed him, and he said, "It is time for another Patton to die." Determined to press forward, he called for volunteers. Six men advanced with him. Five of them died, and Patton himself was wounded in the leg. Still, he continued to direct his tanks, sending them forward to destroy the machine-gun nests before allowing himself to be taken to the field hospital.[17]

* * *

"Advance until the last man drops!"[18] barked Major Charles Whittlesey from the 77th Infantry Division. The bespectacled New York lawyer looked more like a college professor than an Army officer, but he would soon prove his worth. With his command to advance, Whittlesey set in motion a legendary episode in the Meuse-Argonne, that of the Lost Battalion. On October 2, 554 men from the 1st and 2nd Battalions of the 308th Infantry Regiment advanced toward their objective: a key road in the Argonne Forest. When a flanking action went wrong, they found themselves far out ahead of the American lines, and on October 3 the Germans surrounded them. Whittlesey, who commanded the 1st Battalion and was the ranking officer on the scene, and former Rough Rider Captain George Gibson McMurtry, who led the 2nd, told their men to dig in. In all, they had nine depleted companies from the 1st and 2nd and other units—each at about half strength.

Whittlesey attempted to break out of the position with one company of his troops but the attempt failed. He sent out runners with messages asking for reinforcements, but all were captured or killed, leaving the battalion cut off from communications and supply, with little hope for help.

The Germans attacked. Sniper and machine-gun fire poured in from all sides. The enemy hurled grenades, followed by mortars. By the night of October 3, the Americans had lost more than 150 of their men. The haunting "moans and half-suppressed cries"[19] of the dying filled the shrinking pocket of American foxholes. Digging in deeper, Whittlesey and McMurtry told their men, "Our mission is to hold this position at all costs. No falling back. Have this understood by every man in your command."[20] By this time, the Americans were running out of food, and their only source of water was a polluted creek guarded by the Germans.

Desperate to inform his commanders of the battalion's situation, Whittlesey sent carrier pigeons back to headquarters. With radio still in its infancy and telephone wire difficult to lay on the battlefield, the birds provided an essential means of communication within World War I armies. Around fifteen thousand pigeons were trained to carry messages on the Western Front. But carrying a bulky pigeon cage into battle could be tedious. One pigeon handler, apparently annoyed with his job, inserted in a message, "I'm tired of carrying this God damned bird."[21]

Receiving no reply to his messages, Whittlesey continued to obey his most recent orders and kept his men in their defensive position. Tragically, they came under attack from their own artillery. In an attempt to stop the friendly fire, Whittlesey sent his last pigeon, but an exploding shell stunned the bird, causing it to fall to the ground. Eventually, the artillery realized their mistake and halted the barrage, but no sooner had the Allies stopped their attack than the Germans began a fresh assault. They continued to attack relentlessly for five more days as the battalion ran out of food, water, and ammunition.

Several counterattacks nearly broke through. After capturing four Americans in one of the attacks, the Germans sent a prisoner back to the pocket carrying a white flag and carrying a note requesting Whittlesey's surrender. A portion of the note read, "It would be quite useless to resist any more in view of the present conditions. The suffering of your wounded men can be heard over here in the German lines, and we are appealing to your human sentiments. A white flag shown by one of your men will tell us that you agree with these conditions. Please treat Private Hollingshead as an honorable man. He is quite a soldier. We envy him."[22]

Whittlesey showed the note to his officers. McMurtry remembered, "There was a good smile all around among the crowd of us, because we knew that the Germans felt that they could not take us. . . . They had tried to wipe us out every day and had been trying to wipe us out every day since we had been in the position and then had written us a note stating that they would like to have us surrender in the name of humanity."[23]

Still, the Americans maintained their position. In the near distance, US units advanced toward the Lost Battalion. Racing against time, the Germans threw a greatly attenuated *Sturmbataillon* at Whittlesey's men. Flamethrowers spewed liquid fire, incinerating several men before Americans armed with Chauchats and rifles picked the operators off. The doughboys repelled the attack—and the Germans never attacked the Lost Battalion again.

Finally, on the evening of October 7, the first American troops broke through, rescuing the Lost Battalion. What they saw was ghastly. "The sheer horror of the strip of hillside is unimaginable," recalled one member of the relief force. "The stench was unbearable. Bits of flesh, legs, arms, parts of bodies, were all about. The hillside in their position had literally been blown to pieces."[24]

Of the more than five hundred men who had first set out with Major Whittlesey, only 194 were able to walk out on their own, and many of those were wounded. Proud of their gallant stand, the survivors "walked heavily, numbed by utter exhaustion, clothes tattered and filthy, faces like drawn masks of putty with the fixed stare of determination. Worn out, dirty, hungry, thirsty, they would not give in."[25] The rescuers had tears in their eyes as they watched the men depart. One soldier tried to congratulate the members of the Lost Battalion as they passed but held back his words. "There was nothing to say anyway. It made your heart lump up in your throat just to look at them. Their faces told the whole story of their fight."[26] For his heroism in the face of overwhelming odds, Whittlesey received a battlefield promotion to lieutenant colonel and was later awarded the Medal of Honor, as was McMurtry.

On October 4, Pershing was able to resume the Meuse-Argonne Offensive with the same objective as on September 26: penetrate the Kriemhilde Stellung. Progress was difficult, and they were sustaining high casualties. Still, they were moving forward.

Initially, to relieve Whittlesey's Lost Battalion, the 82nd sent Corporal Alvin York and other members of a battalion from the 328th Infantry Regiment north to take out more than thirty machine-gun nests on a nearby ridge and sever a German rail line supporting the front line.

Born in the backwoods of Tennessee, York had attended school only through the third grade, but he knew plenty about farming, blacksmithing, hunting, and fighting. He was also a crack shot, winning numerous local shooting competitions. In his youth, he gained a reputation as a hard-drinking rabble-rouser before becoming a born-again Christian after seeing a close friend killed in a bar fight. Drafted into the army, the devout believer first claimed conscientious objector status. Later, he became convinced that his faith did not forbid participation in war, and the army inducted him into the 82nd Division as a private. York's unit arrived in France at the end of May 1918; the 82nd rotated into and out of quiet sectors of the front and then fought at St. Mihiel. However, the Meuse-Argonne was their first serious trial by fire.

At first, York's unit attempted to cross the valley and seize some high ground. "It 'most seemed as though it was coming from everywhere. I'm telling you they were shooting straight, and our boys jes done went down like the long grass before the mowing machine at home. Our attacks jes faded out." With all of the officers in the group dead or wounded, York took command as the senior noncom present. Rather than ordering the men to cross the valley again, he had them circle the left flank through brush to approach the high ground from behind the German lines. York put his shooting skills to work. He observed that the German machine gunners would lift their heads up above their defenses just slightly before shooting, and he began picking them off one by one. "Every time a head come up, I done knocked it down," he later said. "I was out in the open and the machine guns were spitting fire and cutting up all around me something awful."[27]

Determined to stop the American, a German officer and five men made a headlong charge toward York. Unfazed, the corporal killed them with his pistol "the same way we shoot wild turkeys at home." He dropped the last man first, then the second to last, and so on. As a result, the men at the front kept running toward him without realizing their friends had been killed. In the end, only the officer made it to York's position. The American quickly took him prisoner. York pointed his .45 at the German and told him to make his men cease their fire. Otherwise,

"I would take his head next," York recalled. "He knowed I meaned it." The officer blew a whistle, and the Germans firing down upon York complied. After capturing a German major in the haul, York put a gun to the second officer's back and took him in the front of the line, where he forced the officer to surrender more of his men. The broad-shouldered, red-mustached Tennessean had killed twenty-eight enemy soldiers. He took his long line of prisoners back to the American trenches, where he reported to Brigadier General Julian R. Lindsey. The American flag officer glanced at the strapping corporal and quipped, "Well York, I hear you have captured the whole damned German Army." The Tennessean humbly responded, "I only had 132 men."[28]

For his valor, York received a promotion to sergeant. Later, he received the Distinguished Service Cross and the Medal of Honor.

York's extraordinary actions paralleled those of another legend of the Meuse-Argonne, First Lieutenant Samuel Woodfill.

CHAPTER 23

"I GOT A FEW"

October 12, 1918,
Bois de Pultière, Near Cunel, France

Woodfill's men, sodden in filthy uniforms, rejoiced as the seemingly relentless rain finally stopped falling. Woodfill awoke in a water-filled shell hole after an uncomfortable night's sleep interrupted by the constant roar of machine-gun fire and the blast of shells detonating nearby. "I discovered that if I lay on one side long enough without moving, the water inside my clothes would begin to feel warm, and then I'd drop off for a few winks. If you get tired enough you can sleep anywhere, even with a few hundred cooties to keep you company."[1] When morning came, he found himself "just about to float out of that hole. The water was almost up to the top."

Just a few minutes before 6:00 a.m., Woodfill received his orders. "Zero hour was six o'clock. In other words, over the top and fight!" Woodfill steeled himself for the attack. A vast blanket of heavy fog reduced visibility to yards. *So much the better*, Woodfill thought to himself—the mist would cloak their approach from the Germans. The German resistance was somewhere in the woods in front of them, and the 3rd Battalion, including Woodfill's M Company along with a machine-gun battalion, would conduct a reconnaissance in force to locate the German line. Woodfill and M Company, composed of about two hundred men, left the relative safety of their trenches and crossed the rail line east of Cunel, which sprawled out in front of them, to enter the Bois de Pultière where the enemy lay in wait in the heart of the Kriemhilde Stellung.

The veteran soldier knew the fighting would be savage. "Lots of shootin' in this fight," he told one of the men near him. They had only moments to wipe sleep from their eyes and prepare for what would be one of the bloodiest battles in American history.

At 6:00 a.m., the doughboys advanced, forming long skirmish lines spread out through the woods, sixteen paces apart, rifles ready and bayonets fixed.

"We were partly screened under cover of a low-hanging fog, which aided us on our advance wonderfully and reduced our casualties greatly," Woodfill recalled. Reaching the deeper cover of the Bois de Pultière required traversing a clearing that surrounded the rail line. As the first men stepped into the open area, they were pelted by shells and heavy machine-gun fire. Before they could take another step, German machine guns cut down half a dozen Americans. These were men—boys in many cases—whom Woodfill had led for the past few months.

Woodfill heard the man next to him grunt.

"Hit?" Woodfill asked, poised to guide or carry his friend to safety.

But the man never answered. "He took three more steps, toppled, and fell dead across the railway tracks."

It was an ominous beginning for the battle.

As Woodfill witnessed his friend slump onto the tracks in front of him, he heard the first of many shells whistle overhead. "The Germans were givin' us the whole works, from soup to nuts, before we could even see anything to shoot at," he recalled. For many of the men with him, this was the first real taste of intense combat. With the enemy entrenched and shrouded by the thick foliage and underbrush, the green troops found it nearly impossible to locate the enemy positions.

Another shell exploded between two of the men advancing alongside him, but amazingly, both survived. War can be that random. "The concussion hurled them end over end like a leaf hit by a whirlwind," Woodfill remembered. "I thought they were done for, but before I could get over to them they were back on their hands and knees, grabbin' their guns, and continuing the advance."

Woodfill's company painfully crawled toward the Germans under withering fire. The rat-a-tat of the German Maxim machine guns continued, "spittin' a swath of fire that was cuttin' the men down like a mowin' machine." The whine of shells filled the air overhead, and explosions rocked the ground beneath their feet.

For some of the men, combat was simply too much. One young soldier who had lied about his age in order to enlist fell to the ground, dazed. Woodfill saw him "get up and start firing wildly, back in the direction he'd come from" before another one of Woodfill's men tackled him and hurled him to the ground. All around Woodfill, men were falling, some dead, some just hoping to avoid the deadly rain of machine-gun fire.

Only one option remained for him: "The only thing to do was to find out where that first machine gun was and get it," he recalled. "And I didn't believe in askin' any of my men to do something I wouldn't do myself." Motioning to his men to stay where they were, Woodfill ripped off his pack and made a mad dash toward the woods—and the machine guns.

Flinging his body with all his might, Woodfill aimed for a shell hole in front of him and barely made it. He catapulted himself inside the earthen depression just as the German machine gunners turned their weapons toward him. "There was a rain of bullets so close I could feel the heat of them on my face," he remembered.

Now closer to the action, Woodfill determined that the deadly machine-gun fire was coming not from one direction, but from three: one to his right in an abandoned stable, one directly in front of him, and a third in a church tower to his left. From his current position, the church tower presented the best target. Although Woodfill could not see the Germans inside, he fired a round through the window. The fire from that direction immediately ceased, the gunner either dead or in flight.

Next, he turned toward the stable. As with his view of the tower, he could not visualize the gunner inside; however, he could see where someone had removed a board to have a clear line of fire. Woodfill carefully aimed his Springfield and fired another round through the hole. "Again I couldn't see the result of my shootin', but no more enemy fire came from there," he recalled.

With two gun positions eliminated, Woodfill dashed for the cover of the next shell hole. Again he dove inside just as bullets passed over his body. Feigning death, he waited a long time until the remaining machine gunner moved on to other targets. After a few moments, he quickly scrambled to another hole in front of him.

But this time, the shell hole did not provide the shelter he had sought. "Queer I should feel so out of breath," he recalled. "I was weak and gasping. I knew then I'd run into a patch of mustard gas. My eyes were stinging; my nose and throat felt raw. The air in that hole was full of fumes like you get when you grate horseradish."

Woodfill knew he would have to be decontaminated, but instead of turning back to the rear to receive treatment, he determined to push forward, deeper into the German lines.

He carried a gas mask; however, he knew that if he donned it after exposure to the mustard, his tear-filled, inflamed eyes would impair his vision, making him unable to see well enough to shoot. He had to get out of the hole and into some better cover, but the gas had rendered him too weak to run. Gasping for air, Woodfill crawled out of the shell hole and headed for the only bit of cover he could see: "a clump of old thistle."

More bullets whizzed by overhead. Lying on the ground protected by nothing but the sparse bush, he waited for the gunfire to swing away once more. Then, slowly and carefully, he crawled on his stomach into a ditch near an old roadbed.

Woodfill knew he was close to his target. Inch by inch, he cautiously maneuvered himself. "I quickly slid my rifle forward and placed the butt against my shoulder before exposing any part of my body," he recalled, "then raised on my elbows enough to see the gun." Forty feet in front of him, he spotted the muzzle of a machine gun sticking out from a bush. "There isn't much difference between stalkin' animals and stalkin' humans," Woodfill explained. "It was usin' the same tactics I had used in big-game huntin' in Alaska ten years before. It's all in outwittin' the other fellow. If a bear sees you first, he will charge, tooth and claw. If these German gunners saw me first, the game would be up."

His eyes still stinging from the mustard gas, Woodfill strained for a glimpse of the gunner, but he could not make out anything, save for the bush and the flash of the gun. "*Damn those field-gray German uniforms*," he thought. "Even at such a short distance they were almost invisible against the woods."

In an instant, his luck turned. The clouds shifted, and for a moment the light struck the gunner's camouflaged helmet, allowing Woodfill to catch a glimpse of a face beneath. He pulled his trigger, and the machine-gun fire came to a sudden stop.

But the gunner at this position was not alone. Trained to perform in combat, the German gunners operated like a well-oiled machine. A second man pushed the dead man out of the way and resumed firing. Woodfill took a second shot, which again found its mark. "Four times a dead gunner was pulled away from the gun by a man who took his place, and each time I pulled the trigger of my rifle before he could open fire," Woodfill recalled. "The third and fourth ones must have known what to expect. That was nerve—to take their places knowin' they would be picked off. It was just a sample of the way the German army fought."

However, the next man in line did not feel as brave. Instead of manning the gun, he attempted to crawl away through the bushes. Woodfill fired his rifle once more, emptying his entire five-round clip and dropping him.

His Springfield was out of ammunition, but the machine-gun nest still was not empty. A sixth German scurried into the position. "No time to reload. I picked up my automatic, and just in time," Woodfill said. He killed that man as well.

Seeing no more signs of life from the machine-gun nest, Woodfill now took the time to reload his rifle before heading up to the German position. "There was the gun, and the pile of dead Germans behind it, with the tops of their heads torn off," Woodfill recalled.

"Follow me!" Woodfill yelled to a couple of his men, who bravely trailed behind him; he knew that his troops would kill any other German gunners who approached the machine gun. Woodfill charged forward.

Almost immediately, he stumbled over the body of another German—only this one was not dead. "I started to swerve around him when he sprang to his feet, grabbed my rifle, and threw it into the air," the American remembered. It was an old-fashioned shoot-out. "If his Luger had been in his hand instead of in its holster he could have got me. I snatched my pistol from my belt and fired; got him in the body and he doubled up with a grunt and dropped." The insignia on the German's uniform revealed that he had been an *Oberleutnant*. Woodfill tore off his epaulet and grabbed the officer's Luger.

At this time, some of his men approached the machine-gun nest. Within the woods, the Germans fired incessantly, sweeping the entire area with lethal fire. Despite the deadly hail of bullets, Woodfill motioned for his men to continue forward. Others were scattered throughout the woods looking for enemy troops. "Those soldiers of mine, some of them so green they'd hardly smelled powder before, were on their own now," Woodfill remembered. "Sweatin' and swearin', they kept on toward the German lines. The only thing that stopped their followin' me was a German bullet."

Miraculously, Woodfill had eliminated three machine-gun positions entirely on his own, but his fight was not yet done. As he continued through the woods, more fire erupted from a machine-gun nest two hundred feet away from the first. The veteran immediately dropped to his belly in the mud. However, the machine gun was not the only danger ahead. "Ping! The mud splashed in my face as a rifle bullet struck in the ground six inches in front of me," he said. A sniper was taking aim and soon sent another bullet Woodfill's way.

The lieutenant jumped and rolled behind a nearby tree. Unbeknownst to Woodfill, however, one of his men had progressed much closer to the German sniper, stopping beneath the very tree where the rifleman was hiding above in the branches. The German pointed his weapon straight down and took the shot, which hit the ground between the American's feet. Before the German could fire again, the American shot him with his pistol and watched him tumble from the tree branches.

Meanwhile, Woodfill began crawling toward the machine-gun nest. With the weapon positioned in a shallow pit, the Indiana native could clearly see the head and shoulders of the gunner. Just as he had in the first nest, Woodfill methodically took out the Germans one at a time as they each took a turn on the weapon—five of them in all. "As soon as one dropped, I'd nail the next one when his head appeared as he tried to take over the gun," he explained.

When no additional gunners appeared, Woodfill cautiously approached the Maxim. He put a round into the gun's water-cooled jacket to render it inoperable and then moved deeper into German lines.

After only a few steps, he nearly collided with three enemy soldiers who were bringing ammunition to the machine gun positions. Startled, all three dropped the boxes of ammunition and equipment they were carrying and raised their hands. "*Kamerad, kamerad!*" they yelled, eager to surrender. "Their fright was almost comical," Woodfill recalled. "They were nothin' but boys, and they were surrendering in dead earnest. I made sure they were disarmed."

Woodfill tried to ask the prisoners the location of the other Germans in the woods. "How far? How far?" he asked, gesturing with his hands. They didn't seem to understand. Woodfill thought, "*What wouldn't I have given right then if my mother had only drilled some German into my skull when I was a youngster?*" Frustrated, he motioned for the trio to head toward the other Americans. The ammunition bearers threw their helmets to the ground and did as he asked.

Picking up his pace, the lieutenant continued moving closer to the German positions. A cone of fire engulfed him, and he again found himself the target of a machine gun. Bullets struck the tree next to him, spraying bark in his face; he dropped and crawled to cover. The intense fire obliterated shrubbery just inches away. Peering around a tree, he located the nest by the flash of the muzzle. He crawled on his belly through the soft mud. "I simply wallowed in soup for thirty feet until I could get a better view," he recalled. He saw that this latest machine gun was positioned in a trench line. Woodfill could just make out the top of the gunner's head, but it was enough for the shot. Once again, he took out five men, one at a time, with a single clip of ammunition.

He waited for a while, but when no more Germans came into view, he ran for the trench. Another gun position off to his right opened fire. Woodfill remembered, "As I dashed into the trench for cover, I almost jumped on a German." The enemy soldier had been crawling up the trench to the Maxim and was stunned to see an American come flying in. The space was too tight for Woodfill to use his rifle, but he was ready with his .45. As the officer raised his Luger, the American fired. Woodfill said, "I beat him to it by a split second, and he doubled up and rolled to the ground."

From around a bend in the trench, another German rushed Woodfill. The American fired again, but this time his pistol jammed. Still the Indiana native did not flinch. "My eye fell on a long-handled pick-mattock stuck into the side of the trench," he recalled. "I grabbed it, and as the second German tried to level his rifle, I crashed the pick down on his head with both hands. He fell like an ox." One of Woodfill's men who witnessed the melee stated, "He grabbed a pick laying on the edge of the position and finished him."

Another gunshot sounded. Moving by instinct, Woodfill wheeled around, narrowly avoiding a bullet to his back. The German he had shot with his automatic wasn't dead. The gut-shot soldier had somehow found the strength to aim and fire his Luger, squeezing off a round. The American recalled, "Another blow of the pick, and I finished him and bounded out of that trench."

At this point, the Germans seemed to be in retreat. A few ran through Woodfill's line of sight, and he fired, hitting at least one.

Just then, he heard a noise behind him. With his rifle ready, he turned swiftly.

"Don't shoot, Lieutenant," whispered a familiar voice. It was Blackmore, one of the men from his unit.

"Germans up there ahead," Woodfill informed him.

"Yes, and Germans behind us," came the reply.

They were surrounded. Hemmed in on all sides by German fire, Woodfill and his men took aim at every enemy soldier who came into view. More of Woodfill's men filtered in, joining the small group.

Carrying both his Colt automatic and his captured Luger, Woodfill was better armed than most of his men. He handed the pistol to Blackmore. "Better take this," he whispered. "You might be able to use it when you can't use your rifle."

Nearby, the enemy regrouped, and then their fire intensified. "Rifle bullets were still poppin' all around, a murderous stream of machine-gun fire was mowing down the branches above us, shrapnel was bursting, and the steady roar of the big guns was banging at our eardrums like ten boiler factories."

Unless help arrived soon, Woodfill and his men were done for. He sent a runner to ask for support, but the battalion commander had no additional troops to send. Instead, the messenger returned with orders for the group to retreat several hundred yards to the edge of the wood.

Under constant shelling, Woodfill and his men made their way back toward their original position. Ominously, German planes appeared overhead. Woodfill took aim and fired his rifle at one of the aircraft. He surmised that the Germans had spotted his battalion's horse-drawn machine-gun company. The planes signaled the artillery and called in a massive barrage. "There was a screech of shell, a clap of thunder, the screams from horses and mules and carts, and a half dozen men were wiped clean out."

The German artillery continued hammering away at the American lines. As Woodfill and his men were nearing their foxholes at the jumping-off point, they heard the whine of another shell that landed just fifty feet away. A massive "clod of earth as big as a house flew up and came down" on two men in the shell hole next to Woodfill. The lieutenant and his troops began digging out the men, who miraculously had not been blown to pieces—they were just stunned and gassed.* But their rifles had been torn from their hands and "twisted up like corkscrews." The men a few feet to the right did not fare so well. "Bang: square in a shell hole over to the right—a direct hit," Woodfill remembered. He had also been struck by the shell's hot, jagged shrapnel. "A column of mud and rags, blood and brains and muscle, shot into the air and sprayed us from head to foot. There was nothin' more left of the two men who had been there than of a tomato when you throw it against a brick wall."

Back behind Allied lines, Woodfill, suffering from the searing pain of mustard exposure, and the shrapnel wound to his left leg, reported to his superior officer who asked what the lieutenant had been doing to the Germans.

The Indianan downplayed his contribution, remarking, "I got a few."

* Woodfill later recalled, "On October 12, the enemy shelled with high explosive and gas intermingled. I was always careful in watching out for gas, but under the terrible circumstances I was unable to escape it all. I ran into gas several times, and received enough to burn my eyes, mouth, and throat severely which made me very sick for several weeks. I could not stand a strong light on my eyes for months."

CHAPTER 24

LOUIS RAZGA:
THE BIG GUNS

First Week of November 1918,
Meurthe-et-Moselle, France

"Number One, Ready!"

"Number Two, Ready!"[1]

One by one, the crews of the 58th sounded off, each hoping to be swifter than the others preparing their heavy guns to fire. Then, they waited for the fateful command.

"Commence firing!"[2]

On a cool day in early November 1918, Body Bearer First Sergeant Louis Razga of Battery D, 58th Coast Artillery Corps (CAC), pulled the lanyard on his eight-inch howitzer. Immediately, a high-explosive shell arced high through the air before beginning its descent on the enemy target hundreds of feet below.

Born in Turoczent Marton, Hungary, in 1887, Razga was twenty-two years old when he enlisted in the fall of 1909. He immediately joined the CAC, which was focused on defending America's ports. He served at various forts on the East Coast before shipping over to France. He rose through the ranks quickly, becoming a first sergeant in December 1917. The European immigrant spoke fluent German, Bohemian, and Polish, as well as Hungarian and Slavic, which was an asset on the battlefield.

* * *

Since America's founding, the US harbors required protection from foreign invasion. Prior to the turn of the twentieth century, the country's harbor defenses were becoming obsolete and falling into disrepair, prompting President Grover Cleveland to establish the Endicott Board in 1885 to investigate the issue and make recommendations. Named for its chairman, Secretary of War William Crown Endicott, the group, which included civilians as well as Army and Navy personnel, urged the nation to add fortifications, artillery, and controlled submarine mines to twenty-nine ports. Despite the plan's hefty $127 million price tag, Congress approved it, and the US Army Corps of Engineers spent the decade from 1895 to 1905 constructing the new harbor defense systems.

The US Army recognized that manning these defenses demanded specialized training, and in 1901, it divided the Artillery Corps into two groups: field and coastal artillery. The new Coast Artillery Corps assumed responsibility for coastal, harbor, and anti-aircraft defenses until 1950.

Although the CAC was born as a defensive force stationed in America, many CAC companies were pulled from stateside duty and shipped over to Europe during World War I. Eleven brigades, consisting of thirty-three regiments with twenty-four guns each, joined the AEF. Additional CAC units handled mortars, anti-aircraft guns, and even the AEF's biggest artillery, massive rail guns. Few of these men ever saw action. Most of their weaponry was manufactured in Britain or France. Only one unit—Louis Razga's 58th CAC—possessed American-made eight-inch howitzers.

Formed in December 1917, the 58th consisted of three battalions of two companies each, armed with the eight-inch howitzer M1917, based on the British BL eight-inch howitzer Mk VI. These huge artillery pieces spanned more than twelve feet, and the gun itself weighed more than three tons. The total weight for just one M1917, with its carriage, topped ten tons.

Like all howitzers, the M1917 was a "high-angle fire" artillery piece. The weapon lobbed projectiles at lofty elevations, allowing them to surmount hills, trees, buildings, friendly forces, defensive fortifications, or other obstacles before descending upon the enemy target. The howitzers most commonly shot high-explosive two-hundred-pound shells that could travel a maximum distance of 10,500 yards, nearly six miles. The CAC projectiles had one of two fuse types: instantaneous or time-delay action. As the name suggests, the instantaneous fuse caused the shell to explode upon reaching its target. These fuses created "smaller" craters approximately two- or three-feet deep, but sent fragments flying in every direction. The 58th unit history explained, "Splinters of steel fly in all directions and with killing effect for a radius of 800 yards to the right and left, 600 yards in front and about 250 yards to the rear." These types of shells proved very effective at halting the movement of enemy troops and in taking out enemy guns. The time-delay fuse, by contrast, allowed the shell to penetrate deeply into its target before exploding. The result was dramatic: "A huge crater is formed in the ground, eight or ten feet deep and eight to fifteen feet across the top, depending upon the nature of the soil."[3] The CAC relied on these fuses when it needed to eliminate defensive positions and shelters, such as dugouts and gun emplacements.

Sailing on the USS *Covington* and USS *Leviathan*, the 58th landed in France in May 1918. Upon their arrival, the regiment spent several months in training. Even preparing for battle was not without its hazards. The first man from the 58th to die in Europe was Private Monroe C. Hodge, who was struck by a piece of a gun that accidentally exploded during target practice.

By September, the men had completed their training and were sent to an area near the town of Vignory, about 175 miles southeast of Paris, to await further orders. With little else to do, Razga and the 58th spent a great deal of time sweeping the streets and cleaning up the villages where they were staying. Some joked that CAC stood for "Clean All Cities" or "Come And Clean," and a popular song lamented, "All of the war we've seen so far is cleaning the streets of France."[4] One bright spot during this time was the arrival of a young American woman named Susanna Bottomly, who had been sent over by the YMCA. According to the unit history, "Miss Bottomly managed canteens in the various villages and in many ways made conditions as cheerful as possible for the enlisted men."[5] As a result, the men "became greatly attached to her" and began calling her the "daughter of the regiment."[6]

The 58th's time of rest and repose came to an end in late October when command ordered the regiment to the front. Moving the guns, batteries, ammunition, equipment, and other supplies was no small undertaking, and the 58th used the rail lines to get them as close to the front as possible. They disembarked in the town of Toul, where they joined the newly formed Second US Army for its large-scale offensive scheduled for November 13. The regiment split in two: the 3rd Battalion headed northeast to the town of Saizerais, while Razga and the 1st and 2nd went farther east to Meurthe-et-Moselle.

For the men of the 58th, this was the first taste of war. "Booming of guns was audible day and night; troops constantly on the move back and forth; airplanes always whirring about somewhere in the sky, and sometimes seen in combat. The towns and villages were but heaps of broken masonry—the last undestroyed remains of constructive civilization."[7]

For Razga and his crew, the first task was to establish gun positions. This involved digging huge pits in the ground to shelter the heavy artillery. Fortunately for the 58th, the Germans had recently occupied the areas to which they were assigned, and much of the hard work was already completed. They simply had to move into the dugouts, many of which had concrete walls, gas-proof entrances, and even electric light. The unit history noted that the only small drawback to these facilities was that "they faced the wrong way and had their entrances toward the front."[8] The unit also had to lay down telephone wires to enable communication with headquarters, a task made difficult by the Germans, who often took shots at the men assigned to lay the wire. By October 31, Razga and the rest of his battalion completed the gun positions, and Battery B of the 1st Battalion fired its first shot at the Germans.

The gun crews typically served a four-day rotation on the front before rotating back to the rear for a break. Their time on the front lines was arduous, often requiring extended periods without sleep. "During the days of action there was little or no rest for officers and men. Many of them went more than 36 hours without a moment of rest or sleep. The men spared neither themselves nor their equipment in carrying out the heavy firing program that was laid down for some batteries."[9]

In addition, the Germans maintained a near-constant shelling. Enemy aircraft flew low overhead, firing their machine guns down on the heads of the gun crews. Early on, an enemy shell struck one battery's powder supply, setting off an enormous explosion that killed one of the men. He would be the only man from Razga's battalion to die on the front; seventeen others, including Razga, would be wounded or gassed. On November 9, 1918, just two days before the signing of the armistice, the first sergeant was the victim of a mustard gas attack. He reported to his company surgeon and "was sent back to the Eohelen for treatment and since has been under continual observation."[10] As a result of the attack, Razga received a wound chevron reserved for placement on the sleeve of his uniform—Louis Razga's participation in combat in the Great War was over.

VII

THE FINAL BATTLES
AND COMING HOME

CHAPTER 25

THE FINAL PUSH

The survivors of Belleau Wood, Soissons, and Blanc Mont's deadly "Box" gathered unenthusiastically to hear General Charles Pelot Summerall pontificate. Very few original members of the 49th remained—green troops just off the boat filled the company's ranks. Sitting atop his black stallion, the new V Corps commander addressed the 5th Marines in the final days of October 1918.

Bareheaded, with his helmet tethered to his saddle tie, the general lectured the men regarding what he expected. The son of a Confederate soldier, Summerall was short legged with a long torso. Not mincing words, he motioned with his riding crop, illustrating what lay ahead of the 2nd Division. "You are the troops who taught the world how to take machine guns. . . . Before you are twenty kilometers of machine guns. Go get them."[1]

Despite the blistering, condescending diatribe, Summerall knew modern war and trod on its cutting edge. As an artillerist, he understood that artillery and combined arms had eclipsed the romantic days of the American rifleman fighting without support. At the beginning of the war, he openly challenged Pershing for not having enough artillery, saying, "The infantry would pay dearly in losses for a lack of artillery." Irate, Pershing "viciously attacked" and privately told Summerall to "get together" with his staff. Summerall boldly responded, "Your staff is wrong."[2] Pershing shipped Summerall back to Washington, but despite the rebuke, the Army promoted Summerall to brigadier general and sent him back to France. Remarkably, he soared through the AEF's ranks from artillery brigade commander to commander of V Corps, building his reputation on ruthlessly producing results—at times at the expense of his men.

Corporal Elton Mackin recalled that some of the men sneered under their helmets. Others, combat veterans who understood war, had "bitter memories etched in their faces. They didn't like the picture, yet they would go again."[3]

Summerall pointed the horse in the same direction as his riding crop, "Way up there to the north is a railhead. Go cut it for me! And when you cut it, you will go hungry if you try to feed the prisoners you take. You'll cut the crown prince's army in two. It's the last railroad they hold this side of the Belgian frontier. Men, if you cut it soon enough, you may very well end this damned war. . . . Before you are three ridges. Behind the third, the German artillery is parked almost hub to hub. Go and get them! Don't let them take a single gun!"[4]

He cautioned them against hunting for souvenirs because the Americans would employ toxic gas on a broad scale. Prior to the Meuse-Argonne, the AEF used it sparingly. On this final drive, the Americans planned to drench German positions with mustard and phosgene gas. Both tended to linger in trenches and shell holes alongside prized dough-boy souvenirs such as helmets and Lugers.

The general prattled on: "Now on those ridges, all your officers may be down, but you keep going. And I repeat, you keep going forward while you can still crawl." As the general continued speaking, Mackin reflected upon the Marine officers he fought alongside. *They had a code to live and die by; to never send a fellow where they wouldn't go themselves.*[5] The Marine officers who fought shoulder-to-shoulder with Mackin embodied the principles of leadership.

Summerall continued, "I want to sit back in my headquarters and hear that you carried all your objectives on time." He then delivered his final blow: "And now I say, and you remember this, on those three ridges, take no prisoners, nor should you stop to bandage your best friend."[6] Silence. The general's words hung in the air as he and the Marines studied one another. With those words, he raised his riding crop in a salute and trotted off down a winding forest trail.

One of the Marines then repeated Summerall's plan, mocking the general's desire to sit at headquarters and survey their progress on the map while they fought and died. "Bastard! Bastard!"[7]

Summerall addressed most of the units in the 2nd Division, including Body Bearers Corporal Thomas Saunders and Color Sergeant James W. Dell. After addressing the 5th, he gave the 6th Marines the same pep talk and a tongue-lashing. "[Summerall] lashed out at us as though we were raw, erring recruits," recalled one Marine. "If we failed to take a single objective, he said, he would relieve and send to the rear our regimental commander, our brigade commander, and even our deeply admired and respected division commander. It was a strange performance and one resented by all. Afterward, General Lejeune's call of 'three cheers for General Summerall' was met with stony silence."[8]

By late October 1918, two separate AEF attacks on the German defenses in the Meuse-Argonne had gained the Americans a mere nine miles of enemy territory. During each push, First Army sustained more than one hundred thousand casualties. Pershing cannibalized newly arrived units from the United States to replenish his gored divisions. The AEF suffered, but the Germans were in worse shape. The Allies did not have a complete picture of Germany's dire situation: it was at the end of its rope. The Grand Offensive swallowed up entire units, and influenza ran rampant. The home front teetered on the verge of collapse.

On other fronts, the French and British had advanced deeper into German-held territory. While discussing an end to the war, Field Marshal Haig pointed out that the Germans could shorten their front and make "a very effective stand." He went on to state that the British and French were "pretty well exhausted," and he also jabbed that the American army "suffered a great deal on account of its ignorance of modern warfare. . . . It requires time to get into shape."[9] Haig favored mild terms for the armistice: the Imperial German Army leaving the conquered territories as well as the Alsace-Lorraine seized during the 1870 Franco-Prussian War. Foch disagreed with Haig's assessment.

He noted that victorious armies are never fresh, and he defended the Americans. Believing they had beaten the Germans, he wanted to push hard for an armistice that would include an occupation of Germany up to the Rhine River.

As they had done throughout the war, the Allies once again aimed to marginalize the AEF and take credit for the success. General Tasker Bliss, the US representative to the Allied Supreme War Council, explained, "[Our Allies will] attempt to minimize the American effort as much as possible. They think they have got the Germans on the run, and they do not need as much help as they were crying for a little while ago."[10] Sensing the possibility of the end of the war in 1918, Pershing knew he needed to revive the offensive and achieve a breakthrough.

Unlike the French and British and even his own president, Pershing found Wilson's Fourteen Points* too lenient, and he made it clear that unconditional surrender was the only way to end the war and prevent another. Prescient, Pershing bucked the chain of command. On October 30, 1918, he wrote an unwelcome note to the Allied Supreme War Council that foretold the likelihood of a second world war:

> It is the experience of history that victorious armies are prone to overestimate the enemy's strength and too eagerly seek an opportunity for peace. The mistake is likely to be made now on

---

* In a speech on January 8, 1918, Woodrow Wilson outlined fourteen principles that he believed were essential to peace negotiations. These idealistic principles became known as the Fourteen Points. He called for open peace treaties, freedom of the seas, free trade, and a reduction in arms. In addition, he called for the occupying armies to leave the nations they had invaded, including Russia, Belgium, France, Italy, Romania, Serbia, Montenegro, and Poland. He wanted to set up a League of Nations "for the purpose of affording mutual guarantees of political independence and territorial integrity to great and small states alike." With regard to Germany, he advised restraint, saying, "We do not wish to injure her or to block in any way her legitimate influence or power. We do not wish to fight her either with arms or with hostile arrangements of trade, if she is willing to associate herself with us and the other peace-loving nations of the world in covenants of justice and law and fair dealing. We wish her only to accept a place of equality among the peoples of the world—the new world in which we now live—instead of a place of mastery."

account of the reputation Germany has gained through her victories of the last years. . . . I believe the complete victory can only be obtained by continuing the war until we force unconditional surrender from Germany, but if the Allied Governments decide to grant an armistice, the terms should be so rigid that under no circumstances should Germany take up arms.[11]

Pershing crossed a red line when he meddled in politics and defied the official position of the US government, which was negotiating an armistice based on the Fourteen Points. Secretary of War Baker nearly wrote a letter of reprimand.

Colonel Edward Mandell House, a man who spoke directly for President Wilson, was appalled. A rich Texan who had not served a day in the military but nevertheless held the honorary title of colonel, House was one of Wilson's most trusted advisors. Frail and self-effacing with a gentle voice and soft hands, he often draped a blanket over his legs for warmth. House perfected the art of understanding people and "loved power and politics," earning a reputation as an "intimate man, even when he was cutting your throat."[12]

Pershing quickly retreated from his position after realizing he had gone too far, backpedaling and explaining to House that his letter was just military advice. Wilson considered the matter a misunderstanding and ignored the letter.

In response, Pershing endeavored to beat the German Army so badly that it would never rise again.

Pressure to break out during the Meuse-Argonne rolled onto the shoulders of General Summerall, whose V Corps, specifically the 2nd Division, would spearhead the most important American offensive of the war. James W. Dell, Thomas Saunders, and the surviving combat veterans of Edward Younger's and Ernest Janson's battle-hardened companies led the bloody breakthrough.

As Summerall revealed to his troops, the 2nd Division would have to advance a mind-boggling six miles in one day and ultimately seize several ridges. The first ridge opposite the 2nd Division contained part of the vaunted Kriemhilde Stellung. Although units had pierced a portion of the line to the right of the Marines, there still were plenty of bunkers, mountains of wire, dug-in artillery, and machine-gun nests to overcome. Behind that loomed the fortified Barricourt Ridge and the bunkers and pillboxes of the Freya Stellung. Beyond that, they would encounter the natural defensive barrier of the Meuse River and the Meuse Heights, where the Germans staged hundreds of artillery pieces that had rained fire on the AEF since the opening of the Meuse-Argonne Offensive. The First Army's plan, in which the Body Bearers played a role, comprised three stages: pierce the defensive lines, pursue the Germans, and destroy them as they fell back crossing the Meuse River.

Rumors of an armistice that would end the war had been swirling for weeks. Morale plummeted in the kaiser's army—no one wanted to die in vain during what seemed like the last days of a conflict that was grinding to a halt. A sense of duty often inspired the Germans to keep fighting for what they hoped would be, for each other, or for their commanders, who urged them to battle on.

German diplomatic efforts to achieve an armistice accelerated on October 5, 1918, when the newly appointed chancellor Prince Maximilian of Baden told the Reichstag, the German imperial parliament, to seek an armistice. Field Marshal Ludendorff had become so distraught from news of the American offensive that he had suffered a stroke days earlier; his staff quietly urged the German government to end the war. Maximilian ordered his foreign policy team to disregard the French and British—they were to attempt to negotiate directly with the Americans. Six months earlier, this bold move would have been unimaginable if the Allies had broken up the AEF, instead of allowing it to fight as a unified army. With more than 1.7 million men in the field and still growing, the AEF had enough leverage to dictate terms, effectively neutralizing Britain and France.

Within the military, some were dismayed by the attempts to negotiate peace before the Germans were truly defeated. Color Sergeant

Dell wrote in a letter to a friend, "I have just read of the enemy's offer, or rather suppose a request for an armistice, and our artillery is roaring out what I hope will be the only reply given them until they get out of all invaded territory—and then unconditional surrender should be the only terms."[13] He added, "Let us not ease up one jot nor tittle till they bellow like the curs they are."[14]

However, for those in power, the possibility of peace seemed too tempting to pass up. On October 29 President Wilson, through Colonel House, executed a power play that sent shock waves through the peace process.

House informed his Allied counterparts that the United States might very well negotiate a separate peace with the Germans. In response, Britain and France agreed to support the Fourteen Points as the position from which they would negotiate.

As these events unfolded, the Allies remained unaware that Germany was collapsing from within. The German Empire had employed every means at its disposal to stave off revolt, which had been brewing for years. However, an insurrection began after German sailors were ordered to prepare for one climactic battle with the Royal Navy on October 24. Instead of sailing, they rebelled at Wilhelmshaven, where Body Bearer James Delaney and the crew of *Campana* had disembarked. Sailors mutinied at Kiel, and civil unrest spread throughout Germany. Communism, the virus that the Germans had unleashed in Russia, was spreading inside their own country, undermining the imperial government. Revolutionaries organized strikes that brought industry to a halt. Escalating unrest led to the proclamation of a German Republic on November 9. Kaiser Wilhelm II abdicated and fled to Holland when Hindenburg informed him the troops would no longer follow him.

As bad as the German political situation was, its military was not yet beaten. The Allies still hadn't driven the German Army back out of France, and Berlin remained untouched, hundreds of miles away. The French and British had sustained tens of thousands killed and wounded from what was supposed to be the last offensive.

The AEF's logistical system showed signs of strain as supply shipments from the United States declined and the Allies stretched their own lines of communication. Any Allied attack into Germany would require mountains of supplies. Both the Allies and the Central Powers were near the point of exhaustion. On many levels, the Allies were fortunate that the Germans bowed out of the war when they did.

The influenza pandemic that would last into 1919 had already killed thousands, and now it accelerated. Before it was over, millions more would die. It cut through the Allied and German armies like a scythe, killing and disabling tens of thousands without regard to rank or station. What bullets, bayonets, artillery, and gas failed to do in more than four years of war, influenza accomplished in just weeks. The Body Bearers lived a dog's life with no shelter from the freezing rain that soaked their skin and the knee-deep mud that hampered every step. Saunders, Dell, and their brothers-in-arms slept in water-filled foxholes that fostered the virus and other diseases. In the 6th Marine Regiment alone, influenza rendered 70 percent of the men combat ineffective.[15]

Plague ships filled with infected American troops were hitting the shores of France. For instance, around the second week of October, *Martha Washington* arrived carrying 506 soldiers with influenza and 30 dead. *America* had brought 806 infected men and 30 dead.[16]

The AEF did its best to separate the healthy from the sick. Ambulance crews often brought infected troops back to field hospitals deep behind Allied lines, where they received care in isolated wards before returning to the front after they recuperated. Most influenza deaths resulted from pneumonia. Acute viral pneumonia could kill a victim in hours. According to the US government, 798,509 members of the American military, or roughly one in four doughboys, contracted influenza. Numbers vary, but as many as 44,000 may have died from the disease, almost as many as the total American combat deaths.[17]

Casualties included General Pershing, who contracted the flu in mid-October. In fear of infecting his beloved, he stopped seeing Micheline Resco.

* * *

Dawn broke on November 1, 1918, with a thunderous clash as Color Sergeant James W. Dell's 75s and hundreds of other guns unloaded a deadly and accurate fusillade on Barricourt Ridge.

"The noise was deafening when the 75s and heavy artillery began a bombardment of the hostile lines," one member of the assault recalled. "The bombardment, which was more intense and venomous than any ever before thrown over the heads of the Marines, was still thundering when the 1st Battalion of the 5th passed through the 2nd Battalion positions advancing to attack."[18]

Marines in the 49th began their assault at 5:30 a.m.; a heavy fog masked their advance. On their way to the jumping-off position, the men of the 2nd Division saw the detritus of war: discarded helmets, broken weapons, bodies, and body parts of Germans and Americans alike.

Here in front of the town of Landres-et-Saint-Georges, Lieutenant Colonel "Wild Bill" Donovan, leading the "Fighting 69th," had nearly lost the men under his command during an assault on the Kriemhilde Stellung about two weeks earlier. Donovan, who would later become the United States' spymaster as head of the Office of Strategic Services (OSS),* found that he had to lead from the front to get his inexperienced men to advance. To bolster their morale, he stayed on the front lines as the situation worsened and delivered his orders to the various units in person. He later wrote, "I had walked to the different units and was coming back to the telephone when smash, I felt as if somebody had hit me on the back of the leg with a spiked club. I fell like a log, but after a few minutes managed to crawl into my little telephone hole."[19] Donovan had taken a bullet to his right knee but continued to direct his men for as long as possible. He later received the Medal of Honor for his efforts.

---

* Donovan led the 1st Battalion, 165th Regiment of the 42nd Division, also known as the "Fighting 69th," during World War I. During World War II, Donovan would pioneer America's modern espionage and special operations forces.

The remains of many of Donovan's men were among those the 2nd passed as they made their way forward. The main thrust of the attack lay upon the shoulders of Pershing's elite 2nd Division, which charged Barricourt Ridge, aiming to rupture the main German defenses and force a German withdrawal across the Meuse.

On paper, the AEF's final offensive emphasized fire and maneuver; one group suppressed an enemy position while another flanked and took it out. Combined arms remained the ideal. The AEF deployed artillery, planes, and tanks in concert to destroy enemy positions. However, tanks remained an Achilles' heel—First Army had only eighteen combat-ready Renaults. The Americans attempted to apply the tactics they learned during the dress rehearsal at St. Mihiel. Yet new replacement officers sometimes led the men in costly frontal assaults on machine guns. Doctrine often clashed with expectations as general officers, like Summerall, demanded results. "No man is ever so tired that he cannot take one step forward," he told the men, adding, "The best way to take machine guns is to go take 'em."[20]

George Hamilton's 1/5 and Janson's 49th Company led the attack and, after hard fighting, advanced several miles, which one Army historian described as "one of the most remarkable feats of the war."[21] Corporal Elton Mackin remembered the scale of the offensive: "Looking back we saw lines of men, flowing after us in endless waves, breasting over the crest of the first ridge, following after us as we faced the second hill. Always, always we faced another hill."[22]

The Marines and soldiers of the 2nd Division lost hundreds of men killed and wounded breaching the Hindenburg Line. But the 2nd pierced the line, and in this push, unlike prior engagements, German resistance crumbled. The 2nd advanced a breathtaking six miles and captured the ridge. November 1 was a debacle for the German Army; Gallwitz confessed, "We suffered a defeat!"[23]

CHAPTER 26

THE BRIDGE

With the end of the war less than twenty-four hours away, General Summerall, in command of V Corps, ordered Body Bearer Corporal Thomas Saunders and Company A of the 2nd Engineers to bridge the Meuse River. The 5th and 6th Marines along with several infantry units and the 6th Machine-Gun Battalion were to cross the river and assault the German lines overnight.* The brass had handed the men a perilous and deadly mission that in the end needlessly sent many to their deaths. Crossing the Meuse was complex and difficult. The Germans had emplaced machine-gun nests on the eastern side of the river. Snipers lurked in the heavy woods, and artillery had zeroed in on all the logical crossing points. In an instant, the Germans could call upon several batteries of 77s, 88s, and 150 mm cannons to rain down artillery fire. Since the Germans had destroyed all the nearby bridges, the 2nd had to prefabricate footbridges and assemble them at the crossing point. Using a captured sawmill and wood from a German barracks, Saunders and his fellow engineers built two floating footbridges behind the lines. They constructed the bridges in sections—each flimsy bridge span was roughly the width of a large ladder and twelve feet long. One Marine described them as "like a railway track turned upside down."[1] Teams of mules would transport the heavy sections to an area near the Meuse where they would be floated in the river.

Before approaching the river, the men discussed a possible armistice, rumored to occur the following day, with anticipation and anxiety.

* The other units involved in the attack included elements of the 89th Division.

No man wished to sacrifice life or limb for naught. Corporal Elton Mackin bitterly reflected back on the long evening of November 10–11, when the 2nd Engineers moved the bridges into position and expected the Marines to cross them: "They lied to us that night. It was a patent, flimsy lie. Officers said: 'We're to move a lot of 75mm ammunition over to the 89th Division, to the right of us.' Old hands among us knew the difference at once and were prepared for anything."[2]

To soften up the German defenses prior to the crossing, James W. Dell's men brought their 75s closer to the river to provide support. They would fire for an hour upon a strip of low ground between the river and wooded slopes on the eastern side of the Meuse. Dell's men would then lift the barrage from the riverbank and concentrate on German strong-points along the river with the hope of facilitating the Marines' crossing.[3]

Saunders and the fighting engineers hoisted the rafts and bridge sections over their heads and hiked to the crossing point. The familiar sound of battle—the chatter of machine guns and the thud of exploding shells—reverberated in the background. Commanded by Major George Hamilton, the Marines trailed minutes behind Saunders and the engineers. Soaked through, many of the men forged ahead, plagued by influenza and other maladies. The Leathernecks trudged in single file, groping in the darkness silently—noise and talk forbidden.

A dense, freezing gray fog prevented the engineers from being annihilated as they approached the Meuse. Saunders strained as he and his fellow engineers manhandled the bridge sections and pontoons down a steep railroad embankment, and the men gingerly struggled to maintain their footing on the loose rock. A mere 200 feet separated Saunders and his men from the enemy; the slightest sound could reveal their position to the German snipers and half a dozen machine-gun nests hidden on the German side of the river. Painstakingly, the engineers floated the pontoons into the icy-cold waters of the Meuse. The fog shrouded their movement and deadened sound. The fighting engineers carefully placed the sections on the pontoons and tied them down with heavy rope.

Silently, Company A guided and thrust the bridge across the muddy, freezing Meuse. A brave engineer clung to the front of the contraption, rifle in hand, kneeling on the waterlogged planks as they floated across the river. Miraculously, the current drifted the lone soldier across the Meuse, and he tied the guideline onto a tree on the eastern side. Saunders's Company A was succeeding: a two-by-four-foot path bridged the Meuse. Unbeknownst to Hamilton's Marines, this was a pathway straight into hell.

Not far away, the plan to float the bridge for the 6th Marines' crossing had not gone nearly as well. German artillery spotted one bridge almost immediately and scored a direct hit. As dawn came, the Marine commanders had limited means to get their men across the river and, even worse, their current position left them exposed to enemy fire. Potentially putting their careers in jeopardy, they decided on their own to march their Marines back to the safety of the woods.

However, at the 5th Marines' bridge, the crossing went ahead as planned. Most of the Marines were exhausted after ten days of combat and suffered from lack of sleep, and many were sick with influenza.

A gleaming white star shell arced across the inky sky, silhouetting Saunders and his men, along with members of the 49th Company and the rest of two battalions of Marines. Staccato fire from machine guns obliterated the relative silence. An enemy patrol set up their Maxims on the far bank and fired. Fortunately, the volley sailed above the heads of Saunders and the Marines. Six more machine-gun nests sprayed lead like a fire hose.

Artillery shells exploded and plastered the men with lethal, arm-size, razor-sharp shrapnel. Elements of the 9th Infantry provided security. Several Body Bearers converged in one place on that bone-freezing, windswept, rainy night, the 143rd birthday of the Marine Corps. Sergeant Edward Younger had recovered from his wounds and participated in the battle as men from Janson's 49th Company and elements of George Hamilton's 1/5 moved toward the Meuse.* "Death lashed and tore at the mouth of the ravine"[4] as the Marines navigated the embankment.

---

* George Hamilton had command of the crossing group that included the 1st Battalion 5th Marines and the 2nd Battalion 5th Marines.

Dead and wounded men lay across the heavily wooded path leading to the river. One Marine recalled, "Near the small bridge, the bank of the river was strewn with our dead. I counted about twenty-five within a distance of a hundred yards. Several shells had hit directly where we had laid along the bank of the river. Nearly all of one platoon of one of the other companies had been either killed or wounded. All the dead still lay where they had fallen"[5]

Shadowy figures darted past the Marines, heading away from the Meuse. Darkness and the woods masked the location of the river.

"The bridge, the bridge. Where is the Bridge?! Come on guide us," shouted the Marines as cowardly men dashed past them.[6]

Hamilton captured a fleeing soldier, jammed a .45 into his spine, and forced him to guide them to the bridge. As the column crept forward, exploding shells and machine-gun fire ripped through the area around them. Hamilton slipped on a broken rail. "The guide leaped once or twice into the fog and disappeared. We heard Major [Hamilton] curse as he fired, missing him."

Hamilton and the 49th and other companies within 1/5 charged forward. Outlined in the glow of flares, Saunders and the engineers bellowed, "The bridge! The Bridge! This way, come on, Marines!"[7]

Leading by example, as he had done countless times in the past, Major Hamilton made his way to the vanguard of his men to lead the assault across the bridge; however, a burly Marine forced him aside, perhaps to protect the beloved and esteemed officer. Shells exploded near the footbridge, sending a tower of water that sank the fragile structure and drenched the men. Maxim bullets "ripped a seam through the water, then swung back. They changed their tone abruptly to the *sock, sock, sock* sound bullets make when they hit flesh,"[8] recalled Mackin. Bodies of the first men who attempted to cross the rickety contraption piled up on the western side of the Meuse.

Scores of Marines crossed the water; others died trying when another shell detonated. "The bridge is gone!"[9]

The 49th Company and elements of 1/5 and 2/5 were cut off on the German side of the Meuse. One Marine stripped down and swam through the freezing waters to obtain help. Trapped within German territory, the war still raging all around him, Hamilton ordered his Marines to form a perimeter and dig in on the eastern bank. That the war would be over in hours seemed implausible to these embattled, exhausted warriors. The Germans hit the Marines with a box barrage. Heavy guns pummeled the group, felling enormous trees and killing many of Hamilton's men as enemy infantry attempted to envelop the group. "We lost old friends who had come with us a long and dreadful way," Mackin recalled.[10]

Staring down annihilation, the men did not know the war would end within hours. What the Marines did know is that they had leaders they trusted and followed to the end. They had each other—a fellowship forged only in battle. This bond kept many of the men alive.

Before the Germans signed the armistice, Marshal Foch issued an order on the afternoon of November 9 that the Allied advance should accelerate. Pershing, who had no love for the armistice, eagerly acquiesced and ordered all attacks, including the Meuse crossings, to proceed on November 10 and 11. According to one staff member, Pershing despondently sighed when hearing that the end of the war was near. "What an enormous difference a few more days would have made," he said, placing his finger on a map to indicate the start of the November 14 offensive near Metz.[11] There the remaining men of Body Bearer Louis Razga's Battery D of the 58th CAC now positioned their heavy guns to support the offensive, while Razga writhed in pain in a hospital bed.

Undoubtedly, Razga breathed a sigh of relief after Pershing's offensive with the American Second Army against German-held Metz did not take place. Razga was in a field hospital recovering from the gas attack that had seared his lungs and portions of his body. The 58th's guns had been softening up the defenses at Metz for the planned offensive when the gas shell hit Razga.

Although the Metz offensive did not materialize, Pershing's other planned assaults went forward. According to Pershing's chief of staff,

"[The AEF planned] to take every advantage of the situation."[12] Even when Pershing discovered that the armistice was signed at 5:45 a.m. on November 11 (at which time the 49th and Major Hamilton fought for their lives on the eastern side of the Meuse and other units were engaged in heated battles as well), Pershing merely relayed the order that fighting should cease at 11:00 a.m. Protocol for what happened from 5:45 a.m. to 11:00 a.m. was never addressed to the Marines in the 2nd Division, who clung to and fought for their tiny toehold on the eastern side of the Meuse.

CHAPTER 27

OCCUPATION

Silence.

At 11:00 a.m. the guns finally fell silent.

Immediately afterward, the first joyful shouts rang out from the German lines. In unison, men in the trenches cheered wildly. The juxtaposition of ebullient sounds from the Germans, out of place in the desolate, lunar landscape furrowed with trenches and shell holes, and blanketed with rusted coils of barbed wire, caused the soldiers and Marines of the 2nd Division to gaze at one another and their opponents in confusion.

"The thunder of the guns ceased, and the men, unable to speak, clasped hands in silence," recalled one of the doughboys.[1] Slowly, word spread through the American trenches. The warring parties had signed an armistice. The Great War, which had killed millions, was over.

Marshal Foch communicated the news to the front in a short telegram: "Hostilities will be stopped on the entire front beginning at 11:00 a.m., November 11th (French time). The Allied troops will not go beyond the lines reached at that hour on that date until further orders."[2] Accounts of the day from American war diaries say the announcement was greeted "on the enemy's side with jubilant shouts, by us in silent joy."[3] Another American describing the profound silence could hear his watch ticking the first seconds after 11:00 a.m. passed. The guns, including James W. Dell's 75s that had been supporting the Meuse crossing, ceased their fire.

Wasting no time, the Germans began abandoning their trenches. Stunned by the sudden and unexpected end to the fighting, Body Bearers

Saunders and Dell and the 49th Company watched along with other elements of the 2nd Division as the German Army, in a scene that would be repeated across the Western Front, climbed out of their positions, assembled into formation, and began the long march back to their home country, leaving many of their heavy weapons behind. Slowly, the news sank in; the rumors of an armistice had finally come to fruition. The Americans began taking stock of their supplies, collecting their gear and belongings, and preparing for their next move.

Over the previous eleven days, the 2nd Division had suffered significant casualties. The division lost 97 officers and 3,201 men in the Meuse-Argonne: 11 officers and 391 men killed, another 82 officers and 2,290 men wounded, and 3 officers and 85 men gassed. In addition, 1 officer and 435 men were missing.[4] Influenza had also incapacitated or killed scores of soldiers and Marines. The division history noted, "These corrected figures, however, give no idea of the actual fighting strength of the regiments on the Meuse. The continued exposure to cold and rain, and the lack of hot and properly prepared food, had caused much sickness, and American units on November 11th were a mere fraction of what they had been on October 31st."[5]

After waiting several days to allow the Germans time to withdraw and establish a neutral zone between the armies, the 2nd followed the enemy into Germany, per the terms of the armistice. Body Bearers James W. Dell with the 15th Field Artillery and Thomas Saunders of the 2nd Engineers embarked upon the long march by foot into German territory, along with the 49th Company of the 1st Battalion 5th Marines. As John Thomason looked at the long line of men behind him, very few of the original members of the 49th Company remained. He reflected, "There were very few men in the column who remembered the hike to Verdun, in the early spring of 1918; in one company eight, in another eleven; in the whole battalion the barest handful. It had been a long road. The first waystation was the Bois de Belleau; a lot of people stopped there, and were there yet. And there were more, comfortably rotting in the Foret de Retz, south of Soissons. And more yet, well dead around Blanc Mont. And a vast drift of them back in hospitals. Men walked silent, remembering the old dead. . . . Twelve hundred men hiking to the Rhine, and how many ghosts."[6]

From the 49th Company, Marine Ernest Janson had finally recovered from his severe wounds suffered on Hill 142 at Belleau Wood and rejoined his Marine brothers. On December 13, the division crossed the Rhine into Germany and established control and occupation in the area around Coblenz. French troops were garrisoned in the nearby town of Mayence. Major George Hamilton continued to command 1/5 during the occupation of Germany. Hamilton's battalion included seasoned veterans such as Lieutenant John Thomason and Corporal Elton Mackin, who would receive the Distinguished Service Cross for their actions in the Great War.

While the negotiators had achieved a truce, they had yet to accomplish true peace. The men on the ground maintained a constant state of readiness in the event that the Germans, once again, took up arms. "With all of its training and other activities, the Army of Occupation never forgot that it might resume operations," the division history recorded. "The peace negotiations were followed with close attention, and every delay or gesture of resistance on the part of the German delegates was at once reflected in renewed discussion of advance."[7] For men like Saunders, Janson, and Dell, it was a time of tension and waiting. Any day could be the day when true peace came at last or, alternatively, when they once again resumed the fight against the Germans whose country they now occupied. They also saw firsthand the effects of the Allied blockade. Even after the war, the population was still starving; emaciated children picked through the Allied troops' garbage searching for food.

Still, the longer the men remained in Germany, the more their camps began to seem permanent; they constructed barracks and other buildings. When they were not engaged in training or other duties related to camp life, the soldiers passed the time creating and participating in sports leagues and entertainment groups. They also fraternized with some of the locals; many doughboys would bring home European war brides.

While the 2nd Division occupied Coblenz, Harry Taylor and his 91st Division headed deeper into Belgium. Along with massive numbers of French and British troops, they marched toward Brussels along two different roads. However, as the unit history noted, "The difficulty of handling the transportation of three corps on these two roads proved great."[8] After just two days, the bulk of the division stopped in an area about thirty miles east of the Belgian capital. Just one battery of field artillery from the 91st traveled on to escort the Belgian king for his return on November 22. Twenty-five American officers from other units joined them to witness the event.

Most of the 91st traveled to Dunkirk, on France's northern coast, to await rail transportation to other locations while Harry Taylor's Head-quarters' Troop and division colors traveled into German territory to the tomb of Emperor Charlemagne in a city the French call Aix-la-Chapelle and the Germans call Aachen. There on December 7, a French general delivered a speech that epitomized the venomous feelings the Allies had for the Germans and foreshadowed the treatment of the fallen enemy that would eventually lead to a second world war. "A study of history will show that all the wars and invasions which for the last two thousand years have flooded Europe with blood can be traced to the thirst for conquest of the Teutonic people or of the Germans. Let us not forget this," he told them. He went on to catalog Germany's many offenses before adding, "And now, when the German Emperor, author of this war which has cost humanity twenty million men and France so many sacrifices, so much devastation and mourning, now, when this vanquished and dethroned Emperor awaits nearby a just punishment, the victorious flags and standards of the descendants of Charlemagne's knights bow down before the tomb of their great ancestor."[9]

Wilhelm II waited nearby. On November 10, 1918, he fled in exile to Holland, which refused the Allies' demands to extradite him, rankling the Body Bearers and their brothers-in-arms. Eventually, a quixotic plot to capture the kaiser and bring him to justice unfolded in the dark hours of New Year's Eve and Day. An inebriated Colonel Luke Lea, a former US senator from Tennessee, and several of his officers and enlisted men took matters into their own hands, driving a convoy of cars into Holland. After the American caravan crossed the Dutch border, they stormed into the drawing room of a castle owned by Count Godard von Bentinck and demanded to see the kaiser, who was residing in the fortress. While versions of the story differ, Wilhelm, through Count Bentinck, asked Lea if the American officer represented the official position of the American or Allied governments. Lea responded that his party did not represent the official US position. At this point, "things got a little warm."[10] Wilhelm's guards filtered into the drawing room, and Lea saw a detachment of Dutch soldiers riding motorcycles toward the castle. Lea and his men jumped into their cars and sped away to France, where they received a slap on the wrist but were celebrated as heroes.

As with the raid, occupation duty resulted in several tense moments for the Body Bearers and other men serving in Germany. In May, that activity culminated. "Friction in the peace conference became acute, and the German delegates flatly refused the demands of the Allies."[11] The 2nd Division and other Allied units received orders to prepare to advance further into Germany on June 17. As a result, "all construction work was at once discontinued; athletic teams and entertainment groups were broken up; movement of civilians across the outpost lines was stopped."[12] The division was ordered to "march prepared for action, with all dispositions for security. In case of armed resistance by organized troops, it was to be promptly overcome. Any form of opposition by the civil population was to be suppressed by such means as necessary, and the offenders were to be summarily dealt with."[13]

Ultimately, Germany relented, and the troop movements were suspended. The official end of war between the Allies and Germany materialized with the signing of the Treaty of Versailles on June 28, 1919. Despite the treaty, occupation duty for most of the Body Bearers lingered on for several more weeks, and America garrisoned troops in Germany until January 24, 1923, when the US Army withdrew from the Rhine.

*   *   *

Pershing's Body Bearers from the US Navy were also recovering from their experience in the Great War. Water Tender and Body Bearer Charles Leo O'Connor spent nearly a month in sick bay convalescing from the severe burns that covered his body—the result of the torpedo that struck *Mount Vernon*. He would soon return to duty and resume service with *Mount Vernon*, transporting some of the tens of thousands of US troops from France back to the United States.

A walking scarecrow after being liberated from a POW camp in Germany, James Delaney had lost a significant portion of his body weight on the camp's starvation diet. Despite the harsh conditions, Delaney and his men had managed to survive; when the Germans signed the armistice, everything changed. The Social Democratic Party forced the German soldiers in the camp to relinquish their swords and remove the ranking marks from their uniforms. The soldiers addressed their prisoners, promising to send them home as soon as they could. "They told us to forget all our bad treatment in the prison, as they would now treat us as men," Delaney recalled. He added, "I myself would not listen, as one of these soap box speech makers was the worst German for punishment and making the prisoners work, before the Armistice. He reported to the Count in charge of the camp that I insulted him."[14]

It took nearly a month for the socialists to make good on their promise. The thirty-four Americans from Brandenburg were finally released on December 8 and transported to Denmark. According to Delaney, "the socialists tried to humor us, even giving us a wagon and horses to carry what food and clothes we were taking with us; which had never been done before."[15] Delaney returned to the United States, and the Navy mercifully assigned him to recruiting duty while he recovered.

Samuel Woodfill recuperated from the effects of the toxic gas and the wounds he suffered from his heroic charge in October and marched into Luxembourg for occupation duty with the 60th Infantry Regiment of the 5th Division. The time between the armistice and the period when the troops finally left Europe for home also provided an opportunity to recognize soldiers who had fought with great distinction. That winter, Woodfill received orders to report to General Headquarters in Chaumont, France, to receive the Medal of Honor. The Army also temporarily promoted Woodfill to captain, but the promotion would not last long. Within months, the Army demoted him back to the rank of sergeant—the sort of nonchalant bureaucratic downsizing typical of the time. The large US Army required to fight the Great War was no longer necessary, and the military was returning to peacetime numbers, a shell of its former wartime self. The bureaucracy mercilessly viewed Woodfill and many of the other men who fought in the AEF as statistics.

A military band played as an honor guard lined up in formation. Then General Pershing appeared onstage and announced the names of seventeen men who would receive the medals. Woodfill also met and conversed with fellow Medal of Honor recipient Gunnery Sergeant Ernest Janson, a.k.a. Charles "Charley" Hoffman. Woodfill vividly described Janson's action on Hill 142: "Hoffman saw twelve Germans armed with half a dozen light portable machine guns. They were crawling right toward his outfit. Then Charley gave a yell to warn his buddies and lit right into those Heinies like a charging grizzly. He got two of them with his bayonet and the rest dropped their machine guns and beat it."[16] Captain George McMurtry from Whittlesey's Lost Battalion also received his medal that day; Colonel Whittlesey received the Medal of Honor as well, but on another date. In the months after the war, each of the Body Bearers received medals for his service.

Woodfill recalled that he was "in a bit of a daze" as the commander of the AEF said, "This is the highest honor an American soldier can receive from his government. I am mighty proud of these men." To be praised by a leader they admired was a great privilege. "When he said that, you could almost hear the heads and chests of the lot of us expanding," Woodfill remembered. "At any rate, to an old regular like myself, it meant far more than I have the words to express."[17]

The ceremony also included an opportunity for Medal of Honor recipients to dine with Pershing and many of the other generals. Woodfill later recollected, "'Black Jack' himself was mingling with the crowd, looking every inch a soldier, just as he always does, and chatting with all the men."[18]

The time had come to return home. The Body Bearers embarked upon a transatlantic voyage back to the United States. One of the last divisions to leave was the 2nd. Transportation was first provided by twenty-six trains packed with men of the division. They then loaded onto ships in the waning days of July 1919, landing in New York on August 8. The Marines assembled in Washington Square wearing their forest green uniforms and helmets adorned with the Indian-head logo in the various sizes and colors representing each battalion. The elite 2nd proudly marched up 5th Avenue to 110th Street, passing General John Lejeune at 42nd Street. For most of the men, the end of their enlistments marked the end of their military service; they now made the difficult transition from combat to civilian life.

The end of the war marked a period of turbulent change. The Treaty of Versailles did not put into place the lasting peace that Wilson envisioned. As Colonel House wrote in his diary at the time, "The Treaty is not a good one . . . it is too severe. . . . However, the time to have the Treaty right was when it was being formed and not now. It is a question if one commenced to unravel what has already been done, whether it could be stopped. . . . We desired from the beginning a fair peace, and one well within the Fourteen Points, and one which could stand the scrutiny of the neutral world and of all time. It is not such a peace, but since the Treaty has been written, I question whether it would be well to seriously modify it."[19]

The treaty ended the old world order and created a new one. Monarchies, like the one in czarist Russia, fell away. The rise of communism and Stalin would result in the deaths of millions. In the United States, the Espionage Act and the government encroachment on the Bill of Rights would leave a legacy that persists to this day.

The influenza pandemic continued to spread after the war ended. Between fifty million and one hundred million people, between 3 and

5 percent of the world's population at the time, would perish before it was over.[20]

The world had altered dramatically since the Body Bearers entered the war in 1917. The heavily agrarian lifestyle of the nineteenth century was giving way to the fast-paced, technology-driven society of the twentieth century. America was just beginning to assume its place as one of the great powers and becoming the preeminent military, economic, and social force in the world.

The termination of hostilities did not usher in lasting peace—in fact, in many cases, it had the opposite effect. Revolutions flared throughout Europe. Treaties redrew national borders in Europe and the Middle East. The Sykes-Picot Agreement partitioned the Ottoman Empire, creating artificial divisions that didn't take ethnicity, culture, and religion into account, perpetuating conflicts that would last for generations.

In the United States, four million American workers from industries as diverse as textiles, steel, and meatpacking went on strike. The fear that communism would take hold pervaded the United States. The "Red Scare" led to the formation of various anti-Communist leagues, and law enforcement rounded up labor movement leaders and other suspected Communist sympathizers and deported or imprisoned them.

Immediately following the armistice, the US economy experienced a short but very deep recession in 1919–1920, as factories converted from wartime to peacetime production. However, as soldiers began returning home, the influx of labor led to a quick turnaround, and the "Roaring Twenties" got under way. Newly built factories and emerging technologies—cars, airplanes, motion pictures, radio, and chemicals—boosted incomes and spending, injecting a general feeling of optimism.

American society was also undergoing a dramatic metamorphosis, particularly regarding the role of women. The suffragettes marched to demand equal rights, and in 1920, the United States ratified the Nineteenth Amendment to the Constitution, which granted women the right to vote. More women began working outside the home and attending colleges and universities. The birthrate declined, and the divorce rate climbed. Even styles changed as women cut their hair short and donned flapper dresses, expressing their independence.

This was also the Jazz Age, and dance clubs sprang up across the country. People flocked to hear the modern music and dance the Charleston, the foxtrot, the black bottom, and the shimmy. Art deco was the rage. Partygoers in the age of *The Great Gatsby* drank a variety of cocktails such as the mint julep, the gin rickey, and the French 75, a reference to the WWI artillery piece. Everywhere, a wild and carefree attitude prevailed, and personal expression and individuality seemed more important than adherence to rigid societal mores.

Not everyone was on board with the looser morals of the time, though. Temperance groups advocated for and eventually passed prohibition laws. On January 20, 1920, the Eighteenth Amendment to the Constitution, which prohibited the production, transportation, and sale of alcoholic beverages, went into effect. While the laws did reduce consumption of alcohol, they also led to a rapid rise in criminal activity, especially organized crime; gangsters such as Lucky Luciano and Al Capone defied the government edicts.

The war had also left many people feeling disillusioned and cynical. Writers Ernest Hemingway, F. Scott Fitzgerald, Gertrude Stein, Sinclair Lewis, Edith Wharton, and H. L. Mencken criticized the materialism, greed, and other abuses they saw in society. African American authors, poets, musicians, and artists added their voices to the swelling critique of contemporary life as the "Harlem Renaissance" flourished. But while some Americans were more receptive to the influence of African American culture, this was also a time when the Ku Klux Klan thrived and Jim Crow laws still enforced segregation throughout the South.

Woodrow Wilson, who had been one of the leading advocates for peace, was serving his second term as president. But in September 1919, he collapsed under the stress of bringing an end to the war. Just a few weeks later, he suffered a stroke that left him partially paralyzed and affected his vision. He would never fully recover.

The future Body Bearers, recently back from Europe, were thrust into this rapidly changing culture. They had to transition from being participants in the most deadly war in human history to peacetime garrison life. Adjustment was difficult, as it is for all soldiers returning from all wars. The unimaginable horrors of the trenches and the uncertain peace left several of the men wondering what they had fought for. For most men, the invisible scars lingered. War altered all its participants and left them forever changed.

Americans were not the first to envision the idea of honoring an Unknown Soldier who would epitomize the sacrifice of all those who died, unidentified, in the war. As early as 1916, André Maginot, France's minister of pensions and later the mastermind of France's WWII Maginot Line, began discussing plans to exhume one of his country's unknown dead to be honored as a national hero. On November 11, 1920, his plans came to fruition with the burial of France's Unknown Soldier underneath the Arc de Triomphe. The very same day, the British held a similar ceremony and entombed their Unknown Soldier in Westminster Abbey. Italy and several other European countries followed suit shortly thereafter.

While the French were still planning their ceremony, Brigadier General William D. Connor, who replaced Pershing as commanding officer of the American Forces in France, heard about the project and suggested that the United States plan a memorial to honor one of its unknowns. But Army Chief of Staff General Peyton C. March initially thought it was a terrible idea and dismissed it out of hand. He hoped that the Graves Registration Service (GRS) would eventually identify all the unknown American dead, and moreover, he argued, the United States did not possess as grand a place as the Arc de Triomphe or Westminster Abbey for such a memorial.

However, after Americans saw news coverage of the ceremonies in London and Paris in 1920, Marie M. Meloney, the editor of *The Delineator* a popular women's magazine, also brought the idea to March. "There is in this thing, the way England has done it, the essence of democracy, and the soul of a people," Meloney wrote, attempting to appeal to the general's patriotism. "It is the kind of thing which should have found birth in America. I want you to do the fine, big human thing that no one else in America has initiated. . . . It brings patriotism home to men in a personal way. Nothing lures the mind so much as mystery."[21]

March, still unconvinced, replied with the same arguments he had made to Connor. Leaving the door open, however, he suggested that he would support the idea if it came from Congress.

Then, *The New York Times* got involved. The paper ran a column suggesting that the United States should honor an Unknown Soldier with a tomb at Arlington National Cemetery, "where the bravest lie."[22] A New York congressman, Representative Hamilton Fish, ran with the idea. During the war, Fish, a white man, had served as a captain in the 369th Infantry Regiment, a unit made up of African Americans and nicknamed "Harlem Hellfighters." Fish and his men spent 191 days on the front lines, more than any other regiment, and he received the Silver Star and the Croix de Guerre, as well as a promotion to major, for his service. On December 21, 1920, he introduced legislation that called for "bringing to the United States of a body of an unknown American killed on the battlefields of France, and for burial of the remains with appropriate ceremonies."[23] The House approved the measure by a wide majority, but Newton D. Baker, the secretary of war, convinced the Senate Committee on Military Affairs not to take up the bill because he, like March, believed that all of the unknown dead would eventually be identified.

Meanwhile, public support for the idea continued to mount. General Pershing also got on board, telling the House Committee on Military Affairs, "I favor the idea. It is a fitting tribute for the nation to pay, not only to its unknown dead, but to all who gave their lives or risked their lives in France. There has been no national expression since the war ended to give the people an opportunity to show their appreciation."[24] He also pointed out that 2,148 unknown Americans were still buried in France.

Sensing which way the political winds were blowing, Baker reversed course and backed the idea. But the next big question was where to place the Tomb. While Arlington had been the first recommendation, another option was gaining support. When it was first built, the US Capitol had a small room two stories below the Rotunda (one floor below the room known today as the "Crypt") set aside for the body of George Washington. However, Washington was never buried there. *The New York Times* got behind the idea of using this vault for the Unknown Soldier, writing, "All who visit Washington turn their steps toward the Capitol from an irresistible impulse of interest and patriotism. If the unknown soldier were laid there under an inscription that told the story of his sacrifice, the appeal would have a more solemnizing and reverential effect than if the sepulture were in the cemetery at Arlington across the Potomac."[25] Others argued in favor of placing the body in New York's Central Park.

However, the lawmakers deemed the original plan superior. On February 4, 1921, Congress approved Public Resolution 67, which called for the construction of a simple tomb for an unknown soldier at Arlington. In one of his last acts as president, Woodrow Wilson signed the bill just hours before leaving office on March 4, 1921.

Congressman Fish had pushed for a springtime ceremony to honor the Unknown Soldier, possibly Memorial Day. But John W. Weeks, the new secretary of war under incoming president Warren G. Harding, chose Armistice Day, November 11, 1921, as the most appropriate time for the burial.

Preparations for the ceremony to honor the Tomb of the Unknown Soldier progressed slowly. Congress worked for several months to appropriate funds for the Tomb, and the War Department spent weeks upon weeks finalizing its plans. Finally, on September 9, Brigadier General William Lassiter, assistant Army chief of staff, ordered the Quartermaster Corps to select an American body buried in France "so as to preclude the remotest possibility of future identification as to his name, rank, organization, service, or the battlefield on which he fell."[26]

The bulk of the work for the effort fell on the shoulders of Lieutenant Colonel G. V. S. Quackenbush. He supervised the project, assigning the teams that would exhume the bodies and detailing every aspect of the process to minimize the chance that the body would ever be identified.

Meanwhile, excavators worked to ready the site in Arlington for the burial. Atop one of the most picturesque hills in the cemetery, the men dug down twenty feet by hand and laid massive concrete footings in the burial chamber itself. They also completed a shaft that connected to the Memorial Amphitheater, constructed just one year earlier. This would be the location for the burial ceremonies as well as the monument marking the Tomb of the Unknown.

The initial monument for the Tomb of the Unknown Soldier looked quite different from what exists today. The original monument was a plain rectangular piece of marble lying nearly flat against the ground. This early marker was always intended to be temporary until Congress could appropriate the funds for something more fitting. The seventy-nine-ton Colorado marble sarcophagus sculpted by Thomas Hudson Jones was added to the memorial in the early 1930s.

The planning for the Tomb of the Unknown Soldier included the selection of eight men who would perform a highly visible role in the funeral: they would serve as Body Bearers for the Unknown Soldier, physically carrying the casket containing his remains. The secretary of war sent letters to all branches of the service, asking each to "submit the names of five warrant or non-commissioned officers of the Regular Army . . . to act as Body Bearers at the burial of an unknown American."[27] These men were to represent the finest the American military had to offer, both in their appearance and in their actions on the field. The letters listed the specific requirements: "These warrant or non-commissioned officers must not vary by more than one inch from six feet in height, measured in stocking feet, and must present the finest military appearance possible. Each and every one must have served in battle with a combat branch during the World War and have an exceptional record."[28]

The various service branches culled through thousands of citations and selected one hundred men as possible candidates. They hailed from each major branch of service—the infantry, the cavalry, the field artillery, the big guns of the coast artillery, the combat engineers, the Marine Corps, and the Navy. The collective memories of these exceptional, decorated, enlisted combat veterans representing each branch of service told the story of America's involvement in the war.

The final selection came down to General Pershing, who knew several of the men personally. Pershing reviewed scores of files, eventually choosing enlisted men who told the untellable for those who had never been to war. According to Samuel Woodfill, when Pershing came upon his name in the list, he said, "Why I've already selected that man as the outstanding soldier of the AEF."[29]

Among the thousands of files considered, Pershing chose Woodfill, Thomas Saunders, James Dell, Harry Taylor, James Delaney, Charles O'Connor, Louis Razga, and Ernest Janson to represent America's role in the Great War. The military then began the process of selecting America's greatest unknown: one of America's unidentified soldiers, who currently lay resting in hallowed ground in France.

VIII

AMERICA'S
UNKNOWN SOLDIER

CHAPTER 28

THE UNKNOWN

October 22, 1921,
US Military Cemetery in Thiaucourt, France

The first rays of dawn poked through the trees at the eastern edge of the US military cemetery in Thiaucourt, France, as Lieutenant Arthur E. Dewey and a supervisory embalmer knelt on the muddy earth beside one of the hundreds of crosses in the field. Each white marker designated the final resting place of one of the Americans who had fallen in the battle of St. Mihiel. Bundled against the morning chill, the two men began their grisly task—painstakingly sorting through the remains buried in this plot, searching for anything that could identify the man who had been interred on the site. Nearby sat a gleaming steel-gray Springfield casket, its polished surface contrasting sharply with the gritty russet soil of the grave site.

Having fallen in battle three years prior, the body was badly decomposed. Despite their best efforts to treat the deceased with respect, pieces of fabric and undoubtedly rotting flesh fell away as Dewey and the embalmer carefully exhumed the dead soldier. They sifted through the cold, damp earth with their fingers, searching for dog tags, photographs, scraps of paper, or anything else that could possibly identify who the man had been in life. They combed through the tattered clothing as well, intent upon following their orders thoroughly.

Finding nothing, they gently placed the remains on a blanket they had brought for the purpose. Then they wrapped the body and placed it into the waiting casket.

Dewey had not chosen this grave on his own. When establishing this cemetery, the GRS had assigned to each unknown soldier a unique ID number. Lieutenant Colonel G. V. S. Quackenbush, a senior officer in the GRS, had selected two of those numbers at random and had placed them in two separate envelopes: one marked "Unknown—Thiaucourt" and one marked "Alternate—Thiaucourt." Dewey's orders were clear: if he found anything that could identify the soldier whose number was in the first envelope, he was to move on to the alternate grave and repeat the process.

One day earlier, Dewey first arrived at the cemetery with his entourage, including the embalmer, two technicians, a checker, and a conveyer, traveling in a white Cadillac and a GMC truck. He had opened the "Unknown—Thiaucourt" envelope, read the number inside, and found the assigned grave. In preparation for the next day's exhumation, workers from the cemetery dug down two feet "so that the actual exhumation might be expedited the next day."[1]

At the same time, an identical scene unfolded in three other cemeteries across France. They hold Americans who had fought in three major battles. Dewey later explained, "An unknown was to be exhumed at four American Cemeteries, each of which was considered as representative of . . . one of the four major fronts on which American forces had been engaged in battle: Belleau Wood, where the Marines had added to the fame which has always followed their battle flags; Bony, in the Somme, where the National Guard from New York under their illustrious General [John] O'Ryan broke through the hither-to-fore impenetrable Hindenburg Line; Thiaucourt, that town in the Meurthe et Moselle, which owed its freedom from the oppression of the Germans to the bravery of American soldiers during the bloody St. Mihiel drive; and Romagne-sous-Montfaucon, the final resting place of thousands who gave their lives in the battle in the Argonne, the last decisive battle, which brought peace with victory to the Allied cause."[2]

Quackenbush scripted every detail of the process, even down to the number of screws that were to be used to secure the lid of the casket's wooden shipping case (six) and the tools that the embalmers were to bring with them ("2 braces and screw bits; 2 wrenches for metallic tops, and 2 claw hammers"). [3] The planners were determined that no external sign would allow identification of the body of the Unknown Soldier, or even the cemetery whence he had come. In addition, "The body was to be prepared in the usual manner, wrapped in a blanket and covered with a sheet and placed in the casket with only the corner lugs screwed down. The lid of the shipping case was to be fastened lightly, to permit easy opening." [4] In addition, they were to wrap tape around the casket inside the shipping case and adjust it, so "that it will allow the lifting of the casket from the case without any difficulty." [5]

In keeping with this purpose, Dewey's final task before departing was to destroy the "pick-up card" in the cemetery office so that no one would know which body he had removed. He lit the card on fire, and when nothing remained but ashes, he ground them into the soil beneath his boot.

From there, Dewey and his men transported the body in the truck to Romagne, where they met the crew who had exhumed the body from the Romagne cemetery. The next morning, Sunday, October 23, 1921, they left Romagne in a convoy consisting of the white Cadillac touring car, the two canvas-topped trucks carrying the caskets, and a third truck available in the event one of the other two broke down. Their destination was Châlons-sur-Marne, the capital of the Champagne region in northeastern France. "When a point about four kilometers from Châlons was reached, the convoy halted that the trucks might be cleaned and flags placed over the caskets," [6] Dewey recalled.

With the trucks now gleaming, the convoy arrived at the *hôtel de ville* (city hall) in Châlons at precisely 2:50 p.m., as ordered.

Sergeant Edward F. Younger waited at attention outside city hall at Châlons. French soldiers, "a guard of honor composed of Poilus who saw action," [7] waited in formation as Younger and six other Americans extracted the caskets from the trucks and carried them somberly inside the hall. On their way inside, the flag-draped wooden crates holding the coffins passed "between two lines of French infantry at present arms."[8]

Five minutes later, the two caskets from the other two cemeteries arrived and went through exactly the same ceremony. "The caskets were removed from the shipping cases and with the cases as pedestals, flag draped, were placed in a line in one of the small rooms on the right of the entrance hall of the Hotel de Ville," Dewey remembered.[9] According to *The New York Times*, the room was "a mass of red, white and blue flags and bunting."[10]

A French honor guard took up positions in the room, and for the next two hours, French citizens, including many war widows, passed by the coffins to pay final tribute to the American dead. They heaped flowers in front of the caskets. "Each person in that long, steady line, as he reached the door, bowed the head, offering a silent prayer, a prayer of sorrow and of thanksgiving, for the eternal rest of the souls of those Unknowns, far from home, who had given their lives in assisting France," Dewey recalled. "Hardly a dry eye was to be seen in the crowd, for nearly every French family had lost dear ones during the awful four years of the war."[11]

Later that evening, they went to further lengths to ensure that no one would be able to identify from which cemetery the Unknown Soldier had come. First, a detachment of soldiers shifted around the caskets on their platforms so that no one knew which pedestal held a casket from a particular cemetery. "Then while everyone was out of the room, the two supervisory embalmers from Romagne, who had seen none of the bodies previously, opened all the cases and shifted the remains from one to another. Thus the chance of ever identifying any of the four Unknowns was further eliminated."[12]

That night, Sergeant Edward Younger and the other pallbearers got little sleep "as the full meaning of our assignment bore in upon us," Younger said.[13] After recovering from his leg wound on Blanc Mont, Sergeant Younger had returned to the 9th Infantry. While on occupation duty with the 9th, he had likely become inebriated; the Army fined him a petty 14.98 francs for damage done in "looting a box car on December 28, 1918."[14] After the minor infraction, Younger returned to the United States and reenlisted in the US Army at Camp Travis, Texas. He received an assignment to Company E of the 50th Infantry, which had been on occupation duty since December 28, 1919. He was serving with this unit in Europe when he was chosen to be involved in the selection of the Unknown Soldier.

The night before the ceremony, Younger, a combat veteran who had participated in the heart of all the AEF's major battles, took stock of the profound nature of the event. "I felt a haunting restlessness that was different from anything I had ever known before."[15] The men had learned that very day that they were to play a role in the ceremony honoring the Unknown Soldier. They knew that one of the them would ultimately choose the body that would become the Unknown, but they went to bed not knowing which of them it would be.

The next morning, Monday, October 24, was set aside for the selection of the Unknown Soldier. It dawned bright and glorious, "almost with a note of resurrection in it," Younger recalled.[16]

The six pallbearers reported for duty. "Men, the selection has been made," the major in charge told them. "Younger will have the honor of placing the bouquet of roses on the casket which he will choose from the four assembled here, and by that act, America's Unknown Soldier will be designated."[17] Younger later said that the officer "asked about our war records and decided I had the best one."[18]

Younger, who had fought at Vaux, St. Mihiel, and Blanc Mont, felt completely overwhelmed. A quintessential doughboy, a citizen-soldier from Chicago, Younger had battled and bled for his country; yet like countless grunts from any of America's wars, he was never recognized for his valor with a medal. However, the two wound chevrons on the sleeve of his uniform, a decoration that later evolved into the Purple Heart, demonstrated he had experienced the reality of combat. Upon hearing his newest orders, he reflected on his service: "I had gone over the top many times, had known the agony of waiting for the charge. But nothing had paralyzed me as that simple announcement did."[19]

Although the actual selection would not take place until 11:00 a.m., men and women from the surrounding countryside began arriving in the town square outside the *hôtel de ville* very early in the morning. Dewey later described the scene: "No festal air prevailed, rather one of solemn dignity. The voices were low pitched and often broke with sobs."[20]

At eleven o'clock on the dot, the French military band commenced the weighty strains of Chopin's Funeral March. Above the sober music, Dewey could hear the footsteps of Sergeant Younger as he approached the rooms with the caskets. Nearby, more than fifty French and American officials watched; however, Younger entered the room alone carrying a clutch of white roses. He later described the scene:

> It was dim inside, the only light filtering in through small windows.
>
> For a moment I hesitated, and said a prayer, inaudible, inarticulate, yet real. Then I looked around.
>
> That scene will remain with me forever. Each casket was draped with a beautiful American flag. Never before had the flag seemed to have such sublime significance and beauty. About the walls were other flags, American and French; flower petals had been scattered over the floor, and outside I could hear the band playing a hymn.[21]

He began pacing slowly around the room, his thoughts racing. He wondered if one of the bodies in the room could possibly be one of his own brothers who had fallen in battle. Perhaps this man had even shielded him from a bullet that would have otherwise killed him. Younger circled the four caskets once, twice, three times. "I was numb. I couldn't choose," he recalled. "Then something drew me to the coffin second to my right on entering. I couldn't take another step. It seemed as if God raised my hand and guided me as I placed the roses on that casket. This, then, was to be America's Unknown Soldier, and by that simple act I had started him on his road to destiny."[22]

His solemn task completed, Younger saluted the fallen before leaving the room.

Immediately, that casket was taken to another room, where the remains of the Unknown inside were transferred to an ebony and silver casket in which he was to be buried. The steel casket from which the body had been taken was returned to the original room, where Dewey and the embalmers placed one of the other bodies inside it. "The three caskets were then sealed and forwarded to Romagne-sous-Montfaucon, where they were assigned new unknown numbers and immediately buried," Dewey explained.[23]

The embalmers then sealed the ebony and silver casket containing the selected remains and placed it in the lobby of the city hall. There, "covered with floral offerings from rich and poor, nations, states, and cities, and organizations of all kinds, it lay in state until five o'clock that evening."[24] On one side stood a French honor guard; on the other were representatives of the US Army interspersed with members of the Veterans of Foreign Wars and the American Legion. As members of the public passed by in mourning, the soldiers "paid their silent tribute to their brothers in arms, 'Unknown,' as the plaque on his casket read, 'but to God.' "[25]

At four in the afternoon, the poilus again lined up in a guard of honor, flanked by representatives of the French and US governments. "At five o'clock a caisson drawn by four jet black horses drew up before the steps and the casket," Dewey recalled. Soldiers carried the casket out to the caisson, and they began a slow procession to the train station. Officers mounted on horseback led the way, followed by a military band and the French infantry from the guard of honor. Then came the caisson bearing the Unknown Soldier. Behind emerged a second guard of honor consisting of soldiers from the Army of Occupation in Coblenz, the American officers present, more poilus, and finally, a variety of civilian societies with members of all ages. "The funeral cortege, with measured tread, marched the two kilometers to the railway station, between lines of French soldiers," Dewey recalled.[26] There, the casket lay in state again for another hour, while the various civilian and military groups paid their respects. "Each company as it passed dipped its torn and bloody battle standards," Dewey noted. "The officers presented sabers; the men executed 'eyes right' and presented arms."[27]

After all the mourners had their opportunity to honor the fallen dead, the casket was moved to the train. Dewey later remembered, that the train "pulled out of the station in such a slow and deliberate manner as to make one believe that the train itself realized the solemnity and importance of the occasion."[28]

Younger and the other pallbearers accompanied the Unknown on his trip to Paris, arriving there around 9:30 p.m. to no fanfare whatsoever. An American guard of honor watched over the coffin overnight before it left on the train again at 9:00 a.m. the next day for Le Havre on the French coast.

By 1:00 p.m., the train bearing the Unknown Soldier arrived in Le Havre for another ceremony. As in Châlons, a huge crowd of French citizens carrying flowers and wreaths stood soberly in the square nearby to pay their respects. France's 129th Regiment formed up in two lines, guiding the way from the train station to the city square, where a caisson drawn by six horses waited to carry the remains. First off the train was Major General Henry T. Allen, the officer in command of American forces in Germany, who greeted the various officials at the station. Next came the six pall bearers carrying the casket containing the remains of the Unknown Soldier. They marched in unison, bearing the Unknown to the gun carriage, as the church bells of Le Havre tolled in mourning. A single white rose lay atop the flag-draped casket.

Once again, a throng of French and American soldiers accompanied the Unknown on a slow procession through town. First came a French infantry regiment, then French marines, and then one hundred poilus all carrying flowers. Next came twenty-four unarmed American soldiers who were directly in front of the gun carriage that was bearing the casket. Boys and girls with many more bouquets and wreaths walked alongside the caisson, while various officials, priests, nuns, and representatives of civic organizations brought up the rear. Many had experienced the war firsthand and lost loved ones. An article in *The New York Times* noted, "It was a beautiful tribute to the French people that not one policeman was used to preserve order. With uncovered heads the Havre population showed its deepest respect."[29]

With great dignity, the procession wound through the city streets before arriving at the dock where the USS *Olympia* was berthed. A crowd in front of the ship parted as the carriage neared, making way for the Unknown Soldier.

The French officer in command of the docks at Le Havre introduced André Maginot, who was then minister of pensions. Upon his country's entry into WWI, he had resigned his position as undersecretary of state for war and enlisted in the Army. Known for his coolness under fire, he rose to the rank of sergeant. On this day, Maginot, who had been wounded at Verdun and had been awarded the Médaille Militaire, one of France's highest military awards, limped toward the podium. The sergeant thanked the Americans for their sacrifice. Addressing the coffin of the Unknown directly, he said, "You came over here for no material or selfish purpose, but in exhibition of a noble spirit. American brother, they now take you back to the great country whence you came, but France will conserve you forever in pious memory. And her soil will never forget that to it you confided your last dream."[30]

Similarly, Major General Allen also spoke to the Unknown Soldier. "The great republic which today honors you likewise pays tribute to your comrade in blue who fell with you and lives enshrined in the hearts of his countrymen, as you live in the loving memory of yours," he said. "Whoever you be, your gallant deeds are indelibly inscribed in the pages of history to the glory of your nation, and as long as free States endure will your exploits be sung."[31]

As a sign of their deep respect, France decorated the Unknown Soldier with the National Order of the Legion of Honour, the highest French order for military and civil merits.

The speeches over, the band began to play "La Marseillaise," as the pallbearers lifted the casket from the caisson and carried it across the gangplank to *Olympia*. The music segued into "The Star-Spangled Banner" as the Marines secured the coffin on the deck. As they finished, the mournful sounds of taps rang out across the harbor.

The various officials who had taken part in the ceremony then made way for the common people. "Led by nuns and priests, boys and girls of the city, with representatives of various organizations, marched on board and threw flowers upon the coffin until it was almost buried from sight," said *The New York Times*. "A few moments later, the decks were cleared, orders went around, and softly *Olympia* slipped away from the dock."[32]

A band played Chopin's Funeral March as *Olympia* floated out of the harbor and Maginot saluted the mighty ship. She was accompanied by the USS *Reuben James*; in 1941 the destroyer would fatefully become the first American warship sunk by a Nazi U-boat.* The Unknown capped the end of America's involvement in WWI, and ushered in an even more deadly era.

But that day, another world war seemed impossible. As a final sign of respect, a French battleship fired in salute while two other French warships guided *Olympia* and *Reuben James* out to sea.

---

* Laid down on April 2, 1919, and commissioned on September 24, 1920, the Clemson-class destroyer sank on October 31, 1941, near Iceland. A single torpedo fired by *U-552* hit a magazine on the *Reuben James*, blowing off its entire bow and killing 99 men out of a crew of 141.

CHAPTER 29

COMING HOME

Wednesday, November 9, 1921, Washington, DC

A single cannon boomed in salute as the USS *Olympia* entered the Potomac on a gray November day. Drizzling mist hid the ship from those awaiting its arrival on the pier at the Washington Navy Yard. The only way to mark its passage was the boom of the guns as it passed each fort and post on the river.

Then, all at once, the ship bearing the Unknown Soldier seemed to materialize like a ghostly apparition out of the rain and fog just feet from the wharf. On deck, the crew stood at attention in their dark-blue Navy uniforms as *Olympia* slowly came into port. "Astern, under the long, gray muzzle of a gun that once echoed its way into history more than twenty years ago in Manila Bay, lay the flag-draped casket. Above, a tented awning held off the dripping rain, the inner side of the canvas lined with great American flags to make a canopy for the sleeper below. At attention stood five sailors and Marines as guards of honor for the dead at each corner and the head of his bier," the Associated Press reported.[1]

On the pier, horses tossed their heads impatiently. An entire regiment of mounted cavalry and a military band also on horseback waited solemnly for the Unknown's arrival. The ship clanged out "eight bells," the signal for four o'clock, and bugles summoned the crew into formation. At the head of the gangplank, four side boys and a boatswain carrying his pipe stood ready to recognize the departure of the Unknown Soldier—their presence an honor usually reserved for full admirals.

The Body Bearers from *Olympia* stepped forward to lift the coffin as the band on *Olympia* played the familiar strains of Chopin's Funeral March. Pershing stood at attention on deck as they lifted the casket high above their shoulders and slowly paced across the deck and down the gangway. The boatswain's mournful call rang out as they stepped onto the soil of their native land. *Olympia*'s band began to play "The Star-Spangled Banner," and the gathered dignitaries stood bareheaded in the rain to honor the Unknown as they delivered his body to the waiting gun caisson pulled by six black horses.

The trip across the Atlantic had been far from uneventful. With no room for the coffin inside the ship's cabins, it had made the entire trip lashed to the deck. At one point, a terrific storm threatened to tear the body from its moorings and send it over the side. Frantically, the crew scrambled to keep the Unknown on the boat. Somehow, they managed to keep secured not only the soldier but also the now withered roses that had been placed on the casket in France. As the Body Bearers strapped the flag-draped coffin into place on the caisson, the onlookers could see the yellowed flowers that had accompanied him on his long journey.

With the Unknown Soldier now ready to process through the streets of Washington, a mounted band took over from the players on board the ship. They struck up "Onward, Christian Soldiers" as the horses of the cavalry regiment led the way at a slow trot, "sabers, cap brims, and sodden colors dripping with rain."[2] Behind them came the horse-drawn carriage bearing the Unknown, and then finally the cars carrying the various generals, admirals, and dignitaries who were part of the event.

All along the carriage's winding route, Marines lined either side of the road. Major George Hamilton, Ernest Janson's commanding officer, a hero of the fighting on Hill 142 and a native of Washington, DC, was present at the ceremony, as was Lieutenant General James Harbord, an honorary pallbearer, who later reflected on his mixed feelings, writing, "We now worship at the altar of anonymity. Whether the Unknown Soldier sought the colors eagerly or was driven into it; whether he faced the front or the rear when death came to him, we cannot say; whether he was black, white, red, or yellow—for all those races fought under our flag—we shall never know. . . . His tomb is a shrine on which flowers may be heaped without commitment. Whether an anonymous hero who died, we know not how, is more fitting for commemoration than those whose names we have and whose gallant deaths we can describe, may be a question."[3]

A few years later, Harbord would allude to the difficulties that he and the other veterans experienced after the war was over. Speaking at the bucolic cemetery at Belleau Wood during its dedication as an American battle monument, he encouraged those who survived the war to remember the actions of their brothers-in-arms as a way to combat the feelings of frustration and depression that inevitably follow war. "Now and then, a veteran, for the brief span that we still survive, will come here to live again the brave days of that distant June," he told the crowd at the cemetery. "Here will be raised the altars of patriotism; here will be renewed the vows of sacrifice and consecration to country. Hither will come our countrymen in hours of depression, and even of failure, and take new courage from this shrine of great deeds."[4]

As Harbord walked, row after row of ordinary citizens pressed as close as they could behind the military men lining the streets. Despite the rain and cold, they were determined to show their respect and admiration for their countrymen who had gone off to war, laying down their lives for the cause of freedom.

The clip-clop of the horses' hooves clattered on the wet pavement as the procession made its way to the US Capitol. There, the cavalrymen wheeled their horses into two lines and drew their sabers, creating a path for the fallen hero.

Once again, the Body Bearers hoisted the casket to their shoulders and marched it up the granite steps into the Capitol Rotunda. As they entered the majestic building, their footsteps echoed eerily through the dimly lit, nearly empty space. "The only lights were those high among the pillars above the sculptured walls and the last fading gleams of day through the high windows," wrote an AP reporter.[5] As they laid the coffin on a flag-draped platform, the honor guard took up their positions around the body.

They had been in place only a few moments when a sharp sound from outside announced the arrival of the Unknown's first visitors: President Warren Harding and his wife, Florence. A command rang out and then "the flurry of drawn steel as the sabers of the cavalry leaped out again to present."[6] They passed quietly under the canopy of swords and entered the solemn chamber.

As the president and first lady stepped into the room, photographers began capturing images of the scene, the clicking of their cameras the only sound. Mrs. Harding approached the casket first, laying a wide white ribbon she had stitched herself across the casket. The president stepped forward and pinned to the ribbon a silver shield of the United States bearing forty-eight stars, symbolizing that "the heart of the nation . . . goes with this soldier to his tomb."[7] Then he placed a huge wreath of crimson roses near the head of the coffin.

A few other dignitaries laid more flowers on the casket. Vice President Calvin Coolidge, Speaker of the House Frederick H. Gillett, Chief Justice and former president William Howard Taft, Secretary of War John W. Weeks, and Secretary of the Navy Edwin Denby all set floral tributes around the platform. The last to honor the Unknown Soldier that night was the man who best understood the terrible cost of the war. General John Pershing stepped forward with a "wreath of giant pink chrysanthemums, and as he placed it, the officer paused a moment, then stepped back a pace or two and, drawing his figure to its full height, lifted his hand to cap brim in rigid salute to the dead."[8]

As silently as they had arrived, these first visitors melted away into the fading twilight. Thousands would visit the next day, but for the night, the Unknown Soldier lay alone with only his honor guard and the statues of Abraham Lincoln and Ulysses S. Grant keeping vigil.

Thursday, November 10, 1921, US Capitol, Washington, DC
Workers scurried to place the last rope stanchions in place, preparing for the deluge of visitors who would pay their respects to America's

unknown fallen soldier. The press reported, "The sun drove the last sullen cloud away over the distant hills, to leave a glorious, rain-washed sweep of blue, shot with golden light above the dome and the wakening city."[9] Slowly, people began to assemble outside.

At 8:00 a.m., the colossal bronze doors of the Capitol swung wide. A male choir inside commenced singing "America the Beautiful" as members of the public filed in silently. Thousands of mourners passed by—sometimes as many as one hundred per minute. Among them were representatives of America's allies in the war who brought fresh flowers grown in their native lands. The Knights of Columbus, the National Association for the Advancement of Colored People, the Daughters of the American Revolution, and other civic groups sent official delegates, many of whom brought flowers or delivered short speeches at prescheduled times.

Every mourner passed by the honor guard, five soldiers "still as though carved from bronze in their khaki trappings," wrote the Associated Press. "At the head, arms rigid at his sides, his own head bent forward until the tan brim of his cap hid his eyes, stood the non-commissioned officer, the red of his chevrons coloring his sleeve. At each corner, facing inward toward the center, stood a soldier, rifle butt grounded on the stone flagging, body rigidly erect, but also with the head bent forward until cap brim was level with the point of his gleaming bayonet. These soldiers moved not a muscle except at stated intervals when slight changes of position, made simultaneously, eased the physical strain."[10] Throughout the day, the members of the honor guard alternated several times; however, every soldier who served executed his orders to be silent and motionless in reverence.

Among the most poignant scenes were those when family members of soldiers who had perished in the war paid their respects. Small children laid flowers or handwritten notes near the bier. Grandparents shuffled by, unashamed of the tears streaming down their faces. But the most moving of all were the mothers crying for their lost sons. At one point, "two Hoboken war mothers approached, saluted, and added their wreath," the AP wrote. "The ordeal, however, overtaxed one of them, who sobbingly gave way to her grief and had to be assisted out of the Rotunda."[11]

The Capitol police estimated that between ninety thousand and ninety-six thousand paid their respects to the Unknown Soldier that day—the piles of flowers around the casket growing ever higher until the scent of the blossoms became nearly overpowering. It was almost midnight before the last mourner passed though the great hall under the dome, yet outside remained people who had to be turned away. The Associated Press report painted the scene as the day of mourning came to a close: "The lights in the vaulted chamber dwindled and died to a dim glow, the great bronze doors swung shut, and, alone again with the tireless comrades who kept the last vigil with him, America's Unknown from France was left to await dawn and the coming of the cortege in which the President and all the highest figures in American national life will walk humbly to carry him to the grave."[12]

Friday, November 11, 1921, Washington, DC
The thundering boom of the guns at Fort Myer shattered the early morning silence on the second anniversary of Armistice Day. They would continue to sound intermittently throughout the morning as the body of the Unknown Soldier slowly proceeded to Arlington National Cemetery. The fair weather of the previous day continued, the beaming sunlight a sharp contrast to the somber grief felt by the mourning nation.

At 8:00 a.m., an army band began playing a dirge in the plaza outside the Capitol. In time with the music, the Body Bearers deliberately mounted the steps leading to the Rotunda under the Capitol dome. Sergeant Samuel Woodfill, handpicked by General Pershing for his bravery in battle, led the way, accompanied by Sergeant Harry Taylor of the Cavalry, Sergeant Thomas D. Saunders of the Combat Engineers, Sergeant Louis Razga of the Coast Artillery Corps, Staff Sergeant James W. Dell of the Field Artillery, Chief Torpedoman James Delaney of the US Navy, Chief Water Tender Charles Leo O'Connor of the US

Navy, and Sergeant Major Ernest A. Janson of the US Marine Corps. Undoubtedly, their minds harkened back to the battles where they had fought and watched comrades die, likely wondering if the body they were honoring that day was someone they had known.

Meticulously, they again raised the flag-draped casket, festooned with flowers bestowed by the mourners, and carried it down the east steps to the waiting black-draped caisson drawn by six black horses. Behind the Body Bearers appeared twelve more honorary pallbearers, officers from the US Army, Navy, and Marines who had served in World War I. When they had strapped down the casket, the funeral procession marched onto Pennsylvania Avenue.

The event planners had envisioned General Pershing grandly leading the cortège on horseback; however, he humbly declined, saying that he considered himself a mourner and preferred to walk. His place was with his men, with those who best understood the cost of the war. By graciously choosing to follow the Unknown on foot, he once again displayed the nobility and quiet authority that typified his command. In his place, Major General Harry Hill Bandholtz, commander of the Military District of Washington, rode with several other officers. An Army band and drum corps trailed, playing in quick time, followed by an infantry regiment, a field artillery battalion, and a troop of cavalry. Four chaplains proceeded in front of the caisson that carried the Unknown.

Immediately behind the caisson walked the chief mourner: President Harding. Accompanying him were General Pershing and many of the dignitaries who had paid tribute to the Unknown on the first night his body lay in state in the Capitol, as well as governors of nearby states, congressional representatives, and other officials. All walked except for former president Wilson, who was unable to do so after his stroke; he instead rode in an old-fashioned carriage. Following another drum corps were some of America's most heroic warriors: the soldiers who had received the Medal of Honor. The phalanx of courage and honor marched eight abreast. Its ranks included Sergeant Alvin York, who had single-handedly killed at least twenty-five enemy soldiers and captured 132 more in the Meuse-Argonne, and Lieutenant Colonel

Charles Whittlesey, the hero of the "Lost Battalion." Marching behind the Medal of Honor men were long columns of other veterans from the Great War, nurses from the Red Cross, representatives of various civic organizations, and the Gold Star Mothers, who had lost sons in battle.

Tens of thousands of people lined the streets to witness the procession; members of the infantry stationed along the route assisted with crowd control. Many of the onlookers waved small American flags; some carried handkerchiefs to wipe their tears. From time to time, they erupted in cheers, particularly for President Wilson, the Medal of Honor phalanx, and the Gold Star Mothers.

As the five-mile journey continued, the procession dwindled somewhat. At the White House, President Harding and many of the dignitaries opted to travel by car for the remainder of the journey. The band halted at the Potomac Bridge, and "some of the older officers of the escort fell out, leaving it to the hardy men of today's army to escort their dead comrade up the long hill to the roll only of muffled drums."[13] Pershing, however, made the entire trek on foot.

As the cavalcade reached Arlington, most of the cavalry and artillery stopped and stood at attention. Only one gun battery, primed to fire a final salute, entered the cemetery. A Marine band stationed at Arlington's gate began playing a slow dirge as the cortege entered the cemetery. The pace grew more solemn as the body of the Unknown Soldier approached the amphitheater, the site of the funeral. Although Congress had authorized its construction in 1913, work on the Memorial Amphitheater had not begun until 1915, and its dedication took place on May 15, 1920. The dominant feature of the amphitheater was an extensive colonnade made of Danby marble from Vermont. Across the frieze at the top of the colonnade, artisans had carved the names of forty-four US battles spanning the War for Independence to the Spanish-American War. Front and center was a wide stage with the words of Abraham Lincoln inscribed above: "We here highly resolve that these dead shall not have died in vain." Down the sides of the stage were the names of fourteen US Army generals and fourteen US Navy admirals—all of whom had served prior to World War I. As they entered the somber space and found seats in the many rows of benches, the mourners passed beneath a Latin inscription that would become both famous and infamous given the scale of the Great War's death toll: "*Dulce et decorum est pro patria mori*," which translates as "It is sweet and fitting to die for one's country."

In a now familiar routine, Woodfill, Taylor, Razga, Saunders, Dell, Delaney, Janson, and O'Connor gently lifted the casket of the Unknown Soldier above their shoulders. Step by step they carried him through the high-pillared colonnade. At the front, they laid the Unknown reverently upon a high platform engulfed by flowers. The honorary pallbearers followed behind and took their places surrounding the Tomb, as President Harding prepared to give his address.

Just before noon, the band struck up "The Star-Spangled Banner," ushering in Bishop Charles Brent, an Episcopalian who had been senior chaplain of the American Forces in Europe. He stepped forward to offer the invocation. "Help us fittingly to honor our unknown soldiers who gave their all in laying sure foundations of international commonweal," he prayed. "Help us to keep clear the obligation we have toward all worthy soldiers, living and dead, that their sacrifices and their valor fade not from our memory. Temper our sorrow, we pray Thee, through the assurance, which came from the sweetest lips that ever uttered words, 'Blessed are they that mourn, for they shall be comforted.' Be thou our comforter."[14]

As his prayer concluded, a trumpet sounded the call to attention, and the church bells of Washington, DC, rang out the noon hour, signaling the commencement of two minutes of nationwide silence decreed by presidential proclamation. As one, those in the amphitheater rose to their feet and bowed their heads. Throughout the country, the fledgling telephone service went quiet as people everywhere paid their respects. At the conclusion of the two minutes, the Marine band began the opening bars of "America (My Country, 'Tis of Thee)," and everyone sang along.

Then it was time for President Harding to speak—an address noteworthy not only because he would honor the country's fallen, but also because the sound of his voice would be transmitted electrically for the

first time ever to crowds gathered in New York, Chicago, and San Francisco. It was not a radio address—that would be possible the following
summer. Instead, his voice traveled over wires to special amplifiers in
the three cities, employing technology similar to that of the telephone
service. An artricle in *The New York Times* explained, "The President's
words will travel more than 3,500 miles in its simultaneous trips from
Washington to California and to New York and will be louder at the
end of the journeys than at the beginning."[15]

The article noted, "At the start, the President's voice will enter several
receivers, as the ordinary speaker's voice enters the telephone mouthpiece,
the sound waves are being translated into electrical waves. This current of
electricity carrying the impression of the President's voice is passed into a
vacuum tube. Another current 1,000 times as great is passed through the
tube at the same time."[16] Special repeater stations, set up every 250 miles,
amplified the signal, enabling the long-distance transmission.

The previous day, workers had tested the system, known as the Bell
Loud Talker, and a hundred people who listened from Madison Square
Garden and Madison Square Park had been "amazed at the clarity and
strength"[17] of the transmitted sound. "The words were so clear and the
voice was so strong that a person standing in any part of the Garden
could understand perfectly. Bugle calls transmitted from the cemetery
sounded as if they were being blown in the building."[18] To transmit the
sound, workers had set up twelve horn-shaped speakers inside the building and twelve larger horns outside at Twenty-Sixth Street and Madison
Avenue for the overflow crowds. The outdoor speakers performed so
well that "the voices of a quartette singing could be heard above the roar
of traffic even at the corner of Twenty-Third Street and Broadway."[19]

As Harding prepared to speak, workers fiddled with the equipment
connecting similar amplifiers on-site at the cemetery. The technology,
amazing for its time, broadcast Harding's words for all to hear:

> Mr. Secretary of War and Ladies and Gentlemen: We are met
> today to pay the impersonal tribute. The name of him whose
> body lies before us took flight with his imperishable soul. We

know not whence he came, but only that his death marks him with the everlasting glory of an American dying for his country.

He might have come from any one of millions of American homes. Some mother gave him in her love and tenderness, and, with him, her most cherished hopes. Hundreds of mothers are wondering today, finding a touch of solace in the possibility that the nation bows in grief over the body of one she bore to live and die, if need be, for the Republic. . . .

Sleeping in these hallowed grounds are thousands of Americans who have given their blood for the baptism of freedom and its maintenance, armed exponents of the nation's conscience. It is better and nobler for their deeds. Burial here is rather more than a sign of the Government's favor, it is a suggestion of a tomb in the heart of the nation, sorrowing for its noble dead.[20]

He went on for several minutes, waxing eloquent about the horrors of modern war:

It was my fortune recently to see a demonstration of modern warfare. It is no longer a conflict in chivalry, no more a test of militant Manhood. It is only cruel, deliberate, scientific destruction. . . .

There was the rain of ruin from the aircraft, the thunder of artillery, followed by the unspeakable devastation wrought by bursting shells; there were mortars belching their bombs of desolation; machine guns concentrating their leaden storms; there was the infantry, advancing, firing, and falling—like men with souls sacrificing for the decision. The flying missiles were revealed by illuminating tracers, so that we could note their flight and appraise their deadliness. . . . As this panorama of unutterable destruction visualized the horrors of modern conflict, there grew on me the sense of the failure of a civilization which can leave its problems to such cruel arbitrament. Surely no one in authority, with human attributes and a full appraisal of the patriotic loyalty of his countrymen, could ask the manhood of kingdom, empire, or republic to make such sacrifice until all reason had failed, until every effort of love and consideration for fellow-men had been exhausted, until freedom itself and inviolate honor had been brutally threatened."[21]

Harding concluded with a call that the Unknown Soldier's "sacrifice, and that of the millions dead, shall not be in vain. There must be, there shall be, the commanding voice of a conscious civilization against armed warfare."[22] He added, "As we return this poor clay to its mother soil, garlanded by love and covered with the decorations that only nations can bestow, I can sense the prayers of our people, of all peoples, that this Armistice Day shall mark the beginning of a new and lasting era of peace on earth, goodwill among men."[23] And then he led the entire nation in the Lord's Prayer.

His speech concluded, President Harding had one more remaining task left: awarding the Unknown Soldier two of the nation's highest honors for military service. He presented the Distinguished Service Cross, which is awarded for extreme gallantry and risk of life in actual combat with an armed enemy force. First awarded during WWI, the Distinguished Service Cross is the second-highest military award that a member of the US Army can receive. Harding also pinned to the casket the most prestigious medal awarded to members of the American military: the Medal of Honor.

Next several foreign dignitaries added to the Unknown Soldier's honors. Lieutenant General Jules Marie Alphonse Jacques awarded the Belgian Croix de Guerre. Admiral Earl Beatty bestowed the Victoria Cross of Great Britain, which had never before been given to anyone who had not hailed from Great Britain. Marshal Foch, Supreme Allied Commander, spoke with profound emotion about the Unknown's sacrifice before giving him the French Croix de Guerre with Palm, the highest honor of valor for soldiers or noncommissioned officers in the French Army. General Armando Diaz added the Italian gold medal for bravery; Prince Antoine Bibesco bestowed the Romanian Virtute Militară; Dr. Dedrich Stephenek conferred the Czechoslovak War Cross; and Prince

Kazimierz Lubomirski, the first Polish ambassador to the United States, granted him the Virtuti Militari. All these accolades made the Unknown Soldier America's most decorated World War I soldier.

The awards accorded, the ceremony ended with more hymns, the recitation of Psalm 23, and a Scripture lesson delivered by a chaplain.

As the Marine Band played "Our Honored Dead," the eight Body Bearers proceeded forward one last time to carry the Unknown Soldier to his grave. Flanked by the general officers serving as honorary pallbearers, the men slowly marched less than a hundred yards to the location of the Tomb. The dignitaries, including President and Mrs. Harding, as well as representatives of mothers who had lost sons to the war, followed behind them. The Body Bearers tenderly placed the coffin in position. New York Congressman Hamilton Fish, who had authored the resolution to honor the Unknown Soldier, laid a wreath atop the coffin, as did two mothers representing all those who had lost sons to the war.

As he watched the somber ceremony, Whittlesey, the commander of the "Lost Battalion" sat rigid, his eyes fixed straight ahead. He hardly uttered a word during the ceremony, but at one point he turned to Captain George G. McMurtry, the executive officer of the Lost Battalion and also a recipient of the Medal of Honor, and said, "I keep wondering if the Unknown Soldier is one of my men. . . . I should not have come here."[24] Whittlesey, like many of the Body Bearers and other World War I soldiers, wrestled with the aftereffects of the war. He felt guilt about the men who had died under his command, and the living veterans who visited his law office discussing their wounds and ailments provided a constant reminder of the horror of war. Farley Granger expressed those feelings, writing, "[Are] the brave men who now lay forgotten in our government hospitals, broken in mind and spirit as a result of the war, any less heroes as those who died in battle? Perhaps the sacrifice of the living is even greater. Still they live on forgotten."[25] All this suffering manifested itself in night terrors for Whittlesey. "I'll hear the wounded screaming again," he said. "I have nightmares about them; can't remember when I last had a good night's sleep." During one of his night terrors, he awoke after seeing in his dreams the face of a young soldier, "cold in death," touching his cheek.[26] Tragically, he would take his own life before the month's end.

One final American stepped forward to honor the Unknown on behalf of his people. Chief Plenty Coups, present throughout the ceremony, removed the feathered war bonnet from his head and placed it on the sarcophagus alongside his coup stick. The symbols were meant to honor the sacrifices of the many American Indians who, like Body Bearer Sergeant Thomas D. Saunders, had served their country heroically.

Before being elected chief of the Mountain Crow tribe at the age of twenty-nine, Plenty Coups, then known as "Buffalo Bull Facing the Wind," had lived the life of a traditional Native warrior, which included fighting against the Sioux and Cheyenne. He experienced many visions, including a vision of the elders, interpreted to mean that the white people would eventually take over all Native lands. As chief, Plenty Coups became outspoken in his belief that Indians should cooperate with non-Native people, but he continued to advocate for his people in Washington, DC. He told his fellow tribe members, "Education is your greatest weapon. With education you are the white man's equal, without education you are his victim and so shall remain all of your lives. Study, learn, help one another always. Remember there is only poverty and misery in idleness and dreams—but in work there is self-respect and independence."[27]

On this day, the chief addressed the crowd:

I feel it an honor to the red man that he takes part in this great event, because it shows that the thousands of Indians who fought in the great war are appreciated by the white man. I am glad to represent all the Indians of the United States in placing on the grave of this noble warrior this coup stick and war bonnet, every eagle feather of which represents a deed of valor by my race. I hope that the Great Spirit will grant that these noble warriors have not given up their lives in vain and that there will be peace to all men hereafter. This is the Indians' hope and prayer.[28]

As the casket was lowered into the sarcophagus, the Unknown Soldier again came in contact with earth from the country where he had fallen in battle. "Over the floor of the narrow crypt in which he will sleep forever, soil from France had been spread; earth from the country where his death blood was poured out on a stricken field that it might remain free soil," explained the Associated Press. "It was brought with the casket from France, and forever the nameless one of America who died for France and for America will rest on French soil here in his own home earth."[29]

As the casket of the Unknown Soldier settled into the ground, two artillery pieces sounded in tribute. Then a lone bugler blew the mournful tones of taps, and the burial ceremonies ended with a twenty-one-gun salute.

At long last, the Unknown Soldier had come home to rest.

An AP reporter poetically captured the poignant moment:

Under the wide and starry skies of his own home-land America's unknown dead from France sleeps tonight, a soldier home from the wars.

Alone, he lies in the narrow cell of stone that guards his body; but his soul has entered into the spirit that is America. Wherever liberty is held close in men's hearts, the honor and the glory and the pledge of high endeavor poured out over this nameless one of fame, will be told and sung by Americans for all time.[30]

For most Americans, the Tomb of the Unknown Soldier serves as a symbol of who we are as a nation. For the Body Bearers, it was much more personal. As happens after every war, most fought their own private, hidden wars when the conflict was over.[31] They carried the Unknown home, bearing the burden and honor of the forgotten generation who changed the world.

Afterword

The Tomb of the Unknown Soldier

The Tomb of the Unknown Soldier, America's greatest memorial, began as a simple stone marker placed atop the Tomb in 1921. But this first version was far too humble to serve as the country's homage to the thousands who sacrificed their lives in the Great War. In 1926, Congress set aside funds to envision and construct a more fitting monument.

A new design, the brainchild of architect Lorimer Rich and sculptor Thomas Hudson Jones, replaced the original slab in 1931. While simple, the new marble monument, sculpted from a fifty-six-ton block of Yule marble excavated from a Colorado mountainside, brought a new weight and gravitas to the Tomb. Wreaths representing six World War I battles adorn two of its sides. On the third, Greek figures symbolize Peace, Victory, and Valor. And on the fourth side, an inscription:

> HERE RESTS IN
> HONORED GLORY
> AN AMERICAN
> SOLDIER
> KNOWN BUT TO GOD

From the moment Edward Younger first selected his body to serve as a symbol for the nation's nameless dead, the Unknown Soldier has drawn crowds. The site brings patriotism home in a personal way. In the early days, some of those who came to pay their respects liked to picnic on the site, and some even used the stone marker as a table. To prevent this sort of activity, guards began keeping watch over the Tomb in 1925.

Over the years, the Tomb guards developed elaborate rituals to honor the dead. Today, members of the Army's 3rd US Infantry Regiment, "The Old Guard," stand sentinel over the Tomb twenty-four hours a day, every day, regardless of the weather. They "walk the mat" with honed precision in an endless cycle: twenty-one steps across the black mat that lies across the Tomb; twenty-one seconds standing ramrod-straight while facing the Tomb; twenty-one steps down to the other side of the mat; twenty-one seconds facing the Tomb; twenty-one seconds facing down the mat. Then, the cycle repeats, day and night, without end.

These carefully selected soldiers serve in twenty-four hour shifts. They spend hours preparing themselves and their uniforms for duty. They don't wear rank insignias while guarding the Tomb, so as not to outrank the Unknown Soldier. Thousands have applied for the privilege of serving on the honor guard. Only a select few meet the rigorous requirements and pass the strenuous tests required for service.

The living are not the Unknown Soldier's only companions.

The "War to End All Wars" was far from the last conflict fought by America's soldiers, sailors, airmen, and Marines. Men and women from the US armed forces eventually fought in a second World War.

Then Korea.

Then Vietnam.

In each war, thousands of those who perished evaded identification. After each war, the nation selected another body to represent the Unknowns of that generation. Each time, a war hero chose the fallen soldier who would epitomize the sacrifices made by so many of his comrades.

The process of selecting an Unknown Soldier from World War II began in 1945, but the outbreak of the Korean War delayed the eventual burial. In the spring of 1958, the military exhumed six bodies from three cemeteries where unknowns from the Pacific Theater had been buried. At a ceremony in Hawaii, under unusually gray skies, US

Air Force Colonel Glenn T. Eagleston, an ace fighter pilot who flew nearly one hundred combat missions during the war, placed a lei on a casket he chose to represent a soldier from the Pacific Theater. In a similar process, officials disinterred thirteen soldiers who died in the European Theater and transported the bodies to France. There, US Army Major General Edward Joseph O'Neil, a battalion commander and then a supply and logistical support officer, laid a wreath on the casket that would represent those who fought in Europe, Africa, and the Middle East. With the Army and the Air Force already playing a role in the selection process, it fell to Navy Hospital Corpsman First Class William R. Charette, who at the time was one of its only active duty Medal of Honor recipients, to select between the two Unknowns. Following the tradition established after World War I, he laid a wreath on one of the caskets to signify his final selection.

By the time of the selection of the Unknown from World War II, the Korean War was over. More than thirty-six thousand US troops died in the conflict, many of them never to be identified. The Unknowns were buried in Hawaii, and in an all-too-familiar procedure, military officers exhumed four bodies to serve as candidates for burial in the Tomb of the Unknown Soldier. On the day before the selection of the Unknown from WWII, US Army Master Sergeant Ned Lyle, who had been wounded in Korea and received the Distinguished Service Cross for "extraordinary heroism in action against enemy aggressor forces in the vicinity of Mundung-ni, Korea," placed a wreath of carnations on the casket he selected as the Korean War's Unknown Soldier.

The two Unknowns traveled together to Washington, DC, where they lay in state in the US Capitol. On May 30, 1958, military leaders again headed a procession through the city, concluding with the burial of both bodies at the Tomb of the Unknown Soldier in Arlington. Two sets of six of Body Bearers, from World War II and Korea, many of the men Medal of Honor recipients, each with a unique extraordinary story that represented his war, laid the Unknowns to rest.

A fourth Unknown joined the trio in 1984. The previous ceremonies had involved elaborate measures to ensure that the Unknowns from World War I, World War II, and the Korean War could never be identified; but this time everyone knew that the Vietnam War body, designated "X-26," had fallen near a stream in An Loc, Vietnam. Marine Sergeant Major Allan J. Kellogg, Jr., who received the Medal of Honor after throwing himself on a live grenade to save his fellow Marines, officially designated him as the Vietnam War Unknown.

The body lay in state for three days before the funeral on Memorial Day in 1984. In a moving speech, President Ronald Reagan told the crowds, "We must remember that we cannot today, as much as some might want to, close this chapter in our history, for the war in Southeast Asia still haunts a small but brave group of Americans—the families of those still missing in the Vietnam conflict. They live day and night with uncertainty, with an emptiness, with a void that we cannot fathom. Today some sit among you. Their feelings are a mixture of pride and fear. They're proud of their sons or husbands, fathers or brothers who bravely and nobly answered the call of their country. But some of them fear that this ceremony writes a final chapter, leaving those they love forgotten." President Reagan called on Congress and the nation to help those families. "Our dedication to their cause must be strengthened with these events today. We write no last chapters. We close no books. We put away no final memories. An end to America's involvement in Vietnam cannot come before we've achieved the fullest possible accounting of those missing in action."[1]

Fourteen years later, America kept Reagan's promise to the family of the Vietnam War Unknown. After evidence surfaced suggesting that the Unknown was US Air Force Captain Michael J. Blassie, who had gone missing in 1972, the Department of Defense exhumed the body again and conducted DNA testing that confirmed the Unknown was Blassie. His family laid his body to rest in Blassie's home state, Missouri. In a symbolic gesture, his crypt at the Tomb of the Unknown Soldier was left empty. The marble slab above now reads, "Honoring and Keeping Faith with America's Missing Servicemen."

In this day of technological advances, the servicemen and -women who fall in combat can almost always be identified. We may never again have the need—or the honor—of burying another soldier in the Tomb of the Unknown Soldier.

But that does not diminish the significance of the monument in modern life. If anything, the Tomb has become more poignant for modern Americans who no longer face the possibility of remaining unidentified after dying in battle. We recognize the price paid by the hundreds of thousands of soldiers, sailors, airmen, and Marines who made the ultimate sacrifice. Millions of Americans have visited the Tomb, silently offering gratitude to those who died so that we might be free. As President Reagan proclaimed in his speech at the Tomb, we say to them, "Thank you, dear son. May God cradle you in His loving arms."[2]

Epilogue

General John J. "Black Jack" Pershing: After the Great War, Congress created a new rank specifically for Pershing: General of the Armies of the United States. While some wanted Black Jack to run for president, he chose not to campaign. He continued to serve in the US Army until his sixty-fourth birthday, on September 13, 1924, when regulations required him to retire. He remained active in civic organizations and wrote a memoir, titled *My Experiences in the World War*, for which he received a Pulitzer Prize.

Congress recognized the need for federal oversight of American cemeteries and monuments abroad and created the American Battlefield Monuments Commission. Pershing was elected the organization's first chairman, a role in which he served until his death. As chairman, he did much to construct, maintain, and commemorate cemeteries, monuments, and battlefields, preserving America's memory of WWI.

During the lead-up to World War II, Pershing actively campaigned for the United States to assist the Allies, particularly the United Kingdom.

Pershing remained in contact with his lover, Micheline Resco, and she spent considerable time in the United States after the war. While she lived in France, the two wrote letters to each other in a secret code. During WWII, she lived in America; Pershing later married Resco in a private ceremony performed by a Catholic priest in 1946 at Walter Reed General Hospital, where he was recovering from a stroke. On July 15, 1948, General Pershing died of coronary artery disease and congestive heart failure. The General of the Armies joined the Unknown Soldier and countless other doughboys in Arlington National Cemetery.

Sergeant Edward F. Younger: Younger married Agnes Anna Wasco, the daughter of Eastern European immigrants, in 1923, when both were twenty-five. After the war, he led a quiet life.

The man who selected the Unknown Soldier tried but failed to escape the fame that his involvement with the Unknown brought. He returned to his home in Chicago, where he worked for decades in the post office, and he and Agnes raised a son and a daughter. Community organizations regularly invited him to speak, particularly on Armistice Day and Memorial Day, and he frequently obliged, although with unfailing humility, he downplayed his role in world events. A newspaper story from 1939 explained, "Too many people wanted to make him a hero. . . . He doesn't like war. He doesn't believe in war. He didn't think he was going to get into a war when he enlisted in the infantry in January 1917, and he didn't want to fight anyway. He enlisted for the 'excitement,' he says."[1]

When World War II loomed on the horizon, Younger told a reporter that he and his fellow soldiers "tried to save democracy—at least that's what they told us we were fighting for—and they did save it once. Now it has to be saved a second time. . . . However, I'm against America getting into this war. We have no business fighting in Europe under any circumstances. We should stay at home. War is useless."[2]

Younger visited the Tomb of the Unknown Soldier at least five times. Gold Star Mothers frequently asked him if the Unknown Soldier could be their son. He always told them he didn't know, but that it was possible.

He died of a heart condition in 1942 and was buried in Arlington, not far from the Tomb of the Unknown Soldier.

Body Bearers

Chief Gunner's Mate James Delaney: For his heroism, Delaney received the Navy Cross, the second-highest decoration bestowed by the US Navy and the equivalent of the US Army Distinguished Service Cross. The former POW retired from the military in 1933 but again served his country in WWII. He returned to Beverly, Massachusetts, where he lived with his wife, Eleanor. He died of lung cancer just days after Christmas in 1954.

Gunnery Sergeant Ernest A. Janson: After the war, Janson remained in the Marines, working for several years as a recruiter. He retired with the rank of sergeant major in 1926. A native New Yorker, Janson moved to Long Island after leaving the military and died just four years later of an embolism at the age of forty-nine. He was buried in Evergreen Cemetery in Brooklyn. He was survived by three brothers and a sister.

Color Sergeant James W. Dell: Dell spent thirty-two years in the Army before retiring as a master sergeant. He then continued to serve his country and the US military by working as the superintendent of several national cemeteries in Kentucky, Nebraska, and Texas. His first wife, Pauline, died in 1948, and he later married Viola Browning Hite. He died in Florida in 1967 at the age of ninety-one, and he was buried at St. Augustine National Cemetery.

Corporal Thomas D. Saunders: After the war, Saunders appeared to fade from history. He spent some time in San Antonio, Texas, while fellow Body Bearer James W. Dell also lived there, but little else is known of his life. The Native American hero died in November 1947 and was buried in Golden Gate National Cemetery.

Chief Water Tender Charles Leo O'Connor: Little is known about O'Connor's activities after the war. However, a tombstone in Arlington records that Charles Leo O'Connor of Massachusetts who served in the Naval Reserve died in 1934.

First Sergeant Harry Taylor: The cavalry trooper remained in the Army until at least 1927. He and his wife, Millie, had four children.

Sergeant Samuel Woodfill: Woodfill left the Army in 1923 and returned to Fort Thomas, Kentucky, with his wife, Lorena. The couple bought a farm.

Woodfill became something of a local celebrity, complete with an elementary school named in his honor. However, he struggled financially during much of his life. Farm debts accumulated, and the man Pershing considered the greatest soldier of the AEF was forced to take odd jobs to prevent the loss of his land. Like many of the other Body Bearers, he had mixed feelings about his participation. "I'm tired of being a circus pony," he once said. "Every time there is something doing they trot me out to perform."[3]

When World War II began, the Army awarded Woodfill a commission as a major, and he served as an instructor. In 1944, he retired from the military again and moved to a farm in Indiana. He died of natural causes in 1951 and was initially buried in Indiana before his body was moved to Arlington.

First Sergeant Louis Razga: Eventually promoted to master sergeant, Razga went on to serve out his thirty years with the Coast Artillery Corps. In 1929, he faced a court-martial after being charged with "transporting liquor while also carrying a shotgun" during Prohibition.[4] The judge dismissed the charges after the trial ended with a hung jury. Razga retired in 1935, and he settled in Granogue, Delaware, with his wife, Margaret, and two daughters. Putting his military skills to use, he worked for a time as a guard for the prominent Du Pont family, who lived in the area. One of Razga's daughters shared his enthusiasm for military life and followed in his footsteps by becoming an Army nurse.

In 1941, at the age of fifty-two, Razga endeavored to serve in World War II, but was told he would have to "sit this one out." According to a newspaper account, doctors pronounced him "in splendid physical condition," and he was "chafing at the bit to get back in service again and volunteer his service to the Army in any position or place that the Army might be able to use him. He is particularly desirous of serving in the foreign countries where his knowledge of the people, languages and territory might be of military value."[5]

After his first wife died, Razga remarried and later moved to Florida. He died in 1959.

SUPPORTING WITNESSES

Kapitänleutnant Victor Dieckmann: Under Dieckmann's command, *U-61* sank many more Allied ships. The boat went missing after March 23, 1918, with all hands lost.

Major George Wallis Hamilton: Hamilton, who received the Army Distinguished Service Cross, the Navy Cross, and the Croix de Guerre, did not survive long after the war. He became a Marine Corps pilot, and in July 1922, he was participating in a mock air battle over Gettysburg when the plane he was piloting plummeted to the ground.

Captain John William Thomason, Jr.: Until his death in 1944, Thomason continued to serve in the US Marines, rising to the rank of lieutenant colonel. In 1926, he published the outstanding *Fix Bayonets!*. He authored, and in some cases illustrated, at least a half dozen other books, as well as numerous short stories and magazine articles. He served in Cuba, Haiti, Nicaragua, and China, as well as aboard a Navy ship, and worked in the Office of Naval Intelligence. He and his wife, Leda, had one son, who also became a Marine but died in a plane crash in 1947. The US Navy named a destroyer after Thomason (DD-760).

Corporal Elton Mackin: Following his honorable discharge from the Marine Corps in 1919, Mackin settled in his hometown, Lewiston, New York, and struggled with "shell shock." During the Great Depression, he moved to Ohio, where he spent the rest of his life. He recorded his recollections of the war. Excerpts of his manuscripts were published in several magazines during his lifetime, but his story remained largely unknown until long after his death in 1974.

Lieutenant Farley Granger: As the owner of a Willys-Overland automobile dealership, Granger was initially very successful after the war. But the stock market crash of 1929 and the Great Depression took its toll on the family business, and eventually the bankrupt Granger used his last vehicle to escape his creditors, moving his family to Hollywood, California. The family struggled to make a living. However, his son,

Farley Jr., became a popular film, television, and stage actor. Despite all the hardship he experienced, Granger remained optimistic and even nostalgic for his time as a soldier. As with many combat veterans, part of his spirit remained in Europe.

Colonel John Henry "Gatling Gun" Parker: The veteran of the Spanish-American War remained in the Army, which eventually promoted him to brigadier general. He died in 1942 and is buried in the Presidio in San Francisco.

Sergeant Alvin Cullum York: The Medal of Honor recipient skyrocketed to fame when an April 1919 edition of the *The Saturday Evening Post* reported his heroic actions during the war. When he returned to the United States, fans honored him with numerous banquets and celebrations. Following a victory tour that included meetings with numerous politicians and dignitaries, he returned home to Tennessee, where he married Gracie Williams. Local businessmen purchased a farm for the Yorks, and he remained active in local civic life, raising funds for a vocational school. He later worked for the Civilian Conservation Corps. He and Gracie had six sons and two daughters.

In 1941, Howard Hawks directed the film *Sergeant York*, with Gary Cooper portraying the sergeant, and the film won two Oscars, including one for best actor.

Like Razga, York attempted to reenlist for World War II, but he was too old and—unlike Razga—too unhealthy to serve in combat. However, the Army did take advantage of York's fund-raising prowess, putting him to work selling war bonds.

Throughout his life York remained in poor health, and suffered several strokes. He died in 1964.

Major Charles White Whittlesey: The bookish officer never recovered from the horrors he witnessed as commander of the "Lost Battalion." After the war, the Medal of Honor recipient returned to his career as a Wall Street lawyer, but his status as a war hero led to constant demands for his attention and attendance at various civic events. Just two weeks after the ceremony to honor the Unknown Soldier, Whittlesey boarded a steamship bound for Havana, Cuba. While en route, he committed suicide by jumping overboard, to the surprise and horror of his friends and family. No one knows for certain what motivated him to take his own life; like countless war veterans before and since, he fought his own private battles after the hostilities ended.

Major General John Archer Lejeune: Following his success at St. Mihiel, Lejeune became one of the most highly revered and decorated officers in the US Marine Corps. He received the Army Distinguished Service Medal and the Navy Distinguished Service Medal, as well as the Legion of Honour and the Croix de Guerre from the French government. In 1919, he became commanding general of the Marine installation in Quantico, and just one year later, he was promoted to commandant of the Marine Corps. The man known as a "Marine's Marine" and the "greatest of all Leathernecks," retired in 1929. He died in 1942 and was buried in Arlington. Today, Lejeune is a Marine legend, with countless buildings, ships, and even the Marine Corps Base in North Carolina named in his honor.

Lieutenant Colonel George S. Patton, Jr.: Patton went on to become one of the most famous and infamous officers ever to serve in the US military. After the Great War, he developed a friendship with Dwight D. Eisenhower that would become vital throughout the rest of his career. The irascible officer continued bolstering the United States' nascent tank force. He also served for a while in Hawaii, where he wrote a paper predicting the eventual Japanese attack on Pearl Harbor.

When the United States entered World War II, Eisenhower tasked Patton with planning and leading the successful Allied invasion of North Africa as well as the campaign in Sicily. However, during the Sicilian invasion, Patton, known for his aggressive approach to war and his caustic personality, became embroiled in controversy after slapping two men suffering from PTSD and ordering them to the front lines. He sat on the sidelines for nearly a year before leading the Third Army into action in Europe. There, Patton masterminded the battles that secured his status as a legend—fighting in Normandy, Lorraine, and the Battle of the Bulge, and into Germany.

Patton died on December 21, 1945, less than two weeks after a car accident left him paralyzed from the neck down. He reportedly said it was "a hell of a way to die."[8] He was buried with his men at an American cemetery in Luxembourg. After his death, multiple movies depicted the life of the iconic general, ensuring his place in the American imagination for all time.

Sergeant Stubby: Postwar America fell in love with the heroic mutt, and he starred in numerous parades across the country. He received countless medals and honors, including meeting three presidents—Wilson, Harding, and Coolidge. After he died in his sleep in 1926, a taxidermist preserved his body, which went on display at the Smithsonian. Stubby's story grew until it became nearly impossible to separate fact from fiction. An upcoming movie plans to celebrate his life and service.

ACKNOWLEDGMENTS

Writing this book led me on an astonishing journey that spanned more than seven years. During that time, I combed through archived letters, diaries, memoirs, and official documents that brought the Great War to life through the words of America's forgotten generation, the doughboys. In my research, I not only found the documents from World War I but also walked the grounds where the Body Bearers fought and lived.

This story found me in 2010 on Hill 142 in Belleau Wood. I'd like to thank Ray Shearer, an expert on the Marine Corps and World War I, who was our guide at Belleau Wood. He also took the time to carefully go through this manuscript and the accompanying maps.

I'd also like to thank the many other people I met while writing this book. *The Unknowns* would not have been possible without the help of many valuable repositories of historical information. I'd like to thank the staff at the National Archives and Records Administration in Washington, DC, as well as NARA II in College Park, Maryland, and the New York Public Library, the Library of Congress, Bibliothèque Nationale de France, and other historical societies and libraries that I visited many, many times. I'd especially like to thank the Military History Institute (MHI), which includes many robust records, oral histories, and other memoirs. The staff at the National Personnel Records Center (NPRC) was also extremely helpful.

Every author has many friends on whom he leans for advice and early reads, and I leaned on mine and am most grateful for their time and thoughtful comments. Thanks to Cyndy Harvey for all her wisdom and editorial advice. Thanks to Justin Oldham for looking at many drafts at the drop of a hat and providing priceless feedback. Thanks also to Colonel Willy Buhl. In Fallujah, he led the Marines of 3/1 with whom

I fought house-to-house, and we later traveled together to France with the 5th Marines and Wounded Warrior Regiment on the trip where the seeds of this book were planted. I'm extremely grateful to Glenn F. Williams, historian at the US Army Center of Military History, for reading the manuscript line by line and providing detailed comments and feedback. Thanks to historian Lieutenant Commander Gray Connelly, who examined the book in detail and provided helpful comments. I leaned on T. Gulley at various stages of the project, and I am grateful for his help. I'm thankful to Marine historian Kevin Seldon, who graciously reviewed the book and is writing the definitive history of Belleau Wood. Also thank you, USMC historian Kara Newcomer, David Mitchell, Ben Ibach, James Noel Smith, Dan Gillotti, and professor of writing Theana Kastens, who spent time providing detailed comments and feedback.

I'm grateful to my beautiful daughter, Lily, for her support. I am deeply in debt to my exceptional fiancée, the gorgeous and brilliant Dr. Lori Snyder, an accomplished ophthalmologist who spent countless hours using her discerning eye and provided numerous insightful and cogent recommendations to strengthen the manuscript. Lori has a passion for preserving America's history.

In addition, I appreciate the hard work of my literary, film, and television agents at William Morris Endeavor (WME). I'm most grateful for the brilliant comments and guidance provided by my outstanding editor, George Gibson, a veteran editor with many decades of priceless experience. And this book would never have become a reality without the vision and support of my publisher, the legendary Morgan Entrekin.

NOTES

PREFACE

1   The author was embedded as a combat historian with 3/1 during the Battle of Fallujah. The complete journey is captured in *We Were One: Shoulder-to-Shoulder with the Marines of Fallujah*, which appeared on the USMC Commandants' Professional Reading List.
2   General Pershing deliberately chose men from all of the various service branches.

PROLOGUE

1   Edward Younger, "I Chose the Unknown Soldier," from his personnel file at the National Personnel Records Center (NPRC), a portion of which is reprinted in *Cincinnati Enquirer*, November 8, 1936, 2.
2   Ibid.
3   The ranks listed here are the Body Bearers' ranks in 1921, which weren't necessarily the same as their wartime ranks.

CHAPTER 1: GETTING OVER THERE

1   Leo Grebler, *The Cost of the World War to Germany and Austria-Hungary* (New Haven, Conn.: Yale University Press, 1940), 78.
2   John Mosier, *The Myth of the Great War* (New York: HarperCollins Publishers, 2001), 303; taken from *Times of London*, January 23, 1925, 12.
3   David Stevenson, *With Our Backs to the Wall* (Cambridge, Mass.: Harvard University Press, 2013), 350–1.
4   Ibid., 354.
5   Ibid., 360–61.
6   Mosier, *The Myth of the Great War*, 304; Benedict Crowell, *America's Munitions, 1917–1918* (Washington, DC: Government Printing Office, 1919), 104–8.
7   Admiral Alfred von Tirpitz, *My Memoirs*, vol. 1 (New York: Dodd, Mead and Company, 1919), unnumbered.
8   Zimmerman Telegram.
9   Woodrow Wilson, "Address to a Joint Session of Congress: Request for Authority," February 26, 1917.
10 Robert H. Ferrell, *America's Deadliest Battle: Meuse-Argonne, 1918* (Lawrence: University Press of Kansas, 2007), 4; Stevenson, *With Our Backs to the Wall*, 3.
11 President Woodrow Wilson, speech to a joint session of the Sixty-Fifth Congress, April 2, 1917.

12 Ferrell, *America's Deadliest Battle: Meuse-Argonne, 1918*, 4.
13 The United States seized ninety-seven ships totaling 638,000 gross tons.

CHAPTER 2: THE KAISER'S KILLING MACHINE

1 Gudmundur Helgason, "U-boats of WWI," Uboat.net
2 Dialogue in this section comes from Edgar Von Spiegel, *U. Boat 202: The Diary of a German Submarine* (Portland, Ore.: W. K. Hawthorne, 2012), location 440, Kindle.
3 Uboat.net. Sources disagree on the number of torpedoes carried by *U-61*. It was either six or seven, but the present author has used the lower number.
4 Gudmundur Helgason, "WWI U-boats: U 61," German and Austrian U-boats of World War I—Kaiserliche Marine, Uboat.net.

CHAPTER 3: JAMES DELANEY AND THE SS *CAMPANA*

1 Andrew Mellgard, formerly First Officer, Report on the Sinking of the SS *Campana*, Office of Naval Intelligence, August 29, 1917, National Archives and Records Administration, Washington, DC (hereafter NARA I), Record Group 45, Entry 520, Box 607. Located in Washington, DC, NARA I contains many US Navy records from WWI. National Archive II (hereafter NARA II), located in College Park, Maryland, contains most of the records of the AEF. The National Personnel Records Center (NPRC) in St. Louis, Missouri, contains personnel files and military records for America's veterans. Note that pages are not numbered in most government records for this period.
2 Service Record of James Delaney, Personnel File, NPRC.
3 History of the Armed Guard Section, October 25, 1918, NARA I, Record Group 45, Entry 520, Box 612.
4 Ibid.
5 *Manual for Instruction and Training of Special Broadside Crews for Armed-Guard Duty*, NARA I, Record Group 45, Subject File 1911–1927, Entry 520, Box 612.
6 General Instructions for Commanding Officers of the Armed Guard, NARA I, Record Group 45, Subject File 1911–1927, Box 612.
7 History of the Armed Guard Section, October 25, 1918.
8 Statement of H. M. Lusk, Seaman 2nd Class from the Armed Guard on the SS *Campana*, NARA I, Record Group 45, Entry 520, Box 612.
9 Mellgard, Report on the Sinking of the SS *Campana*.
10 Ibid.
11 R. A. Voight, Cox, Member of the Armed Guard for the SS *Campana*, NARA I, Record Group 45, Entry 520, Box 607. (Hereafter, Voight.)
12 Statement of H. M. Lusk, Seaman 2nd Class from the Armed Guard on the SS *Campana*, NARA I, Record Group 45, Entry 520, Box 607.
13 Edgar Von Spiegel, *U. Boat 202: The Diary of a German Submarine* (Portland, Ore.: W. K. Hawthorne, 2012), location 266, Kindle.
14 Quotes in this and the three preceding paragraphs from War Diary of U-61 (Concerning sinking of SS *Campana* on 6 August 1917), NARA I, Record Group 45, Entry 520, Box 1466.
15 Voight.

16   Mellgard, Report on the Sinking of the SS *Campana.*
17   Voight.
18   Extract from War Diary of U-61 (Concerning sinking of SS *Campana* on 6 August 1917).
19   Dialogue and other quotes in this section come from Voight.
20   "American Gunners Lost on Submarine," *New York Times*, August 23, 1917.
21   Voight.
22   Mellgard, Report on the Sinking of the SS *Campana.*
23   Ibid.
24   Extract from War Diary of U-61 (Concerning sinking of SS *Campana* on 6 August 1917).
25   Statement of H. M. Lusk, Seaman 2nd Class from the Armed Guard on the SS *Campana.*

CHAPTER 4: Q SHIPS AND DEPTH CHARGES: *DAS BOOT*

1   Dialogue comes from Report of James Delaney, COAG SS *Campana*, January 11, 1919, from the Armed Guards Report, NARA I, Record Group 45, Entry 520, Box 612.
2   Edgar Von Spiegel, *U. Boat 202: The Diary of a German Submarine* (Portland, Ore.: W. K. Hawthorne, 2012), location 407–8, Kindle.
3   Allied propaganda often demonized the Germans and highlighted atrocities that occurred in order to rally support for the Allies' own war efforts.
4   Lowell Thomas, *Raiders of the Deep* (New York: Doubleday, Doran and Company, 1928), 86.
5   Ibid.
6   Report of James Delaney, COAG SS *Campana*, January 11, 1919.
7   Von Spiegel, *U. Boat 202: The Diary of a German Submarine.*
8   Report of James Delaney, COAG SS *Campana*, January 11, 1919.
9   Ibid.
10   Ibid.
11   Ibid.
12   Ibid.
13   Ibid.
14   Ibid.
15   Ibid.
16   Ibid.
17   Ibid.
18   Ibid.
19   Von Spiegel, *U. Boat 202: The Diary of a German Submarine.*
20   Thomas, *Raiders of the Deep*, 211.
21   Ibid.
22   Report of James Delaney, COAG SS *Campana*, January 11, 1919.
23   "American Gunners Lost on Submarine," *New York Times*, August 23, 1917.
24   Von Spiegel, *U. Boat 202: The Diary of a German Submarine.*
25   Report of James Delaney, COAG SS *Campana*, January 11, 1919.
26–52   Ibid.

CHAPTER 5: PERSHING AND THE AEF

1   *Baltic* delivered the Americans to England. Another vessel took them the rest of the way to France, where they arrived on June 14.

2   John J. Pershing, *My Experiences in the World War*, vol. 1 (New York: Frederick A. Stokes Company, 1931), page unnumbered.

3   US Army Center of Military History, "The U.S. Army in World War I Fact Sheet." As of April 1, 1917, the Regular Army had 127,588 men (5,971 officers; 121,797 enlisted); 5,523 men served in the Philippine Scouts; and 181,620 men served in the National Guard (80,446 in federal service and 101,174 in state service). That brings the total available to 213,557.

4   *New York Sun*, March 10, 1902, as quoted in Stuart Creighton Miller, *Benevolent Assimilation* (New Haven and London: Yale University Press, 1982), 234.

5   John Perry, *Pershing: Commander of the Great War* (New York: Thomas Nelson, 2011), 34.

6   At the time, only members of the 10th Cavalry were known as "Buffalo Soldiers." Today, people use the term to describe all African Americans who fought in mostly black Regular Army units.

7   Perry, *Pershing: Commander of the Great War*, 34.

8   Frederick Palmer, *John J. Pershing: General of the Armies* (Ann Arbor, Mich.: Military Service Publications, 1948), 24.

9   Donald Symthe, *Guerrilla Warrior: The Early Life of John J. Pershing* (New York: Scribner, 1973), 52.

10 Ibid., 84.

11 Jim Lacey, *Pershing* (New York: Palgrave Macmillan, 2008), 54.

12 Nimrod Thompson Frazer, *Send the Alabamians: World War I Fighters in the Rainbow Division* (Tuscaloosa: University of Alabama Press, 2014), 18.

13 *War Department Annual Report 1919*, vol. 1 (Washington, DC: Government Printing Office, 1920), 7.

14 Maj. Gen. James G. Harbord, *Leaves from a War Diary* (New York: Dodd, Mead, and Company, 1925), 125.

15 Lacey, *Pershing*, 98.

16 All three groups were known as the US Army.

17 Jami L. Bryan, "Fighting for Respect: African-American Soldiers in WWI," Army Historical Foundation website, January 20, 2015.

18 John Mosier, *The Myth of the Great War* (New York: HarperCollins Publishers, 2001).

19 Ferdinand Foch (translated by Maj. Grasset), *Precepts and Judgments* (New York: Henry Holt, 1920), 21.

20 Thomas Fleming, *The Illusion of Victory: America in WWI* (New York: Basic Books, 2003), 115.

21 Col. Oliver Lyman Spaulding and Col. John Womack Wright, *The Second Division: American Expeditionary Force in France 1917–1919* (New York: Hillman Press, 1937), 29. Referred to hereafter as *Second Division History*.

CHAPTER 6: ERNEST AUGUST JANSON: FIRST TO FIGHT

1   Name change noted in Hoffman/Janson's Service Record Book, NPRC. Note that some records mistakenly spell Janson as "Jansen," but Janson himself preferred the other spelling. By 1921 the Medal of Honor recipient referred to himself as Janson, and his name change is reflected in newspaper articles chronicling the event.

2   Ernest Janson personnel records, NPRC.

3   Frank Hunt Garvin, "A History of the 49th Company of the Marine 2nd Division," Library of Congress, 3.

4   Ibid.

5   Maj. Edwin N. McClellan, *The United States Marine Corps in the World War* (Washington, DC: US Marine Corps Historical Branch, 1920), 9.

6   Dick Camp, *The Devil Dogs at Belleau Wood: U.S. Marines in WWI* (Minneapolis, Minn.: Zenith Press, 2006), 14.

7   McClellan, *The United States Marine Corps in the World War*, 15.

8   Albertus W. Catlin, *With the Help of God and a Few Good Marines* (New York: Doubleday, 1919), 19.

9   Ibid.

10 McClellan, *The United States Marine Corps in the World War*, 25.

11 Dick Camp, *Leatherneck Legends: Conversations with the Marine Corps' Old Breed* (Minneapolis, Minn.: Zenith Press, 2006), 12.

12 Ibid., 12.

13 Camp, *The Devil Dogs at Belleau Wood: U.S. Marines in WWI*, 17.

14 Malcolm Aitken, "Letters from a Marine to His Mother," WWI Veterans Surveys, 2nd Division, 5th Marines, Military History Institute, Carlisle, Penn.

15 Camp, *The Devil Dogs at Belleau Wood: U.S. Marines in WWI*, 18.

16 Quoted from the original report. Jon Hoppe, "The Destruction of the S.M.S. *Cormoran* and the First U.S. Shot Fired in the First World War," US Naval Institute Naval History Blog, October 1, 2015, https://www.navalhistory .org/2015/10/01/the-destruction-of-the-s-m-s-cormoran.

17 Ibid.

18 Ibid.

19 Ibid.

20 Ibid.

21 Garvin, "A History of the 49th Company of the Marine 2nd Division," 3.

22 Leroy Hunt, *History of the 1st Battalion 5th Regiment US Marines* (Printed in Occupied Germany: Battalion Exchange), 7.

23 Garvin, "A History of the 49th Company of the Marine 2nd Division," 3.

24 William Arthur Carter, *The Tale of a Devil Dog* (Washington, DC: Canteen Press, 1920), 33.

25 Ibid., 34.

26 The 2nd Division (Regulars) was the only American division formed in France. The rest were formed in the United States and shipped overseas.

27 Garvin, "A History of the 49th Company of the Marine 2nd Division," 3.

28 The shoulder sleeve insignia was not officially adopted by most units until after the war ended.

29   Benedict Crowell, *America's Munitions, 1917–1918* (Washington, DC: Government Printing Office, 1919), 204. The belt-fed 430 heavy machine guns included 282 Maxim machine guns and 148 Colt machine guns. The United States also had 353 of the lighter Lewis guns and 670 Benét-Mercié machine rifles.

30   Theodore Roosevelt, *The Rough Riders* (New York: Charles Scribner's Sons, 1899), 567–68.

31   Ibid.

32   Terrence Finnegan, *A Delicate Affair on the Western Front: America Learns How to Fight a Modern War in the Woëvre Trenches* (Staplehurst, UK: Spellmount, 2015), location 724, Kindle.

33   George Raach, *A Withering Fire: American Machine Gun Fire in WWI* (Bradenton, Fla.: Booklocker, 2015), 39.

34   United States War Department, *Machine-Gun Firing Manual* (Washington, DC: Government Printing Office, 1917), 192.

35   Bruce I. Gudmundsson, *Stormtroop Tactics: Innovation in the German Army, 1914–1918* (Westport, Conn.: Praeger, 1995), Location 1363, Kindle.

36   Erich Ludendorff, *Ludendorff's Own Story, Vol. 2* (New York and London: Harper and Brothers, 1919), 238.

37   Margarethe Ludendorff, *My Married Life with Ludendorff* (London: Hutchinson, 1929), 25.

38   Dennis Showalter and William J. Astore, *Hindenburg: Icon of German Militarism* (Washington, DC: Potomac Books, 2005), 6.

39   Emil Ludwig, *Hindenburg and the Saga of the German Revolution* (London: W. Heinemann, Ltd., 1935), 86.

40   The Combined Arms Research Library Digital Library has a translation of the original by the Great Britain War Office, 1918.

41   Williamson Murray, *War, Strategy and Military Effectiveness* (New York: Cambridge University Press, 2011), 207.

42   Special Order of the Day, Field Marshal Sir Douglas Haig, General HQ, April 11, 1918.

43   British losses come from *Statistics of the Military Effort of the British Empire During the Great War* (London: HMSO, 1922), 24–25.

CHAPTER 7: TRENCH WARFARE

1   Doughboy accounts after the war also make this reference, which seems like an American reference.

2   The personal account comes from storm trooper Paul Coelestin Ettighoffer in his autobiography, cited in "Landsknechte v Sportsmen: Operation Kirschblüte-Seicheprey, 20 April 1918," Western Front Association, http://www.westernfrontassociation.com/the-great-war/great-war-on-land/battlefields/2039-landsknechte-v-sportsmen-operation-kirschblute-seicheprey-20-april-1918.html, accessed May 1917. The website translated Ettighoffer's original memoir, *Verdun, das große Gericht* (Verdun, the Great Court), which is located at https://archive.org/details/EttighofferPaulCoelestinVerdunDasGrosseGericht1936303S.ScanFraktur.

3   Ibid.

4 Ernst Junger, *Copse 125: A Chronicle from the Trench Warfare of 1918* (New York: Howard Fertig, 2003), 252.

5 Ettighoffer, autobiography cited in "Landsknechte v Sportsmen: Operation Kirschblüte-Seicheprey, 20 April 1918."

6 Ibid.

7 Terrence Finnegan, *A Delicate Affair on the Western Front: America Learns How to Fight a Modern War in the Woëvre Trenches* (Staplehurst, UK: Spellmount, 2015), location 7300, Kindle.

8 Ibid., location 5394, Kindle.

9 Ibid.

10 Ettighoffer, autobiography cited in "Landsknechte v Sportsmen: Operation Kirschblüte-Seicheprey, 20 April 1918."

11 "Two Long-Separated Washington Brothers Meet in German Trench," *Washington Post*, June 2, 1918, 11.

12 William A. Carter, *The Tale of a Devil Dog* (Washington, DC: Canteen Press, 2016), 34.

13 Robert Asprey, *At Belleau Wood* (Denton: University of North Texas Press, 1965), 27.

CHAPTER 8: BELLEAU WOOD

1 Nearly every WWI Marine account I encountered recalled defeated French soldiers saying this to the Marines.

2 Levi Hemrick, *Once a Marine* (New York: Carlton Press, 1968), 94–95.

3 Marshal Pétain, *Report, 1918*, Defensive Campaign Part 5, 16; *Second Division History*, 40.

4 The bulk of the 3rd Division moved up several days later to reinforce Château-Thierry. The American machine guns were able to cross the railroad bridge, as did the Germans, but the Germans were repelled with heavy losses. The area around the bridge became a kill zone.

5 John Toland, *No Man's Land* (Old Saybrook, Conn.: Konecky and Konecky, 1996), 268.

6 Edward H. Simmons and Joseph Alexander, *Through the Wheat: The US Marines in WWI* (Annapolis, Md.: Naval Institute Press, 2011), 36.

7 *Second Division History*, 42.

8 Robert Asprey, *At Belleau Wood* (Denton: University of North Texas Press, 1965), 89.

9 Dick Camp, *The Devil Dogs at Belleau Wood: U.S. Marines in WWI* (Minneapolis, Minn.: Zenith Press, 2006), 68.

10 S.L.A. Marshall, *World War I* (New York: Houghton Mifflin Company, 1964), 380.

11 Elton E. Mackin, *Suddenly We Didn't Want to Die: Memoirs of a World War I Marine* (Novato, Calif.: Presidio Press, 1993), 6.

12 Robert Ferrebee, "Retreat, Hell! We Just Got Here," *American Legion*, December 11, 2014.

CHAPTER 9: HILL 142

1   John W. Thomason, *Fix Bayonets!* (New York: Charles Scribner's Sons, 1926), 14.
2   Ibid., 12.
3   Ibid., 13.
4   Kemper F. Cowing and Courtney Cooper, *Dear Folks at Home* (New York: Houghton Mifflin Co., 1919), 126.
5   Ibid.
6   Thomason, *Fix Bayonets!*, 14.
7   Ibid.
8   Ibid., 17.
9   Ibid.
10 Ibid.
11 Ibid., 18.
12 Cowing and Cooper, *Dear Folks at Home*, 126.
13 Thomason, *Fix Bayonets!*, 19.
14 Ibid.
15 Cowing and Cooper, *Dear Folks at Home*, 126.
16 Asprey, *At Belleau Wood*, 155.
17 Cowing and Cooper, *Dear Folks at Home*, 127.
18 Ibid., 128.
19 Ibid.
20 Medal of Honor Citation for Ernest August Janson, Gunnery Sergeant, 49th Company, NARA II.
21 4th Marine Brigade Field Messages, 2nd Division Records, NARA II, Record Group 120, Entry 1241, Box 35.
22 Thomason, *Fix Bayonets!*, 23.
23 Ibid.
24 Maj. Allan C. Bevilacqua and Nancy Lee White Hoffman, "1918: Voices from Belleau Wood," *Leatherneck Magazine of the Marines* 98, no. 6 (June 2015): 14.
25 Brown's mention of infiltration is located in 2nd Division Records, vol. 4, and also in the 2nd Division records in the National Archives. The Marines had limited training in this area from the chasseurs, and their most recent training involved open warfare and moving in larger formations.
26 Albertus W. Catlin, *With the Help of God and a Few Marines* (New York: Doubleday, 1919), 114.
27 Ibid.
28 Ibid., 115.
29 David Bonk, *Chateau Thierry and Belleau Wood 1918: America's Baptism of Fire on the Marne* (Oxford: Osprey Publishing, 2012), 62.
30 The 73rd Machine Gun Company was interspersed throughout 3/5. Major Maurice Edwin Shearer commanded the 73rd before taking over 3/5 after Maj. Berry was wounded.
31 Floyd Gibbons, *And They Thought We Wouldn't Fight* (New York: George H. Doran Company, 1918), 304.
32 Ibid., 304-13.

CHAPTER 10: "THE MARINES ARE FIGHTING LIKE TROJANS"

1 Floyd Gibbons, *And They Thought We Wouldn't Fight* (New York: George H. Doran Company, 1918), 313.

2 James Harbord, *The American Army in France*, 1917–1918 (New York: Little Brown and Company, 1936), 291.

3 "U.S. Marines Smash Huns," *Chicago Daily Tribune*, June 6, 1918, 1.

4 Ibid.

5 Ibid.

6 "Valor of Marines Stirs All America," *New York Times*, July 9, 1918.

7 Ernst Otto, *The Battles for the Possession of Belleau Woods, June 1918* (Annapolis, Md.: U.S. Naval Institute Proceedings, 1928).

8 United States General Staff, Military Intelligence Division, *Histories of Two Hundred and Fifty-One Divisions of the German Army Which Participated in the War (1914–1918)* (Washington, DC: Government Printing Office, 1920), 376.

9 Cpl. Elton Mackin, interview conducted by Carl D. Klopfenstein, transcribed and published at the Rutherford B. Hayes Presidential Library, http://www.rbhayes.org/research/corporal-elton-mackin-wwi-5th-marine-regiment-interview-1973.

10 Haber later converted to Christianity.

11 Warren R. Jackson, *His Time in Hell: A Texas Marine in France* (Novato, Calif.: Presidio Press, 2001), 101.

12 Levi E. Hemrick, *Once a Marine* (Staunton, Va.: Clarion Publishing, 2013), 106.

13 Cates to his mother, June 14, 1918, Marine Corps Personal Papers Collection, US Marine Corps University, Quantico, Va.

14 Center of Military History, *United States Army in the World War, 1917–1919: Military Operations of the American Expeditionary Forces* (Washington, DC: US Army, 1989), 531.

15 Laurence Stallings, *The Doughboys* (New York: Popular Library, 1964), 128.

16 Cylburn Otto Mattfeldt, *Records of the 2nd Division, Vol. 5* (Washington, DC: Army War College, 1924), 322.

17 "French Launch New Attack: Yankees Force Hun Retreat," *Cincinnati Enquirer*, September 15, 1918, 1.

18 The author toured Belleau Wood many times and had the honor of returning to France with the Fighting 5th, to visit Belleau Wood for the first time as a unit since 1918. Our guide was Ray Shearer, who uttered the same words his great-uncle had ninety-two years earlier.

19 Col. Frederic May Wise as told to Meigs O. Frost, *A Marine Tells It to You* (New York: J. H. Sears and Company, 1929), 222.

CHAPTER 11: EDWARD YOUNGER: VAUX

1 1940 U.S. Federal Census.

2 Marcia Winn, "Picked Unknown Soldier, but He Tries to Forget," *Chicago Tribune*, November 12, 1939.

3 S. L. A. Marshall, *The American Heritage History of WWI* (New York: American Heritage, 1964), 404.

4   W. C. McMullon, 2nd Division 9th Regiment, "Memoirs of World War One," WWI Veterans Survey, MHI, 40.

5   Robert Asprey, *At Belleau Wood* (Denton: University of North Texas Press, 1965), 336.

6   From the diary of Frank Hodson, Pvt., Btry. "F," 15th FA, in Historical Committee of the 2nd Division Association, *The 2nd Division, American Expeditionary Force in France, 1917–1919* (New York: Hillman Press, 1937), 7478.

7   Albertus Wright Catlin, *With the Help of God and a Few Marines* (New York: Doubleday, Page and Company, 1919), 177.

8   Robert Lee Bullard, *American Soldiers Also Fought* (New York: Longmans, Green, and Co., 1936), 39.

9   Robert H. Ferrell, *Woodrow Wilson and World War I, 1917–1921* (New York: Harper and Row, 1985), 72.

10 American Battle Monuments Commission, *American Armies and Battlefields in Europe* (Washington, DC: US Government Printing Office, 1938), 31.

11 The 38th Regiment in the Second Battle of the Marne, Records of the 3rd Division, 38th Infantry Regiment, NARA II, Record Group 120, Entry 91, Box 31. Also, J. W. Woolridge, commanding officer G Company, *The Rock of the Marne: The Chronological Story of the 38th Regiment U.S. Infantry*, privately published, presented to the men and officers of the 38th Infantry regiment, 1919, NARA II, Record Group 120, Entry 91, Box 31.

CHAPTER 12: TURNING POINT: SOISSONS

1   From the diary of Frank Hodson, Pvt., Btry. "F," 15th FA, in Historical Committee of the 2nd Division Association, *The 2nd Division, American Expeditionary Force in France, 1917–1919* (New York: Hillman Press, 1937), 255.

2   Field Artillery School, *Instructional Memorandum: History of the Development of Field Artillery Materiel* (Fort Sill: Field Artillery School, 1939), 56.

3   Kelly DeVries et al., *King of Battle: Artillery in World War I, History of Warfare Services* (Boston: Brill, 2015), 197.

4   James W. Dell, "Life in Vera Cruz, Mexico," *Breckenridge News*, November 18, 1914, 6.

5   Report of Operations, Second Division, in the Attack of the 20th Army Corps, 10th French Army, July 17–21, 1918, NARA II, Record Group 120, Entry 91, Box 5.

6   Maj. Elliott D. Cooke, *We Can Take It and We Attack* (Pike, N.H.: Brass Hat Historical Reprint, no date), 22. Originally published in *Infantry Journal*, November–December 1937.

7   Report of Operations, Second Division, in the Attack of the 20th Army Corps, 10th French Army, July 17–21, 1918, NARA II, Record Group 120, Entry 91, Box 5.

8   From the diary of Frank Hodson, in *The 2nd Division, American Expeditionary Force in France, 1917–1919*, 259.

9   Cooke, *We Can Take It and We Attack*, 25.

10 Ibid.

11 John Eisenhower, *Yanks: The Epic Story of the American Army in World War I* (New York: Touchstone, 2001), 168.

12 John W. Thomason, *Fix Bayonets!* (New York: Charles Scribner's Sons, 1926), 98.

13 Report of Operations, Second Division, in the Attack of the 20th Army Corps, 10th French Army, July 17–21.

14 John Thomason, *Red Pants and Other Stories* (New York: Charles Scribner's Sons, 1927), 7.

15 Douglas Johnson II and Rolfe Gilman, Jr., *Soissons, 1918* (College Station: Texas A&M Press, 1999), 64.

16 Thomason, *Red Pants and Other Stories*, 8.

17 James Harbord, *The American Army in France, 1917–1918* (New York: Little Brown and Company, 1936), 331. Harbord drew from Thomason's recollections for this section of his book.

18 From the diary of Pvt. John A. Hughes, Btry. "C," 15th FA in Historical Committee of the 2nd Division Association, *The 2nd Division, American Expeditionary Force in France, 1917–1919* (New York: Hillman Press, 1937), 260–61.

19 Thomason, *Red Pants and Other Stories*, 8.

20 W. C. McMullon, "Memoirs of World War One," MHI, WWI Veteran Survey Project, 2nd Division, 9th Infantry, 54.

21 "History of 15th Field Artillery, 31 December 1918," 2nd Division 15th FA, NARA II, Record Group 120, Entry 1241 Box 65.

22 Matthew J. Davenport, *First Over There: The Attack on Cantigny, American's First Battle of WWI* (New York: Thomas Dunne Books, 2015), 112.

23 Turrill's after-action report specifically mentions his interaction with General Ely.

24 Elton E. Mackin, *Suddenly We Didn't Want to Die: Memoirs of a World War I Marine* (Novato, Calif.: Presidio Press, 1993), 109–10.

25 Ibid.

26 Report of Operations, Second Division, in the Attack of the 20th Army Corps, 10th French Army, July 17–21, 1918.

27 General Robert Denig, Diary, personal papers, Alfred M. Gray Marine Corps Research Center, Quantico, Va.

28 Ibid.

29 2nd Division Casualties, NARA II Record Group 120, Entry 91, Box 5.

30 Capture numbers come from Report of Operations, Second Division, in the Attack of the 20th Army Corps, 10th French Army, July 17–21, 1918.

31 George C. Marshall, *Memoirs of My Services in the World War, 1917–1918* (Boston: Houghton Mifflin, 1976), 123–24.

32 Ibid.

33 Report of Operations, Second Division, in the Attack of the 20th Army Corps, 10th French Army, July 17–21, 1918.

34 David C. Shanks, *As They Passed Through the Port* (Washington, DC: Cary Publishing Co., 1927), 153.

CHAPTER 13: CHARLES LEO O'CONNOR: USS *MOUNT VERNON*

1 All naval records obtained from NARA I, Washington, DC. Note that Army and USMC records are from NARA II, College Park, Md.

2 Lt. Cmdr. James Madison Doyle, *War Log of the USS* Mount Vernon *"Queen*

of the Transport Fleet," 132, NARA I, Record Group 45, Entry 520, Box 1238. Referred to in short-form citations as USS *Mount Vernon*.

3 Ibid., 130.

4 Engineer Officer to Commanding Officer, memo, September 12, 1918, USS *Mount Vernon*, NARA I, Record Group 45, Entry 520, Box 139. Referred to in short-form citations as USS *Mount Vernon*, Box, 139.

5 Uboat.net, "WWI U-Boat Commanders," http://uboat.net/wwi/men/commanders.

6 Gunnery Officer to Commanding Officer, memo, September 8, 1918, USS *Mount Vernon*, Box 139.

7 Ibid.

8 Executive Officer to Commanding Officer, memo, September 8, 1918, USS *Mount Vernon*, Box 139.

9 USS *Mount Vernon*, 99.

10 Ibid., 100.

11 Executive Officer to Commanding Officer, memo, September 8, 1918, USS *Mount Vernon*, Box 139.

12 USS *Mount Vernon*, 112.

13 Ibid., 103.

14 Ibid.

15 Gunnery Officer to Commanding Officer, memo, September 8, 1918, USS *Mount Vernon*, Box 139.

16 Senior Medical Officer to Commanding Officer, memo, September 9, 1918, USS *Mount Vernon*, Box 139.

17 Ibid.

18 Ibid.

19 Richard F. Faulkner, *Pershing's Crusaders* (Lawrence: University Press of Kansas, 2017), 178.

20 Carol R. Byerly, "The U.S. Military and the Influenza Pandemic of 1918–1919," *Public Health Report 125* (Supplement 3) (2010), 82–91. According to this analysis, 115,660 Americans died in the war. Of those, 43 percent (50,280) died in battle, and 50 percent (57, 460) died of disease, primarily influenza.

21 David M. Morens and Anthony S. Fauci, "The 1918 Influenza Pandemic: Insights for the 21st Century," *Journal of Infectious Diseases* 195, no. 7 (April 2007). The number is an estimate, and the real total is likely to have been much higher because deaths in Asia were not fully recorded.

22 Peyton C. March, *The Nation at War* (Garden City, NY: Doubleday, Doran and Company, 1932), 360.

23 Richard Collier, *The Plague of the Spanish Lady: The Influenza Pandemic of 1918–1919* (London: Allison and Busby, 1996), 75.

24 Senior Medical Officer to Commanding Officer, memo, September 9, 1918, USS *Mount Vernon*, Box 139.

25 USS *Mount Vernon*, 113.

26 Ibid., 132.

27 Ibid., 154.

28 Ibid., 188.

CHAPTER 14: JAMES DELANEY: BRANDENBURG

1 All information and quotes for this chapter come from Report of James Delaney, COAG SS *Campana*, January 11, 1919, from the Armed Guards Report, NARA I, Record Group 45, Entry 520, Box 612.

CHAPTER 15: ST. MIHIEL

1 All quotations in this chapter come from John J. Pershing, *My Experiences in the World War* (New York: Frederick A. Stokes Co., 1931), 244–48.

CHAPTER 16: THOMAS DANIEL SAUNDERS: BREACHING THE WIRE

1 William A. Mitchell, *Official History of the Second Regiment of Engineers and Second Engineer Train* (Regimental Headquarters, Second Engineers, 1920), 40; "A Brief History of the Second U.S. Engineers During Its Service with the Second Division," December 21, 1918, NARA II, Record Group 120, Entry 91, Box 70.
2 There was also a 2nd Engineer Train, which provided logistics support to the division, as well as construction support for rear areas.
3 The actual number of Native Americans who volunteered is a matter of some dispute. See Thomas A. Britten, *American Indians in World War I* (Albuquerque: University of New Mexico Press, 1997), 59.
4 Ibid., 62.
5 Ibid., 79.
6 Elton Mackin, *Suddenly We Didn't Want to Die: Memoirs of a World War I Marine* (Novato, Calif.: Presidio Press, 1993), 155.
7 Carl Andrew Brannen, *Over There: Marine in the Great War* (College Station: Texas A&M University Press, 1996), 41.
8 Mitchell, *Official History of the Second Regiment of Engineers and Second Engineer Train*, 40.
9 Ibid., 147; Thomas D. Saunders, Medal of Honor Citation. Note that the medal citation says that Saunders took prisoners in the "caves" of Jaulny. This is likely to have been related to a translation error. The French word *caves* means "cellars" in English.
10 Michael Keane, *George S. Patton: Blood, Guts, and Prayer* (Washington, DC: Regnery History, 2014), 153.
11 George S. Patton, Jr., "Comments on 'Cavalry Tanks,'" *Cavalry Journal* 30, no. 122 (January 1921): 252.
12 Martin Blumenson, ed., *The Patton Papers*, vol. 1, 1885–1940 (Boston: Houghton Mifflin Co., 1972), 584.
13 Ibid.
14 William A. Cohen, *The Art of the Strategist* (New York: AMACOM, 2004), 53.

CHAPTER 17: THE SKIES ABOVE AND VICTORY

1 Roger G. Miller, *Billy Mitchell: "Stormy Petrel of the Air"* (Washington, DC: Office of Air Force History, 2004), 3–5.

2   Brig. Gen. William Mitchell, "The Air Service at St. Mihiel," in Walter Hines, ed., *The World's Work: A History of Our Time*, vol. 38, *May 1919 to October 1919* (New York: Doubleday, Page and Co., 1919), 365.

3   Ibid.

4   Robert J. Serling, *From the Captain to the Colonel: A History of Eastern Airlines* (New York: Dial Press, 1980), 90.

5   Eddie Rickenbacker, *Fighting the Flying Circus* (New York: Frederick A. Stokes Co., 1919), 233.

6   War Diary of Private Clarence Richmond, 2/5, www.robinrichmond.com.

7   Elton E. Mackin, *Suddenly We Didn't Want to Die: Memoirs of a World War I Marine* (Novato, Calif.: Presidio Press, 1993), 151.

8   Donald Smythe, *Pershing: General of the Armies* (Bloomington: Indiana University Press, 2007), 186–87.

CHAPTER 18: "A NATURAL FORTRESS . . . BESIDE WHICH THE WILDERNESS IN WHICH GRANT FOUGHT LEE WAS A PARK": THE MEUSE-ARGONNE

1   The quote comes from George Crile, founder of the Cleveland Clinic, in Robert H. Ferrell, *America's Deadliest Battle: Meuse-Argonne, 1918* (Columbia: University of Missouri Press, 2007), 39.

2   Subsequently awarded the American Legion of Honour for his transport efforts, Doumenc enjoyed a long military career, rising to the rank of general and serving in an important cabinet position. He continued to serve until World War II and tragically died in a mountaineering accident in 1948.

3   Hunter Liggett, *A.E.F.: Ten Years Ago in France* (New York: Dodd, Mead, and Co., 1928), 167.

4   Edward Coffman, *The War to End All Wars: The American Experience in WWI* (Frankfort: University of Kentucky Press, 1998), 300.

5   James Harbord, *The American Army in France, 1917–1918* (New York: Little Brown and Co., 1936), 433.

6   *Heeresgruppe Gallwitz* included the German 5th Army.

7   John J. Pershing, *My Experiences in the World War*, vol. 2 (New York: Frederick A. Stokes Co., 1931), 290.

CHAPTER 19: HARRY TAYLOR AND THE WILD WEST DIVISION

1   Harold H. Burton, *600 Days' Service: A History of the 361st Infantry Regiment of the United States Army* (Portland, Ore.: James, Kerns and Abbott Co., 1921), 61.

2   Taylor personnel file, NPRC.

3   91st Division Publication Committee, *The Story of the 91st Division* (San Mateo, Calif., 1919), 9.

4   Burton, *600 Days' Service: A History of the 361st Infantry Regiment of the United States Army*, 63.

5   Ben Meldrum, *History of the 362nd Infantry* (Ogden and Salt Lake, Utah: A. I. Scoville Press, 1920), 28.

6   Ibid.

7   Ibid., 30.
8   Ibid.
9   Ibid., 31.
10 Farley Granger Army Service Experience Questionnaire, Farley Granger Papers (separate box), WWII Veterans Surveys, 91st Division, Military History Institute.
11 Farley Granger's account of his war experiences, Farley Granger Papers, Military History Institute.

CHAPTER 20: THE CHARGE OF THE LIGHT BRIGADE AT GESNES

1   Col. John Henry Parker, "Report of Operations of the 362 Infantry During the Offensive 25th to 29th September (Both Dates Inclusive)," Military History Institute.
2   Ibid.
3   Johnson account, Farley Granger Papers, Military History Institute.
4   Parker, "Report of Operations of the 362 Infantry During the Offensive 25th to 29th September (Both Dates Inclusive)."
5   Granger Account, Farley Granger Papers, Military History Institute.
6   According to Johnson's bitter letter to Pershing after the war, the 91st faced the 1st and 5th German Guards Divisions and elements of five German divisions.
7   Granger Account, Farley Granger Papers, Letter from Granger describing the attack, WWII Veterans Surveys, 91st Division, Military History Institute.
8   Ibid.
9   Ibid.
10 Hutchinson account, Farley Granger Papers, Military History Institute.
11 Granger Account, Farley Granger Papers, Letter from Granger describing the attack.
12 Ibid.
13 Ibid.
14 Parker, "Report of Operations of the 362 Infantry During the Offensive 25th to 29th September (Both Dates Inclusive)."
15 Hutchinson, in Granger Papers, 16.
16 Ibid., 17.
17 Ibid.
18 Ibid.
19 Ibid.
20 Ibid.
21 Ben Meldrum, *History of the 362nd Infantry* (Ogden and Salt Lake, Utah: A. I. Scoville Press, 1920), 38.
22 Ibid.
23 Granger Account, Farley Granger Papers, Military History Institute.
24 Richard Faulkner, "Disappearing Doughboys: The AEF's Straggler Crisis in the Meuse-Argonne," *Army History*, no. 83 (Spring 2012): 7. Faulkner cites a straggler estimate from Maj. Gen. Hunter Liggett.
25 Inspection of the 37th, NARA II, Record Group 120, Entry 590, Box 2.
26 Faulkner, "Disappearing Doughboys: The AEF's Straggler Crisis in the Meuse-Argonne," 7.

27 Ibid., 9.

28 Granger Account, Farley Granger Papers, Letter from Granger describing the attack, MHI.

CHAPTER 21: MISSION IMPOSSIBLE: BLANC MONT RIDGE

1 Maj. Edwin N. McClellan, *The United States Marine Corps in the World War* (Washington, DC: Historical Branch HQ, USMC, 1920), 80.

2 John W. Thomason, *Fix Bayonets!* (New York: Charles Scribner's Sons, 1926), 153.

3 Ibid., 157.

4 "History of the 15th Field Artillery Regiment," NARA II, Record Group 120, Entry 1241 Box 64.

5 From the diary of Pvt. John A. Hughes, Btry. "C," 15th FA in Historical Committee of the 2nd Division Association, *The 2nd Division, American Expeditionary Force in France, 1917–1919* (New York: Hillman Press, 1937), 277.

6 Ibid.

7 Thomason, *Fix Bayonets!*, 171.

8 Ibid., 180.

9 Ibid., 171.

10 Ibid., 180.

11 John Ausland, 55th Company, 5th Marines, "Goodbye World," October 5, 1918, MHI WWI Veterans Survey Project, 2nd Division 5th Marines.

12 2nd Division, 5th Marines Field Msgs 1918–1919, NARA II Record Group 120, Entry 1241, Box 52.

13 Major Leroy P. Hunt's official report July 1919, NARA II. Also see George P. Clark, *The Fourth Marine Brigade in World War I* (MacFarland and Co.: Jefferson, N.C., 2015), 52.

14 Ibid.

15 Thomason, *Fix Bayonets!*, 184.

16 Hunt's official report July 1919, NARA II. Also see Clark, *The Fourth Marine Brigade in World War I*, 52.

17 David J. Bettez, *Kentucky Marine: Major General Logan Feland and the Making of the Modern USMC* (Lexington: University Press of Kentucky, 2014), 112.

18 Ausland, "Goodbye World."

19 George B. Clark, *The Second Infantry Division in World War I* (Jefferson, North Carolina: McFarland & Company, 2007), 149.

20 Leroy Hunt, *History of the 1st Battalion 5th Regiment US Marines* (Printed in Occupied Germany: Battalion Exchange), 7.

21 Cates papers, Marine Corps Personal Papers Collection, U.S. Marine Corps University, Quantico, Va.

22 Editha L. Watson, "The Fighting Race," *Plumas Independent*, November 3, 1932.

23 Clark, *The Fourth Marine Brigade in World War I*, 129.

24 John W. Thomason, *Salt Winds and Gobi Dust* (New York: Charles Scribner's Sons, 1934), 46.

25 Elton E. Mackin, *Suddenly We Didn't Want to Die: Memoirs of a World War I Marine* (Novato, Calif.: Presidio Press, 1993) 207–8.

26 Ibid.

CHAPTER 22: WOODFILL OF THE REGULARS

1   John J. Pershing, *My Experiences in the World War* (New York: Frederick A. Stokes Co., 1931), 197.

2   Michael Clodfelter, *Warfare and Armed Conflicts: A Statistical Encyclopedia of Casualty and Other Figures, 1492–2015* (Jefferson, N.C.: McFarland and Co., 2017), 406; in his memoirs, Pershing mentioned that ninety thousand replacements were required.

3   "The Meuse-Argonne Offensive: Part II: Pershing's Report," Great War Society, http://www.worldwar1.com/dbc/bigshow2.htm.

4   Lowell Thomas, *Woodfill of the Regulars: The True Story of Adventure from Arctic to the Argonne* (New York, Doubleday, Doran and Co., 1929), 266.

5   Ibid., 265.

6   Ibid., 267.

7   Ibid., 268.

8   Ibid., 269.

9   Ibid., 270.

10 Ibid.

11 Ibid., 274.

12 Ibid., 276.

13 Ibid., 277.

14 Brig. Gen. Samuel D. Rockenbach was Chief of Tank Corps for the American Expeditionary Forces.

15 John Eisenhower, *Yanks: The Epic Story of the American Army in World War I* (New York: Touchstone, 2001), 168, 217.

16 Michael Keane, *George S. Patton: Blood, Guts, and Prayer* (Washington, DC: Regnery History, 2014), 84.

17 Ibid., 81.

18 Alan D. Gaff, *Blood in the Argonne: The "Lost Battalion" of World War I* (Norman: University of Oklahoma Press, 2005), 144.

19 Ibid., 166.

20 Ibid., 157.

21 Byron Farwell, *Over There: The United States in the Great War, 1917-1918* (New York: W.W. Norton & Co., 2000), 225.

22 Edward Lengel, *To Conquer Hell: The Meuse-Argonne, 1918—The Epic Battle That Ended the First World War* (New York: Henry Holt and Company, 2008), 271.

23 Ibid.

24 Gaff, *Blood in the Argonne: The "Lost Battalion" of World War I*, 253.

25 Ibid., 260.

26 Ibid.

27 Alvin C. York, edited by Tom Skeyhill, *Sergeant York: His Own Life and War Diary* (Garden City, N.Y.: Doubleday Doran, 1930), 220-27.

28 Ibid., 228-35.

CHAPTER 23: "I GOT A FEW"

1   All quotations in this chapter from Lowell Thomas, *Woodfill of the Regulars: A True Story of Adventure from Arctic to the Argonne* (Doubleday, Doran and

Co., 1929), 277–290; Woodfill personnel file, "Personal Military History of Sergeant Samuel Woodfill, 30th Recruit Co. D.E.H.L. Late Captain, 60th Infantry," 4, NPRC; Sworn statement of John P. Riley, Sergeant, Company M, 60th Infantry, NPRC.

CHAPTER 24: LOUIS RAZGA: THE BIG GUNS

1 *History of the 58th Artillery, CAC, American Expeditionary Forces* (New York: Regimental History Board), 46.
2 Ibid.
3 Ibid., 42.
4 Ibid., 26.
5 Ibid., 27.
6 Ibid., 26–27.
7 Ibid., 28–29.
8 Ibid., 31.
9 Ibid., 46.
10 Noel B. Leggett, Surgeon, 2nd Battalion, 58th Arty, C.A.C. to C.O. Btry "D," 58th Artillery C.A.C., memo, April 25, 1919, NARA II, Record Group 165, Entry 210, Box 331.

CHAPTER 25: THE FINAL PUSH

1 Elton E. Mackin, *Suddenly We Didn't Want to Die: Memoirs of a World War I Marine* (Novato, Calif.: Presidio Press, 1993), 225.
2 Matthew Davenport, *First Over There* (New York: St. Martin's Press, 2015), 63–65.
3 Mackin, *Suddenly We Didn't Want to Die: Memoirs of a World War I Marine*, 225–27.
4 Ibid.
5 Ibid.
6 Ibid.
7 Ibid.
8 James Hopper, *Medals of Honor* (New York: John Day, 1929), 142.
9 Edward Lengel, *To Conquer Hell: The Meuse-Argonne, 1918—The Epic Battle That Ended the First World War* (New York: Henry Holt and Company, 2008), 382; Center of Military History, *United States Army in the World War, 1917–1919: Meuse-Argonne Operations*, vol. 10 (Washington, DC: Center of Military History, 1988), 19–25.
10 Paul Braim, *The Test of Battle: The AEF in the Meuse-Argonne* (Newark: University of Delaware Press, 1989), 130.
11 *United States Army in the World War, 1917–1919: Meuse-Argonne Operations*, vol. 10, 19–25.
12 Barbara MacMillan, *Paris 1919: Six Months That Changed the World* (New York: Random House, 2003), 17.
13 James W. Dell, "Wouldn't 'Let Up Till They Bellow,'" *Daily Arkansas Gazette*, November 10, 1918, 5.
14 Ibid.

15 Peter Owen, *To the Limit of Their Endurance: A Battalion in the Great War* (College Station: Texas A&M University Press, 2007), 194.

16 Richard Faulkner, *Pershing's Crusaders: The American Soldiers in World War I* (Lawrence: University Press of Kansas, 2017), 178–79.

17 Ibid., 587; Charles Lynch, *Medical Department in the World War*, vol. 9 (Washington, DC: Government Printing Office, 1923–1929), 67–69. According to the US Department of Veterans Affairs, the United States had 53,402 combat deaths in WWI.

18 Diary of Sgt. Karl McCune, 55th Company, in *Second Division History*, 280.

19 Lt. Col. William Donovan, letter, reprinted in "The Fighting 69th at Landres-et-St. Georges," in *Roads to the Great War*; letter also found through the author's connection with the OSS Society. The author is a member of the board of directors for the organization.

20 George H. English, Jr., *History of the 89th Division, U.S.A. 1917, 1918, 1919* (Denver, Colo: War Society of the 89th Division, 1920), 168.

21 Capt. Shipley Thomas, *The History of the AEF* (New York: George H. Doran Company, 1920), 600.

22 Mackin, *Suddenly We Didn't Want to Die: Memoirs of a World War I Marine*, 236.

23 George Viereck, *As They Saw Us: Foch, Ludendorff and Other Leaders Write Our History* (New York: Doubleday, 1929), 275.

CHAPTER 26: THE BRIDGE

1 Edwin Howard Simmons, *Through the Wheat: The U.S. Marines in World War I* (Annapolis, Md.: Naval Institute Press, 2008), no page.

2 Elton E. Mackin, *Suddenly We Didn't Want to Die: Memoirs of a World War I Marine* (Novato, Calif.: Presidio Press, 1993), 251.

3 *Second Division History*, 220.

4 Mackin, *Suddenly We Didn't Want to Die: Memoirs of a World War I Marine*, 252.

5 Clarence Richmond, "Episode 1: The Shooting Stops November 11–16, 1918," *The War Diary of Clarence Richmond*, robinrichmond.com.

6 Mackin, *Suddenly We Didn't Want to Die: Memoirs of a World War I Marine*, 252.

7 Ibid.

8 Ibid., 256.

9 Ibid., 258.

10 Ibid., 260.

11 Stanley Weintraub, *A Stillness Heard Round the World: The End of the Great War, November 1918* (New York: Dutton, 1985), 176.

12 *United States Army in the World War, 1917–1919: Meuse-Argonne Operations*, vol. 10 (Washington, DC: Center of Military History, 1988), 28–30.

CHAPTER 27: OCCUPATION

1 Col., Oliver Spaulding, Col. John Wright, et al., *2nd Division, American Expeditionary Force in France, 1917–1919* (New York: Hillman Press, 1937), 232.

2 Ibid., 224.

3 Ibid.

4 *Second Division History*, 226.

5 Ibid., 226–27.

6 John W. Thomason, *Fix Bayonets!* (New York: Charles Scribner's Sons, 1926), 232.

7 *Second Division History*, 233.

8 *91st Division American Expeditionary Force, World War I* (San Mateo, Calif.: 91st Division Publication Committee, 1919), 76.

9 Ibid., 79.

10 "Lea Nearly Presented the Kaiser to President Wilson for Xmas," *Editor and Publisher*, April 3, 1919.

11 *Second Division History*, 233.

12 Ibid.

13 Ibid., 234.

14 Report of James Delaney, COAG SS *Campana*, January 11, 1919, from the Armed Guards Report, NARA I, Record Group 45, Entry 520, Box 612.

15 Ibid.

16 Lowell Thomas, *Woodfill of the Regulars: The True Story of Adventure from Arctic to the Argonne* (New York, Doubleday, Doran and Co., 1929), 312.

17 Ibid., 304-5.

18 Ibid., 305.

19 G. J. Meyer, *The World Remade: America in the World War* (New York: Random House, 2017), 523.

20 Jeffery K. Taubenberger and David M. Morens, "1918 Influenza: The Mother of All Pandemics," *Emerging Infectious Diseases* (January 2006), Centers for Disease Control and Prevention.

21 Letter from Marie Meloney to Gen. Peyton March, November 13, 1919, NARA II, Record Group 407, Box 563

22 "Leaders for Honor to Unknown Dead," *New York Times*, February 2, 1921.

23 Burial of an Unknown American Soldier Killed on the Battle Fields of France, H. J. Res. 426, 66th Congress (1921).

24 "Leaders for Honor to Unknown Dead."

25 "The Unknown Soldier's Tomb," *New York Times*, February 3, 1921.

26 Memo from Brig. Gen. William Lassiter, "Body Bearers of an Unknown American to Be Buried at Arlington, November 11, 1921," September 8, 1921, NARA II. Record Group 407, Entry 37-1, Box, 564.

27 Ibid.

28 Ibid.

29 Thomas, *Woodfill of the Regulars: The True Story of Adventure from Arctic to the Argonne*, 317.

CHAPTER 28: THE UNKNOWN

1 Captain Arthur E. Dewey, QMC, US Army, *Selection of the Unknown Soldier*, unpublished manuscript, US Army Military History Institute, 1935, 3.

2 Ibid., 1–2.

3 Memo from Operations Division to Officer in Charge of Operations, Romagne-sous-Montfaucon, October 15, 1921, NARA II. Record Group 407, Entry 37-1, Box, 564.

4   Dewey, *Selection of the Unknown Soldier*, 3.

5   Memo from Operations Division to Officer in Charge of Operations, Romagne-sous-Mountfaucon, October 5, 1921.

6   Dewey, *Selection of the Unknown Soldier*, 4.

7   Associated Press, "America's 'Unknown' to Be Chosen Today," *New York Times*, October 24, 1921.

8   Dewey, *Selection of the Unknown Soldier*, 5.

9   Ibid.

10   Associated Press, "America's 'Unknown' to Be Chosen Today."

11   Dewey, *Selection of the Unknown Soldier*, 6.

12   Ibid.

13   Edward Younger, "I Chose the Unknown Soldier," from his personnel file at the NPRC; a portion is reprinted in *Cincinnati Enquirer*, November 8, 1936, 2.

14   "Charge to Be Entered on Service Record and Pay Card in the Case of Edward Younger," NPRC.

15   Younger, "I Chose the Unknown Soldier."

16   Ibid.

17   Ibid.

18   "Man Who Selected Unknown Soldier Says He Didn't Die in Vain," *Journal Gazette* (Mattoon, Ill.), November 10, 1939, 6.

19   Younger, "I Chose the Unknown Soldier."

20   Dewey, *Selection of the Unknown Soldier*, 6.

21   Younger, "I Chose the Unknown Soldier."

22   Ibid.

23   Dewey, *Selection of the Unknown Soldier*, 7.

24   Ibid., 8.

25   Ibid.

26   Ibid., 9.

27   Ibid.

28   Ibid.

29   Edwin L. James, "Body of America's Unknown Soldier on Its Way Home Aboard the Olympia," *New York Times*, October 26, 1921.

30   Ibid.

31   Ibid.

32   Ibid.

CHAPTER 29: COMING HOME

1   Kirk Larue Simpson, *The Unknown Soldier: Complete Texts of the Service of the Associated Press on "The Unknown Soldier," as Sent from Washington, D.C., on Wednesday, Thursday and Friday, November 9, 10 and 11, 1921* (New York: Associated Press, 1921), 2. The events of this chapter are drawn from the articles in the endnotes.

2   Ibid., 3.

3   James Guthrie Harbord, *The American Army in France, 1917–1919* (New York: Little, Brown and Company, 1936), 574.

4   Address of Maj. Gen. James G. Harbord, US Army Dedication of Belleau Wood, July 22, 1923.

5   Simpson, *The Unknown Soldier: Complete Texts of the Service*, 4.
6   Ibid.
7   Ibid.
8   Ibid.
9   Ibid., 5.
10 Ibid., 7.
11 Ibid.
12 Ibid., 9.
13 Ibid., 13.
14 Ibid., 17.
15 "Millions to Pray for Peace Today," *The New York Times*, November 11, 1921.
16 Ibid.
17 "Amplifiers Tested for Armistice Day," *The New York Times*, November 10, 1921.
18 Ibid.
19 Ibid.
20 "President Harding's Address at the Burial of an Unknown American Soldier," *The New York Times*, November 12, 1922.
21 Ibid.
22 Ibid.
23 Ibid.
24 Slotkin, *The Lost Battalion: The Great War and the Crisis of American Nationality*, 475–80; Gaff, *Blood in the Argonne: The "Lost Battalion" of World War I*, 281–85.
25 Farley Granger Papers, account to his son, Military History Institute.
26 Slotkin, *The Lost Battalion: The Great War and the Crisis of American Nationality*, 475–80; Gaff, *Blood in the Argonne: The "Lost Battalion" of World War I*, 281–85.
27 Quote is widely attributed to Chief Plenty Coups.
28 "Solemn Journey of Dead: Ceremonial Procession in Which Nation's Leaders Walk Stirs Capital," *The New York Times*, November 12, 1921.
29 Simpson, *The Unknown Soldier: Complete Texts of the Service*, 14.
30 Ibid., 195.
31 Each of the Body Bearers and principal witnesses dealt with the war in his own personal way. Shortly after the ceremony to bury the Unknown Soldier, Capt. Whittlesey bought a one-way ticket on a ship to Cuba. While en route, he jumped overboard, taking his own life. Corporal Elton Mackin battled shell shock, now known as PTSD, for the rest of his life. Others moved on and led prosperous, full lives.

AFTERWORD: THE TOMB OF THE UNKNOWN SOLDIER

1   Ronald Reagan, "Remarks at Memorial Day Ceremonies Honoring an Unknown Serviceman of the Vietnam Conflict," May 28, 1984.
2   Ibid.

EPILOGUE

1   Marcia Winn, "Picked Unknown Soldier, but He Tries to Forget," *Chicago Tribune*, November 12, 1939.
2   Unknown author, "Man Who Selected Unknown Soldier Says He Didn't Die in Vain," *Journal Gazette*, Mattoon, Ill., November 10, 1939.

3   Quote from Woodfill, public domain.
4   Williamsburg Bureau, "Razga and Bands Case Not Pressed," *Daily Press*, Newport News, Va., October 15, 1929, 9.
5   "Army Veteran of 26 Years' Service Wants to Reenlist," *Morning News*, Wilmington, Del., February 15, 1948, 36.
6   Granger Account, Farley Granger Papers, Letter from Granger describing the attack, MHI.
7   Granger Papers, 17.
8   Alan Axelrod, *Patton: A Biography* (London: Palgrave Macmillan, 2006), 168–69.

INDEX

Note: Military units are arranged in order of unit size from smaller to larger.